EARL SCRUGGS
AND THE 5-STRING BANJO

REVISED AND ENHANCED EDITION

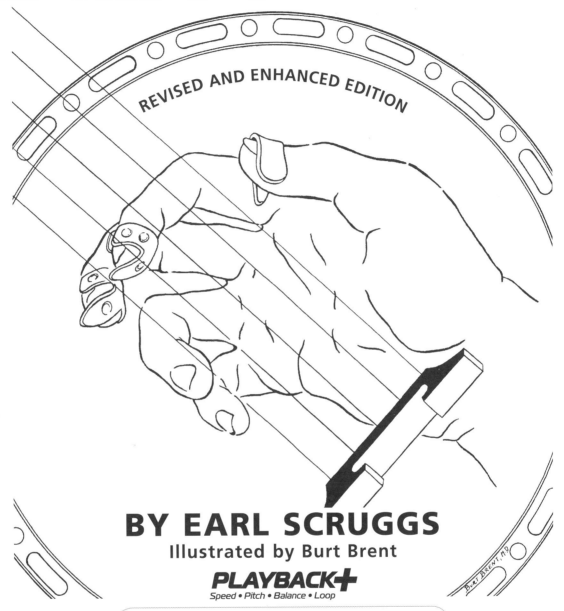

BY EARL SCRUGGS
Illustrated by Burt Brent

Speed • Pitch • Balance • Loop

To access audio visit:
www.halleonard.com/mylibrary

Enter Code
1668-1846-3429-1875

ISBN 978-0-634-06042-7

HAL•LEONARD®

Visit Hal Leonard Online at
www.halleonard.com

Contact us:
Hal Leonard
7777 West Bluemound Road
Milwaukee, WI 53213
Email: info@halleonard.com

In Europe, contact:
Hal Leonard Europe Limited
42 Wigmore Street
Marylebone, London, W1U 2RN
Email: info@halleonardeurope.com

In Australia, contact:
Hal Leonard Australia Pty. Ltd.
4 Lentara Court
Cheltenham, Victoria, 3192 Australia
Email: info@halleonard.com.au

I dedicate this book to
my wife, Louise,
our sons, Gary and Randy,
our grandchildren and great-grandchildren,
and to the memory of Steven Earl Scruggs

TABLE OF CONTENTS

Earl picking at the sound check for "The Three Pickers" CD and DVD, December 2002
– Photo by Louise Scruggs

PREFACE

By Earl Scruggs

THROUGHOUT MY YEARS OF PLAYING MUSIC professionally, one of my goals has been to promote interest in the 5-string banjo, which I began playing at the age of four.

When the book *Earl Scruggs and the 5-String Banjo* was first published in 1968, I had hopes it would be helpful to anyone wanting to learn, or learn more about, my approach to banjo picking. Over the years I've received a lot of positive feedback regarding the book. I've also heard some good suggestions on how to make it even better and easier to understand.

Most of the people I've heard from have told me they prefer tablature to standard sheet music notation. Many have said that they wished the tablatures were larger in size. So with all that in mind, standard music notation has been omitted from this enhanced edition in order to allow more space for the tablature, making it easier to read.

Warren Kennison, Jr., a great picker and banjo instructor, is back on board for this revised edition and worked on the tablatures. The tablatures now include timing indicators so that the time value of each note picked is shown. There are other changes in the format of the tablature which I believe will be user-friendlier to the reader.

Warren, who resides in Golden, Colorado, also did the tablature for the new songs that have been added to the Song Section.

Dr. Burt Brent introduced me to Warren back when the original edition was being written.

I met Burt in 1964 when he was stationed for six months in Fort Campbell, Kentucky with the 101st Airborne Division. There were others who had approached me with the notion of writing an instructional manual teaching my style of picking, but I had doubts that it could be done properly and thoroughly. Burt convinced me that it was possible to do and for those six months that he lived nearby we worked on the book whenever our schedules allowed us to get together.

For this enhanced edition, Burt wrote the Introduction and also redesigned the front and back covers of the book. His step-by-step chapter, "How To Build a Banjo" is again included as well as several of his illustrations and photographs seen throughout the book.

In the years since the original edition first came out, Burt has achieved world-renown in the field of plastic surgery, pioneering many of the ear reconstruction techniques used today.

Special thanks go to my oldest son, Gary Scruggs, for his help with the editing and rewriting of this updated enhanced edition.

When he was growing up, Gary always had a great interest in music. He took band courses in elementary school and continued to do so in both junior and senior high school. He went on to study more music during his college years at Vanderbilt University in Nashville, Tennessee.

Gary performed with me throughout the years of the Earl Scruggs Revue, singing lead and playing electric bass. He now continues to perform with me in my "Family & Friends" band.

The teaching chapters are more detailed and cover new ground in this enhanced edition. A description of what is known as the "Nashville Number System," which is used by many studio musicians when reading chord charts, has also been added to Chapter 4, "Chords."

The original LP and cassette recording that corresponds with certain lessons in the original edition is now available in MP3 format, making it easier to zero in on those audio lessons described in this enhanced version of the book. Audio icons with track numbers are placed with those lessons found in Chapter 9, "Exercises in Picking."

～

While working on this edition, it occured to me that many of you who already know how to play banjo probably enjoy picking with other players in jam sessions. And many of you who are beginners are probably looking forward to the day when you can join in on some jams with your friends that play music. Some of you might even be thinking of someday getting into the music business as a professional musician.

Whether you want to pick just for fun or pick for a living, (which is also fun!), I would like to share some thoughts with you.

There are no hard and fast rules written in stone for playing music with other players, but I do believe there are some things about playing with other pickers that make the music more enjoyable and entertaining for everyone involved, including their listeners.

Once you have learned how to play lead breaks I encourage you to always be conscious of when not to play them. I've heard some bands and I've heard some jam sessions where one or two players played nothing but lead parts, even when others were taking their own lead breaks. To me, that sounds like Babylon must have sounded when everyone was talking all at once and in different languages.

Try not to lose sight of the fact that your backup roles in a group are no less important than your lead banjo rolls. Know when to back off and let other players shine and hope that they will extend the same courtesy to you when it's your turn to step up front and center. I believe this formula for musical interaction makes a player's lead breaks have an even greater impact on the listener.

I also encourage you, especially if you are a beginner, to not be overly concerned with how fast you can play a tune when it comes to picking breakdown-type tunes.

Early on in my professional career, I was often referred to as "the world's fastest banjo player." To me, that didn't mean all that much. I have always been much more concerned with the tone of my playing and how I could pick so that each and every note can be heard clearly and cleanly, not how fast I could play those notes.

I also believe the three most important words in mastering any musical instrument are *practice, practice, practice*. A strong, positive attitude toward learning to play an instrument also works wonders.

There might be times when you feel bogged down by a particular lesson and left with the feeling that you will never get it right. Try not to think of those times as stumbling blocks; instead, think of them as simple hurdles and challenges that you will eventually overcome with more and more practice.

A lot has happened since the original edition of this book was first published. My longtime musical partnership with Lester Flatt ended in 1969. From there I went on to form the Earl Scruggs Revue with my sons, Gary and Randy. My youngest son, Steve, later joined the Revue when he came of age. In recent years I have enjoyed touring with "Family & Friends."

Many people have encouraged me to update the autobiographical section of the book, which I have done in Chapter 11. There are also several other remembrances scattered throughout other parts of the book that I hope you will enjoy reading.

Once again it is my hope that this book will be helpful to all of you wanting to learn or learn more about Scruggs-style banjo playing. The best of luck to you and have a lot of fun with your picking!

Earl in concert at the Telluride Bluegrass and Country Music Festival; Telluride, Colorado – 1999

(Left to right) Earl, Marty Stuart, and Gary Scruggs – Photo by Louise Scruggs

ACKNOWLEDGMENTS

In addition to Gary Scruggs, Burt Brent, and Warren Kennison, Jr., who are mentioned in the Preface, I would also like to thank the following for their efforts:

My wife, Louise, for her photographs and for writing the chapter "A Brief History of the 5-String Banjo."

Dr. Nat T. Winston for writing the Foreword.

Kathy Spanberger, President and Chief Operating Officer at Peer Music.

Jeff Schroedl, Vice President of Popular and Standard Publications at Hal Leonard Corporation.

Brad Davis for re-mastering the recorded instructional material that corresponds to the book. (Brad's website is braddavismusic.com).

Carolintone Music Co., Inc.; Chappell & Co., Ltd.; J. Albert & Son Music Publishers and Paul Henning for permission to reprint "Ballad of Jed Clampett."

Martha White Mills, Inc. for permission to reprint "You Bake Right with Martha White."

Pamper Music, Inc. for permission to reprint "Hot Corn, Cold Corn."

My brother Horace Scruggs and his wife, Maida, radio station WSM, the History Division of the Los Angeles County Museum, the Country Music Hall of Fame® and Museum (Kyle Young, Director), David Schenk, Dan Loftin, Donn Jones, and the Gibson Musical Instruments Company (Henry Juszkiewicz, Chairman and CEO) for photographs. (Dobro guitars are mentioned in this book. Dobro® is registered and owned by Gibson. Gibson's website is gibson.com).

There are several others who contributed to the original edition of this book that have since passed away. They are:

Louis "Grandpa" Jones, David "Stringbean" Akeman, DeWitt "Snuffy" Jenkins, Dorris Macon, and Thomas B. Allen, who provided photographs.

Harold "Shot" Jackson, who offered his insight concerning wood finishing for musical instruments.

Gene Autry, of Golden West Melodies, Inc., who granted permission to reprint "Blue Ridge Cabin Home" and "Shuckin' the Corn."

And last but not least, I dedicate this Acknowledgment page to the memory of Roy Horton, a wonderful "song man" who worked at Peer Music in New York, NY for many years, pitching songs and making people smile. Roy played a major role in encouraging Peer to publish the original edition of the book.

MY FATHER'S BANJO

My father, George Elam Scruggs, worked as a bookkeeper and a farmer. He loved music and he played a frailing style of 5-string banjo. He also played fiddle.

He passed away in 1928 when I was four years old. It was in that year when I began learning to pick on his open back banjo.

My father's banjo is a factory-built instrument but there is no brand name or serial number on it so I have no way of knowing in what year it was built. I do know it was already considered to be old by the time I started learning to play it.

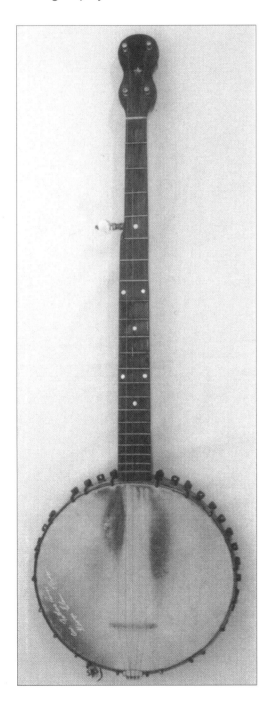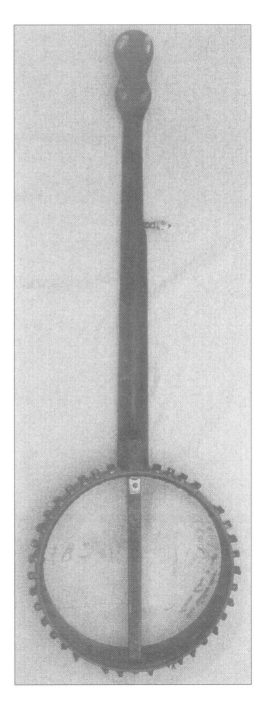

Earl's father's banjo
Photos courtesy of The Country Music Hall of Fame® and Museum

FOREWORD

By Nat Winston, M.D.

Until Earl Scruggs' nationwide debut on the Grand Ole Opry in 1945, banjo players were traditionally a rowdy lot—were comedians of a sort—and most often didn't take their banjo playing seriously. Played mainly by extroverts, whose handling of a tune was to throw it at you, the banjo itself had become the extrovert of musical instruments. It was strictly for fun, nothing to be taken seriously, nothing to be thought about, and certainly nothing to be loved except with the "rough-em-up" form of affection you might bestow on a friendly pup.

Even the four-string, or tenor banjo was only for loud strumming while square-dancers pounded their feet to a coarse rhythm or while crowds whooped it up in a noisy honky-tonk.

The nearest any banjo came to being admitted to polite society was as a single piece in an orchestra, at which times it had to be "toned down" in order to blend in with the more respectable instruments.

In the Southern Appalachians, no decent woman would let her husband associate with a banjo player, and certainly no father would see that fate befall his innocent daughter. The habitat of the banjo was the moonshine still.

My father, who loved this instrument despite its reputation, wrote this poem in connection with the prevailing attitude:

ODE TO A BANJO

Nat T. Winston, Sr.

(1918)

Alas! My banjo, thou art broken,
I quietly lay thee down to rest
Accept these lines, an humble token
From one who deems that thou hast blest.

I know hard things were said of thee—
My once vivacious friend;
And those who hate high revelry,
Rejoice at thine end.

But still to me a friend thou wert,
For with thy cheerful song;
Ye could the darkest hours convert,
And bid care flee along.

For they were songs I understood,
Not high-class throbs and moans;
Real human songs, not angel's food,
Were in thy lively tones.

I loved you not for virtue's sake,
For naught of her ye knew;
Ye ever were a shameless rake,
And yet I loved ye true.

I loved you for your very sins,
You merry hearted knave;
I loved you for those wicked dins,
That made the parsons rave!

He wrote this incidentally, even after having been told by a mountain minister that, "you might as well give your son a ticket to hell as give him a five-string banjo!" This is what can happen to the good name of the most delicate instrument before an artist adopts it for his own.

Fortunately, an artist did. Earl Scruggs restored dignity and the intricate beauty we now enjoy in the five-string banjo, one of music's finest instruments. If I were to settle upon one word to describe Earl, the man and the musician, I might choose "perceptive."

As his vast audiences know, Earl doesn't use many words. He doesn't really need them, as he's as finely at-tuned as any musical instrument. He picks up the nuances of a song or a situation, his acknowledgement of them and his reply are in his music. Like his approach to the world around him, Earl's approach to a musical passage can have a complexity of shading. The sensitivity of the artist shows in the sensitive overtones and undercurrents of his interpretations.

After many years of personal friendship with Earl, I can notice times in our conversation when our words are playing second fiddle to his mental involvement with a new pattern of sound. He may be talking to me about yesterday's weather, but his thoughts are on tomorrow's modification of a particular lick on the banjo.

The five-string banjo has become almost synonymous with the genius of the first man who gave it its right-ful place, and who continues through his relationship with it to earn his title of "The World's Most Imitated Musician." The style is now known throughout the world as "Scruggs-Style Banjo Picking."

To be sure, the five-string banjo is still for fun, but consists of a new type of fun, intricacy, and beauty in its melodies rather than slam-bang roughness.

Like a complete person, like the person who plays it, its approach to life is not limited to one mood. It can rollick with joy; but it can also mourn. It can speak of love or hate, show tenderness or anger. And, it can sound a wistfulness that words have not captured. This is the five-string banjo today, yours to enjoy.

Bumper sticker featuring registered trademarks of the Country Music Foundation, the not-for-profit educational organization that operates the County Music Hall of Fame® and Museum. Used by permission.
Lester Flatt and Earl Scruggs were inducted into the Country Music Hall of Fame in 1985.
The Country Music Hall of Fame® and Museum is located in Nashville, Tennessee.

Kris Kristofferson, Earl Scruggs, "Cowboy" Jack Clement, and Gary Scruggs in the dressing room of the Country Music Hall of Fame® and Museum's Ford Theater following a "picking party" concert by Earl with special guests in 2004. Fourteen musicians took part in the concert and sat in a semi-circle, entertaining the sold-out audience with picking, singing, and stories of the past. – Photo by Donn Jones

INTRODUCTION

By Burt Brent

HE STORY OF THIS BOOK goes back some four decades. The 1950s had ended, the sixties were taking hold, there was a folk music revival, and the popularity of Scruggs-style banjo playing was exploding on college campuses and in cities across the country. Everyone wanted to create these magical finger-picking banjo sounds, but emulators of his style readily admitted that although they felt they were playing the same notes, "it still just didn't sound like Earl." Fans and aspiring players began asking the banjoist extraordinaire to consider writing a teaching book. Generous practically to a fault, Earl never has been one to guardedly hide his technique and would readily share his methods to help any would-be "banjo-picker" learn. He considered writing the book, but the demands of recording commitments and an arduous performing schedule criss-crossed him from coast to coast practically nonstop. It seemed nearly impossible to find the time.

Earl Scruggs already had devoted fans and followers scattered across the country, but now there was a new legion of aspiring banjo players *everywhere*, clamoring to learn his style. I was one of them.

Playing the banjo gave me great joy during the few breaks I got from the strenuous hours of medical training, and I was fortunate to have met Warren Kennison, Jr., a student at University of Michigan where I was interning. Warren was one of the dedicated young musicians who had also been inspired by the folk music revival and he had an uncanny ability to listen to Earl's recorded music and mimic it; he had worked out the tablature to much of Earl's music and taught me to play many of his great songs on the decorative banjo I had built.

The more I played Scruggs' tunes, the more determined I became to *understand* his magical sound. I found that I didn't want to just memorize a bunch of instrumental pieces; rather, as a medical student, I wanted to dissect Scruggs' banjo picking to elucidate and understand the *anatomy* of his style. I discovered that Earl's method was comprised of various patterns and that it could be broken down—perhaps even systematically taught. As much as I enjoyed playing and learning about his music, I found myself wanting to spread the joy of playing the 5-string banjo and to pay homage to Earl Scruggs. I wanted to memorialize for future generations of banjo players the techniques, magical sounds, rhythms, and songs of this legendary genius.

I was thinking about a format for such a book when I received my Army draft notice to serve as a medical officer. It was the peak of Vietnam, and like some predestined twist of fate, I landed in the 101st Airborne Division at Fort Campbell, Kentucky—just fifty miles from the Scruggs' home near Nashville!

I soon met Earl and Louise Scruggs, who graciously invited me into their home to talk. Within several hours of our pleasant first visit, we decided to embark upon this teaching book together. Earl described various right-hand "rolls," touching upon some of the patterns I thought I had "discovered" when I first dissected and analyzed his playing style! We discussed a number of these "picking patterns" and other banjo "licks" he used and how they might be taught. Earl and I began to collaborate on a teaching book the very next week.

During the ensuing months, Louise took time from her busy schedule (of booking and managing *Flatt and Scruggs*) to write a superb history of the 5-string banjo while Earl and I worked out the extensive teaching section of the book. We arranged the format based upon my own perspective as a recent student of the banjo as to how one could best learn the instrument; first the basics about becoming acquainted with the banjo and with music; then how to read tablature, chord composition, and the all-important section on understanding the "anatomy" of Scruggs-style banjo picking. After some additional instruction on banjo tuning and playing hints, we would embark on the "heart" of the book—the "exercises in picking." After we began by teaching the basics of working with the right thumb and using some slides, I suggested to Earl that it would be very effective to use a basic Scruggs' tune and take the student through multiple variations of the song, serially adding techniques to each new variation as the student progressed through the practice exercises within the book. Earl agreed that this plan should help to build the students' confidence and suggested that "Cripple Creek" would serve this purpose well. Earl and I worked diligently during the countless hours we spent together creating the exercise section of the book over a six-month period. During this enjoyable time, we were both amused by the difficulties we encountered when trying to slow down Earl's playing so that I could transcribe it into tablature on paper.

If the student adhered to these exercises, he/she would be armed with Scruggs' technique so that his songs would come naturally and wouldn't seem like compositions to be arduously memorized by rote. This was followed, appropriately, with a large section devoted exclusively to songs, so that the banjoist could learn a number of Earl's classic instrumental pieces. For this section of the book, we solicited contributions from the capable banjo players, Warren Kennison, Jr. and Bill Keith, who individually worked out the tablature for songs from *Foggy Mountain Banjo* and other classic recordings.

The chief purpose of this particular book edition is to greatly enhance the learning experience for students. We are achieving this with a number of improvements to make it even easier to understand Scruggs' singularly unique style, and these are elaborated upon in Earl's Preface. A number of new songs have also been added to the song section, and for this, we again sought my old friend, Warren Kennison, Jr., who transcribed the added songs from Scruggs' original recordings; he also re-worked the original book songs to match their tablature with specific cuts from Earl's albums.

During the decades that have passed since the inception of this book, I have had time to reflect on my friendship with the Scruggs "team" and marvel at their contribution to the musical world. When we began this book, Louise was raising three musically gifted, wonderful sons while simultaneously coordinating thousands of miles of travel, performing engagements, recording sessions, interviews, and publications to promote her husband's unique music. Louise's love and devotion to Earl and his music has been instrumental in disseminating the knowledge, exposure, and love of the Scruggs banjo sound worldwide. I have come to know how much Earl appreciates his fans, how he has inspired legions of musicians, and how much he has done to encourage, assist, and instruct them.

Earl and Burt in 1965

During the years, thousands of banjo students have learned from this book and have come to know the pleasure of banjo playing. While working on this Enhanced Edition, it gave me great pleasure to think of the thousands more who will enjoy this marvelous instrument and the unique and magical sound Earl Scruggs creates with it. Earl's generous efforts with this book ensure that future generations of musicians can learn and enjoy his unique style of banjo playing for many years to come.

Burt Brent
Stanford, California
Winter 2004

Earl and Warren Kennison, Jr. picking in 1965
– Photo by Burt Brent

 # GETTING ACQUAINTED WITH YOUR BANJO

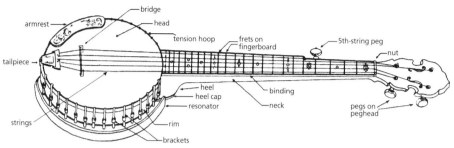

Know the parts of your banjo

PURCHASING A BANJO

I have met a lot people over the years looking to purchase a new or used 5-string banjo or wanting to trade up to a better one. I've been asked many times, "What banjo should I buy?" and "What banjo would work best for me?"

There are no quick and easy answers to those questions because personal preferences have so much to do with deciding on which instrument is right for any one individual.

If you are asking those questions, my advice is to do a little research. Learn as much as you can about a banjo and its parts. Shop around and compare different banjos within your price range. Go to music stores and spend some time trying out what they have in stock.

If you have friends who play banjos, ask them what they like about their instruments. Also ask them if there is anything they don't like about their instruments. Then ask yourself a couple of important questions: Which banjo sounds best to you? Which banjo feels best to you?

Once you have done all of that, it generally gets down to economics. Keep in mind that a cheaply built banjo will be harder to play than a good quality banjo. It can become very frustrating for someone attempting to learn to play an instrument if they're learning on a "clunker."

If you're not happy with your current banjo, then buy or trade up to what you consider to be the best banjo affordable to you.

There are several high quality brand names from which to choose. Gibson manufactures six "Earl Scruggs Signature Models" that I endorse. They are shown on certain pages in Chapter 10. You can also see them along with other Gibson banjos on Gibson's website (gibson.com).

YOUR BANJO AND ITS PARTS

I've known of some players who constantly make adjustments on their banjos to the point of often taking them completely apart and then putting them back together. I'd rather spend all that time watching a good baseball game or a good movie!

I like getting my banjo set up properly and then leaving it alone until something needs adjustment; and with most good quality banjos it really isn't all that often, except of course for changing strings.

Let's talk about the parts of your banjo and what to do and what not to do if certain things get a bit out of kilter.

Fingerboard and Neck

The fingerboard, which is also called the *fretboard*, is glued to the top of the neck.

A fine-grained hardwood is the best material for making a good, smooth-sliding fingerboard. Instrument builders often use ebony or rosewood.

The sliding action on a clean fingerboard is smoother than on a dirty one. Run a soft cloth over it frequently to keep it clean. A good finish on the neck will also give you smoother sliding action.

The decorative designs seen on most fingerboards and pegheads are called *inlay*. *Position markers* are the small dots that are placed into the neck's binding at certain fret positions.

The neck and fingerboard should not be badly bowed, or curved. ("Bowed" is pronounced with a long "o," as in "fiddle bow" and "Mr. Bojangles.") If the neck is bowed, the strings will not play in tune up and down the neck.

One simple test to determine if the neck is bowed is to sight down the length of the fingerboard as if you were aiming a rifle.

If the visual test still leaves you wondering whether the neck is significantly bowed, play the strings at each of the frets. If the other banjo parts are set up correctly and the strings play in tune up and down the neck, then don't worry about the neck possibly having a very slight bow—as I said earlier, I leave things alone when they're working properly.

If the neck is bowed to the extent that the strings play out of tune and there is a *truss rod* in the neck, the rod can straighten out the bow. The adjusting nut for the truss rod is beneath a removable plate mounted on the peghead.

Tinkering around with the truss rod can lead to serious trouble because it can easily be broken if you don't know exactly how to adjust it. A broken truss rod will require expensive repair work.

A banjo will constantly play out of tune if the neck isn't fastened tightly to the rim. Most banjos have either one or two *coordinator rods* located inside the rim that are used to attach the neck to the rim.

The angle at which the neck meets the rim should be approximately 3°. The angle is one factor that determines the distance between the fingerboard and the strings. Slightly increasing the angle lowers the strings; slightly decreasing the angle raises the strings.

When neck work is needed, I strongly advise you to get someone who is very experienced with neck adjustments to do the work for you if you don't thoroughly understand the correct procedures. I take my banjo to a professional repairperson when the neck needs adjustment. (And it rarely does.)

Frets

Most 5-string banjos have twenty-two frets with the first fret being the one closest to the peghead.

Good frets are properly rounded to provide smooth sliding action. If the frets are set too high or too low, the strings are likely to play out of tune or rattle and buzz when fretted.

Frets may eventually have to be replaced because the strings can groove them too low over the course of time. Frets that are set too high can be filed down.

Professional instrument repair shops have the tools needed for such repairs. They also have a systematic method of tapping down new frets into the fingerboard.

Pegs on Peghead

The tuning pegs secure the four long strings at the peghead, which is also called the *headstock*. The part of a peg that you twist when tuning a string is called the *button*.

A peg should turn easily when tuning a string, but not slip freely while picking. Adjust the give and take of a peg's hold on a string by tightening or loosening the button's screw. If the screw tends to loosen from tuning, a very thin lock washer can usually hold it in place.

Fifth-String Peg

There are two basic types of fifth-string pegs, *friction* pegs and *geared* pegs.

I once preferred a friction peg because it made changing a string easier and faster if it broke during a performance. I later switched to a geared fifth-string peg because of its advantages over a friction peg.

A friction peg is only pressed into its hole and can wear the hole larger over time. The peg will then no longer be held securely in place. I've fixed worn pegholes in the past with plastic wood.

A friction peg is subject to not turn smoothly. Dismounting and cleaning it with metal cleaning fluid or silverware polish will improve its action. If the inside parts of the peg are scarred, rough spots can be smoothed away with emery paper or fine-grained sandpaper. Loosen the button's screw when changing a string to avoid stripping it.

Geared pegs are more precise and easier to use than friction pegs when fine-tuning the fifth string. They come in different ratios and are less likely than friction pegs to break a string when tuning it.

With both types of fifth-string pegs, set the button's screw with just enough tightness to keep the string from slipping out of tune while you are playing.

Nut

The nut has four small grooves, or slots, in which the long strings anchor before reaching their respective tuning pegs.

The strings should rest at the same height with each in a tight fitting groove. If the depth of the grooves is too deep or too shallow, the strings will not fret properly.

Rubbing a small amount of pencil lead into the grooves from time to time will allow the strings to slide easier when tuning them.

Heel and Heel Cap

The heel is the thick part of the neck that joins the rim. How the back of the heel is shaped, or trimmed, affects the angle of the neck to the rim.

The heel cap is most often made of wood and covers the bottom of the heel. Some heel caps are ornate and/or made of material that contrasts with the wood of the heel for decorative purposes.

Rim

The rim, which is also known as the *shell*, is the round body of the banjo. Rims are made out of metal or wood.

The rim, tension hoop, tone ring, resonator, and other components of the round part of the banjo are referred to collectively as the *pot*.

Head

There are two basic types of banjo heads: those made of Mylar plastic and those made of calfskin.

Your banjo head should fit tightly to get the best tone and volume out of your banjo. If it loosens and your banjo has a resonator, remove the resonator to access the bracket nuts.

Use a banjo wrench to tighten each of the brackets a little at a time while proceeding clockwise. Keep repeating the process until the head is tightened to the degree you prefer. Pay attention to the bridge when you're close to finishing the work—when it's standing up fairly level, the head is about as tight as it will go without bursting.

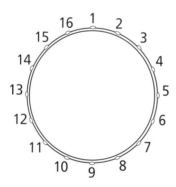

The number of brackets vary with different banjos

When the head has been properly tightened, there shouldn't be any loose brackets and the tension hoop should be level all the way around the rim.

A calfskin head is easily affected by changes in the weather. On damp, humid days the head will loosen, resulting in a dull, lifeless tone. You will then need to tighten it. But if you then forget to loosen the brackets on a dry day, the head will tighten even more and be likely to burst.

A plastic head is much easier to deal with because it will hold practically the same level of tightness through changes in weather conditions.

The first time I used a plastic head, I was playing an outdoor show at a drive-in theater. Fog rolled in and it was so heavy that beads of water were soon forming on the head. I was amazed that I could still pick away with the tone unchanged.

I use a Remo "Weather King" high collar head on my banjo.

Brackets

Clean and lightly oil the threads of the brackets whenever you change the head to prevent their wearing and stripping. I use a very thin oil, such as sewing machine oil.

Tension Hoop

The tension hoop, which is also known as the *stretcher band*, exerts pressure on the head when the brackets are tightened. Because of the shape of a plastic head, I file down a portion of the hoop to avoid tearing the head's mounting band.

Tone Ring

The tone ring is located inside the rim and supports the head. There are two basic types of tone rings: *flathead* rings and *archtop* rings.

The tone each type of ring produces differs from one another because of the difference in their shapes. You can see how the head rests upon both types of tone rings in the illustrations:

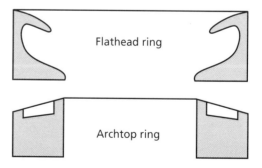

With an archtop ring, there is less surface area of the raised head free to vibrate. Thus, an archtop ring produces a relatively brighter tone, and a flathead ring produces a relatively deeper tone.

Because a banjo is by nature a bright sounding instrument, I prefer a flathead tone ring. Playing styles should be considered when deciding which type tone ring is best suited for any given player.

I often pick hard on the strings, so an archtop banjo in my hands would sound overly bright to my ear when compared to a flathead. Again, it comes down to personal preferences. What sounds bright to one person's ear may sound dull to yours.

The tone ring should fit snug against the rim. If it's loose, tone quality and volume will be diminished.

Resonator

The resonator covers the bottom of the rim. It amplifies a banjo's volume by reflecting the sound coming from the head and directing it forward.

The backs of some resonators are shaped flat, and others are slightly rounded, or bowl-shaped. The resonator on my banjo is rounded.

Banjos that don't have resonators are called *open back* banjos.

Binding

Binding is the trim around certain parts of most banjos such as the resonator and the fingerboard. Binding is not only decorative, but functional as well in that it helps protect the edges of an instrument from bumps and scratches.

Binding is often made of plastic or a hard wood. Mother-of-pearl and abalone are also used. Plastic binding can have different looks, such as ivory, tortoise shell, and gold dust.

Armrest

The armrest makes playing more comfortable by keeping your arm off the tension hoop and the brackets.

Tailpiece

The tailpiece secures the strings to the banjo at the banjo head.

If the tailpiece sits too high off the head, the bridge is likely to slip off center, and the strings will then play out of tune.

If the forward part of the tailpiece is too close to the head, there will be too much pressure on the head, and volume will be lowered—and so will the strings. They will fall too close to the fingerboard and be likely to rattle and buzz when played.

I like having just enough tension on the tailpiece to firmly hold the bridge in place.

Bridge

Banjo bridges are made in different heights, weights, and styles. Each of the five strings rests in its own small groove at the top of the bridge.

I prefer a three-footed bridge to a two-footed bridge as the third foot provides more support to the strings, which prevents sag in the middle.

three-footed bridge   *two-footed bridge*

Bridge placement is critical when it comes to the strings playing in tune. The twelfth fret should be at the approximate midway point between the bridge and the nut.

When the bridge is properly placed, each of the four long strings fretted at the twelfth fret will produce the same note as the harmonic chime sounded when that string is chimed at the twelfth fret.

If the fretted notes ring sharp (or higher in pitch) to the chimed notes, move the bridge toward the tailpiece. If they ring flat (or lower in pitch) to the chimed notes, move the bridge toward the neck. (How to play chimed notes is taught on page 67).

The height of the bridge affects the distance between the strings and the fingerboard. I use Grover bridges that are 5/8-inch in height.

Strings

Strings should be changed when their tone starts sounding dull. String life can last as little as a day or two or as long as several months, depending on how much and how hard you pick.

Strings that have lost their tone quality are said to be "dead." Dead strings are harder to tune and are less likely to stay in tune than vibrant strings.

String life can be lengthened considerably by wiping them off with a soft, clean cloth when you are finished playing.

The distance from the strings to the fingerboard is referred to as *action*. Action is determined by several factors, such as bridge height, tailpiece placement, and the angle of the neck to the rim.

There is no one "right" or "correct" action. Personal preference comes into play as to how the strings feel to your fingers when picking and fretting them. Your friend might love the action on his banjo while you might consider it too high or too low.

I use Gibson "Earl Scruggs Signature" medium gauge strings on stage and in the studio. The strings are also available in light gauge.

If I'm just sitting around the house picking for fun or jamming with friends at picking parties, I sometimes use light gauge strings since they are easier on the tips of the fretting fingers.

If you are a beginner and have never played a fretted stringed instrument, you might want to start out practicing with light gauge strings until your fingertips toughen with more and more practice.

Let's now take a look at a few other items you should know about such as thumb picks, finger picks, and shoulder straps.

Picks

I use a plastic thumb pick and two metal finger picks for my index and middle fingers.

Thumb Pick: A light gauge thumb pick with a point similar to the one in diagram A produces a thinner tone than a heavier gauge thumb pick that I use. I trim off the point to make it a bit rounder as shown in diagram B. Doing so results in a fuller and more balanced tone.

Many three-finger banjo players (and many Dobro players as well) have experienced the terrible feeling that comes when a pick suddenly flies off the thumb or fingers while picking.

I lessen the chances of that happening with the thumb pick by cutting parallel grooves in the inside of the pick with the sharp point of a pocketknife, as shown in the illustration:

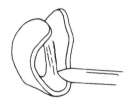

The raised edges grip to the inside of the thumb and make the pick less likely to slip off.

Most new thumb picks fit either too loosely or too tightly to suit me. I reshape them by using boiling water and a pair of pliers. The process is simple.

If you want to reshape your thumb pick so that it will better fit your thumb, hold the tip of the pick with pliers and dip the pick into rapidly boiling water for about one second of time. Then remove it from the water and widen or narrow the thumb slot for a few seconds to the shape you desire. The pick will remain in that approximate position. If you're still not happy with how it fits your thumb, repeat the process.

Finger Picks: I use the old-style National metal finger picks for two reasons: I like the gauge of the picks, and they have holes in them that help prevent the picks from slipping off while picking.

The metal is flexible and can easily be bent to the shape that fits best on your fingers. You can also bend the point of the pick if you don't like its angle.

Wear your finger picks and thumb pick as shown in the illustrations:

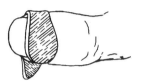

Shoulder Strap

Some musicians wear their instruments relatively high and others wear theirs relatively low. Adjust your shoulder strap so that your banjo will be positioned in your own comfort zone relative to your arms and hands when you are playing while standing.

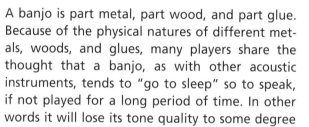

A banjo is part metal, part wood, and part glue. Because of the physical natures of different metals, woods, and glues, many players share the thought that a banjo, as with other acoustic instruments, tends to "go to sleep" so to speak, if not played for a long period of time. In other words it will lose its tone quality to some degree and not sound as lively as it once did.

Simply playing it a lot will restore that loss of tone quality.

If your banjo hasn't been played in a long time and your picking time is limited, one way of helping to "wake it up" is to set it in front of a stereo speaker while music is being played. The sound coming from the speaker will vibrate the banjo and help bring its tone quality back to life.

If you own a good quality used banjo, feel good knowing that it has been tried and tested.

If you own a good quality new banjo, feel good knowing that it will sound even better the more you play it.

Be good to your banjo, and your banjo will be good to you. With proper care and maintenance your banjo can last for generations to come.

2 SCRUGGS TUNERS, HOOKS & CAPOS

I once heard someone say, "Some boys never outgrow their toys." I suppose that statement holds true for me to a certain extent. I still play with a few things that were of interest to me as a child, and they are all related to the 5-string banjo—namely tuning pegs, fifth-string hooks, and capos.

SCRUGGS TUNERS

The idea for Scruggs tuners can be linked back to my childhood days. When we were kids, my brother Horace and I spent a lot of time playing music when we weren't going to school or working on the farm. Our jam sessions were often more like fun and games.

Sometimes while picking a fast song I would play a few long notes while twisting my tuning pegs to bend those notes. A banjo doesn't have a lot of sustaining power and I often noticed that Horace would play his guitar softer and lean in closer to better hear what I was playing.

The tempo would stay the same, but the drive in the picking would relax a bit during those tuning passages. And then we would again be bearing down and driving the music when I started back on my rolls. It was just the two of us picking, laughing, and having fun, but I believe I learned valuable lessons about band dynamics during those times.

As I grew older, playing around with the tuning pegs developed into ways to change tunings in mid-song while keeping the flow of a melody going. I would re-tune my second and third strings from G tuning into D tuning and vice versa. I would sometimes end up getting a string or two a little sharp or flat in pitch, which was always a bit aggravating to me. I began trying to think of ways to make the tuning more accurate.

By 1951, an idea kept floating around in the back of my mind of adding two tuners on my peghead with "stops" for the second and third strings. I liked the design I had in mind but I kept debating with myself over whether it would be wise to drill holes in my peghead, which had pearl inlay. Eventually, I wrote an instrumental that became the deciding factor in making me want to build the tuners.

"Earl's Breakdown" was the tune, and I recorded it on October 24, 1951 for a Flatt & Scruggs record. I played the tuning sections by ear, using my standard second-string peg to bend the notes.

We began receiving a lot of requests for that tune, so I built and installed the tuners that I had in mind in the summer of 1952. They were cam-type tuners and worked fairly accurately. The second-string tuner made the tuning sections of "Earl's Breakdown" much easier to play, to say the least.

The only drawback was thinking I had created an eyesore—the peghead looked way too busy to me with six pegs mounted. I covered the tuners on the front side of the peghead with a small tin box made from an old floor waxer, (which wasn't all that attractive either!)

Original Scruggs tuners covered with a tin box

Later in the year I wrote "Flint Hill Special." We recorded it on November 9, 1952, and I used the new tuners on both the second and the third strings.

I set the tuners so that the second-string B would stop on the note A when tuned down and then stop on B when tuned back up. The third-string G would lock on the note F# (F sharp) when tuned down and then lock back on G when tuned up. That combination made going from G tuning to D tuning much quicker and easier.

In the next few years I featured the tuners in "Foggy Mountain Chimes" and "Randy Lynn Rag." For "Randy Lynn Rag," I set the stops on the B string so that it would tune up to the note C and then lock on B when tuned back down.

Many other cam-type tuners have been made over the years based upon my invention. They are often referred to as "Scruggs tuners" or "D tuners." If you want to make your own cam tuners, it isn't a very difficult job *(see Chapter 14)*, but I encourage you to think twice before drilling through your peghead because there is the risk of damaging the finish and inlay work.

I haven't used cam tuners in many years. There are now several types of tuners known as mechanical D tuners, which I use that are more versatile and more accurate than cam tuners.

Mechanical D tuners are self-contained, with both the tuning peg and the tuner mechanism for each string combined in a single housing. They can easily be installed in the standard pegholes, which eliminates the risks of drilling additional holes in the peghead. The tuners can also be used for the first and fourth strings.

An example of mechanical D tuners

BANJO CAPOS

My first capo was one that I made out of a pencil and two rubber bands wrapped tightly around both ends of the pencil.

I soon learned that the capo had a serious design flaw—rubber bands can snap suddenly when under stress, and pencils can go flying through the air. I decided that a cotton string tied tightly around both ends of the pencil was a much more reliable (and safer) way to go!

There were a couple of commercial banjo capos being sold when I was growing up, but in truth they weren't all that much better than my pencil and cotton string contraption.

In 1945 when I was working in a cotton mill in Shelby, North Carolina, I designed and built a banjo capo that I used until 1971. I had access to the mill's machine shop, and in my spare time I made the capo which is seen resting on the peghead in the photograph on the previous page.

It was some time after I settled in Nashville, Tennessee that it occured to me to market capos made from that 1945 design, but I could find no machine shops in the area that had the equipment needed to make them.

I mentioned that problem to a friend of mine, the late Jim Faulkner, who lived in Ohio. He told me of a machine shop near his home that had the machinery required to make the capo.

Jim took a scale drawing of my capo to the machine shop, and they began manufacturing the capos in 1971. Plastic tubing was added to the original 1945 design. They were sold through a mail order company that my wife, Louise, and I had founded in the mid-1960s and were called "Scruggs-Ruben" capos.

A good capo provides a quick and easy way to "re-tune" the four long strings without having to use the tuning pegs.

If a song you want to sing plays well in the key of G while in G tuning but the higher key of A is better suited for your voice, you can capo at the second fret and then raise the fifth-string G to A. You can then play the song as if you were in the key G even though you'll be picking and singing in the key of A.

When I say to capo "at the second fret," I'm referring to the fingerboard area between the first and second frets and not upon the second fret itself. Position your capo close to the second fret.

Once you've capoed at the second fret you'll want to raise the fifth-string G to A, which is one whole step. You could try raising it by tuning it up in pitch with the fifth-string peg, but doing so puts a great deal of tension on the short fifth string. If you attempt to tune it up more than one half step, the string is likely to break.

That problem can easily be solved by use of a small L-shaped spike, or "hook" as I call it, inserted into the fingerboard at the seventh fret. When the fifth-string G is hooked there, it sounds the note A when played unfretted.

FIFTH-STRING HOOKS

When we were kids, my brother Horace liked playing and singing certain songs in the key of A on his guitar. That meant I had to get out my pencil and cotton string to capo at the second fret if I wanted to pick along as if I was still playing in the key of G.

The downside to moving to the key of A was the good chance that my fifth string would break if I tried to tune it up the equivalent of two frets—and I much preferred playing on all five strings as opposed to only the four long strings.

The problem with tuning the fifth-string G up to the note A inspired the idea for the fifth-string hook when I was ten or eleven years old. It occurred to me that the fifth string could, in a sense, be capoed.

My childhood invention of the fifth-string hook was about as simple as it gets. I made my first hook out of a hairpin that I bent at the sharp point in a right angle ( ). I cut it short to the length needed.

I practiced gently tapping the hairpin into a scrap piece of wood before installing it on my banjo. When I was confident I could install it correctly, I tapped it into my fingerboard at the seventh fret.

Today's fifth-string hooks, or spikes, are made out of metal or bone. The right angle at the top of the hook should be parallel to the fret, and the hook's slot can face down toward the long strings or face up toward the fifth string. (My hooks face down.)

The top of the hook should stick out above the fingerboard with just enough room to easily slide the fifth string under it so that it will catch and hold in place.

My fingerboard has two hooks. One is at the seventh fret for songs I play in the key of A and for songs played in the key of D while in G tuning. I also use it when I'm playing in D minor tuning.

The other hook is at the ninth fret for songs I play in the key of B while capoed at the fourth fret. For songs in the key of B♭ (B flat), I can hook my fifth string at the seventh fret and then tune it up one half step to B♭ or I can hook it at the ninth fret and then tune the string down one half step to B♭.

Small screws can also be used instead of hooks, as shown in the illustration:

I prefer hooks because I find them easier to work with and they're less noticeable to the eye than screws. HO scale model train railroad spikes are often used as fifth-string hooks.

Adding a hook to the fingerboard is a simple job. I recommend pre-drilling a hole slightly smaller than the spike's width at the fret where you want the hook to be on your fingerboard. Be careful not to drill all the way through the neck!

Drill the hole under the fifth string. Be sure to drill straight down, and not at an angle. If you want a hook at the seventh fret, for example, install the hook closer to the seventh fret than the sixth fret as shown with the screw in the previous illustration (3/8-inch from the seventh fret is a good distance).

HO scale model railroad spikes can be found in many hobby stores. If you want to use them as hooks, practice gently tapping a few into their pre-drilled holes on a scrap piece of wood before trying it on your fingerboard. Brace the neck and be careful not to strike your fingerboard when you're tapping the hook.

If you are hesitant to install the hooks yourself, get someone experienced with such work to do it for you.

A variety of fifth-string capos are also on the market as an alternative to hooks. As with other parts of a banjo, the choice between using a fifth-string capo or using fifth-string hooks usually boils down to personal preferences.

Below is a graph that shows where to position your capo for certain keys when playing in G tuning. The second and third vertical rows show the fingering positions for two chords often played along with the root chord shown in the first vertical row.

If you capo at the first fret for the key of G♯, simply tune your fifth-string G up one half step to G♯.

Always raise your fifth string slowly and gradually when tuning it up in pitch. Sudden upward twists on the fifth-string peg can break the string.

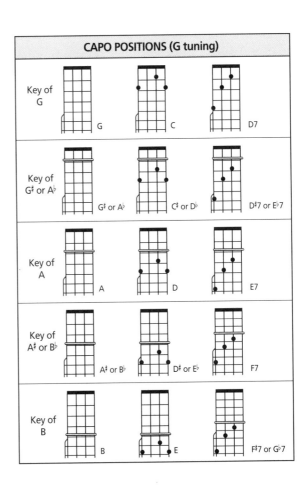

3 TUNING THE BANJO

G tuning is the most commonly used tuning for Scruggs-style banjo. When the unfretted strings are played together in G tuning, a G chord is sounded. The illustration below shows the notes on a piano that correspond to the banjo's open string notes in G tuning. When writing out tunings, many banjo players name the notes from the fifth to the first strings, using a lower case letter for the short fifth-string note and capital letters for the four long-string notes. If you have the audio that corresponds to this book, listen to Track 2 to tune to my banjo:

G Tuning (gDGBD)

TRACK 2

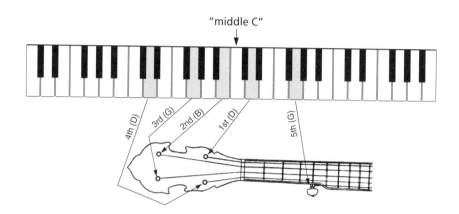

If you don't have the track or a piano to tune to, a good pitch pipe or a G or C harmonica can be handy to have. Exhaling breath while playing a chord on a G harmonica results in a G chord. Inhaling breath while playing a chord on a C harmonica results in a G chord as well. Better yet, a small battery-powered electronic tuner is great to have. Electronic tuners are sold at most music stores. They enable you to "see" if a note is in tune.

If nothing is available to tune to, you can get your banjo in tune with itself by using the following method:

1) Tune the fourth string by ear to the approximate note of D. (And let's assume the string is actually sounding the note D when played open, or unfretted.)

2) Fret the fourth string D at the fifth fret and tune the open third string to match the pitch of the fretted fourth string, which is the note G.

3) Fret the third string at the fourth fret and tune the open second string to match the pitch of the fretted third string, which is the note B.

4) Fret the second string at the third fret and tune the open first string to match the pitch of the fretted second string, which is the note D.

5) Fret the first string at the fifth fret and tune the fifth string to the fretted first string, which is the note G. The fifth-string G is an octave higher than the third-string G.

The late David "Uncle Dave" Macon used to show his audiences how he was taught to tune the four long strings on his banjo to G tuning by singing the melody of a song called "Children, Children, Come Home:"

Strings:	1	2	1	2	3	4
	Chil - dren,		Chil -dren,		come	home (or)

Notes:	D	B	D	B	G	D
	Chil - dren,		Chil -dren,		come	home

You can also play the melody to bugle calls such as "Reveille" ("Oh, You Can't Get Them Up"), and "Taps" ("Day Is Done") on the four unfretted long strings when in G tuning, starting on the fourth-string D.

TUNING TO A GUITAR

1) To get into G tuning by tuning to a guitar that is in standard tuning, tune your open second, third, and fourth strings to the same pitch as the open second, third, and fourth strings of the guitar.

2) You can then use the previously mentioned method to tune your first and fifth strings.

C Tuning (gCGBD)

I like how the fourth string sounds a little more lonesome when tuned down for certain songs played in C tuning, such as "Home Sweet Home" and "Old Folks." C tuning differs from G tuning only in that the fourth-string D is tuned down a whole step to the note C. When the fourth-string C is fretted at the seventh fret, it will match the same pitch as the open third-string G.

D Tuning (f♯DF♯AD)

When I was ten years old, I was playing a tune called "Reuben" in D tuning when I noticed that my right hand was picking with three fingers. Up until that time since the age of four, I had played a two-finger style using my thumb and index finger. I was thrilled when I noticed that my right-hand middle finger was in the mix of the rolls because I had wanted for a long time to pick three-finger style. To get into D tuning:

1) The fourth string is tuned to the same D note as in G tuning.

2) Fret the fourth string at the fourth fret and match the third open string to it, which is the note F♯.

3) Fret the third string at the third fret and match the second open string to it, which is the note A.

4) Fret the second string at the fifth fret and match the first open string to it, which is the note D.

5) I tune my fifth string down to F♯ in order to match it to the first string fretted at the fourth fret. You can also match it to the first string fretted at the seventh fret, which is the note A.

If you raise the fifth string to A, I recommend hooking the string at the seventh fret or using a fifth-string capo at the seventh fret as described in the "Fifth-String Hooks" section of the previous chapter.

D Minor Tuning (aDFAD)

I use D minor tuning for "Nashville Blues," which is in the Song Section. The second and third strings are lowered a whole step, or the equivalent of two frets below their G tuning pitch to the notes A and F, respectively:

1) The fourth string is tuned to the same D note as in G tuning.

2) Fret the fourth string at the third fret and match the third open string to that pitch, which is the note F.

3) Fret the third string at the fourth fret and match the second open string to it, which is the note A.

4) Fret the second string at the fifth fret and match the first open string to it, which is the note D.

5) Fret the first string at the seventh fret and match the open fifth string to it, which is the note A.

Again, it's best to use a fifth-string hook or a fifth-string capo at the seventh fret when raising the fifth-string G to A.

G Modal Tuning (gDGCD)

G modal tuning differs from G tuning only in that the second-string B is raised one half step to the note C. When in G tuning, fret the third string at the fifth fret and tune the open second string to that same pitch, which is the note C.

〜

There are other tunings that can be used on the 5-string banjo. The tunings described in this chapter are the ones found in the "Song Section" chapter of this book. Learn to play in different tunings in order to add to the variety and excitement of your picking.

4 CHORDS

There are many different kinds of chords. Major, minor, sixth, and seventh chords are used in my music, with major chords by far the most often played. By learning to make three *full*, or *closed*, major chord positions while in G tuning, you can play all the major chords three different ways by progressing up the banjo's neck. When making a full chord, all four of the long strings are fretted. An *open* chord position is a chord made with one or more of the long strings unfretted. Fretted open chords are made at the low fret positions.

Chord changes occur quickly when backing up singers and other instrumental leads in up-tempo songs. Drill the chord fingerings into your mind until you can go from one chord position to another with no hesitation.

Below are the three closed fingerings for major chords used in the chart on the following page. In the fingering boxes, "I" = Index finger, "M" = Middle finger, "R" = Ring finger, and "L" = Little finger. From left to right, the four vertical lines represent the fourth, third, second, and first strings. The horizontal lines represent frets.

When making the chord positions shown in the second and third boxes below, only one string should be touched by each of your fretting fingers. Your fingertips should come down perpendicular to the strings. Press the strings down with enough pressure against the fingerboard so that each string will ring clearly when plucked. Don't press down too hard; doing so will make the string's note sharp in pitch. Fret the strings in the fingerboard areas in front of the frets—not directly on the frets or directly between two frets. For example, when fretting a string at the third fret, the fretting finger should be closer to the third fret than the second fret.

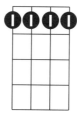 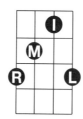 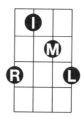

The first fingering position shown in the box above shows the index finger fretting all four long strings by making a *barre* chord. ("Barre" is pronounced as "bar" and is often spelled as "bar.") When making a barred chord, think of your index finger serving as a capo of sorts and barre across the strings at the fret with the bottom of your index finger. When making a sixth or seventh chord out of a barred position, simply reach up with your little finger to fret the added note.

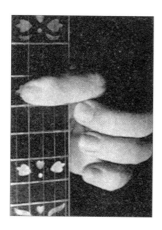

Barred

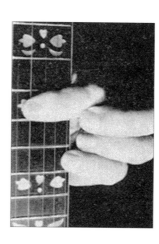

6th

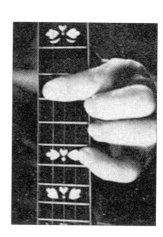

7th

Notice in the following chart that when the closed chord positions are held, the name of the major chord changes as you move up the neck. Each successive fret position raises the chord by one half step. In other words, as you advance one fret up, each note you play in a chord goes up one half step in pitch.

Try forming each of the chord positions starting at the first fret. Brush down on the four long strings with your right thumb as you move up the neck. Avoid striking the open fifth string as you focus on the chord fingerings for the four long strings.

The thick, black line across the top of several chord diagrams indicates the nut, and these diagrams therefore begin with the first fret. When the nut is not present in a diagram, a number indicates what the first fret is.

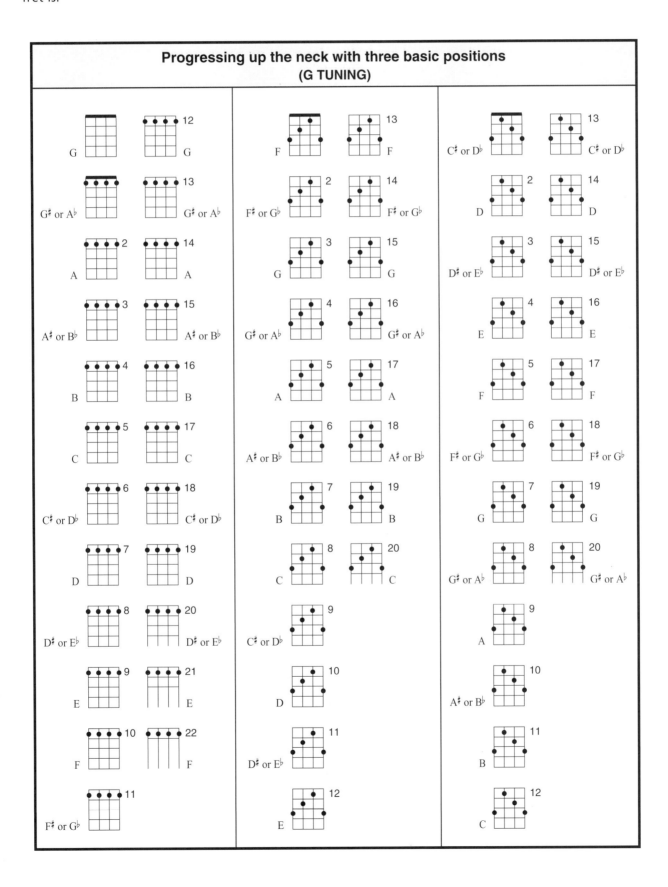

SCALES

To better understand chords, it's helpful to know a few things about musical scales. A chord is a combination of at least three notes. Not just any three notes constitute a chord. A basic major or minor chord is a *triad* consisting of the *first, third,* and *fifth*, which are the 1st, 3rd, and 5th notes, or intervals, of a major scale. The 1st of a chord is also called the *tonic* or *root* note. An illustration of a few notes on a piano keyboard is a good visual tool to learn the difference between whole steps and half steps that exist between certain notes in major and minor scales.

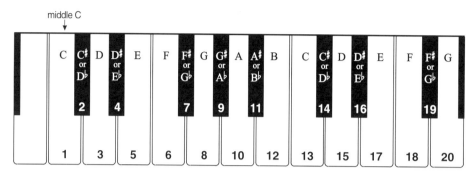

There are twelve different notes in a *chromatic* scale. Starting at middle C, count the piano keys up to the next C note, which is one octave higher, noting that it is twelve half steps up from middle C.

There are seven different notes on the numbered white keys of the keyboard named after the first seven letters of the alphabet, A, B, C, D, E, F, and G. Those notes are called *natural* (♮) notes, meaning they are neither *sharp* (♯) nor *flat* (♭) notes. The notes of the five numbered black piano keys are all referred to as sharp or flat notes. Each black key is positioned between two white keys that are a whole step apart from one another. White keys that do not have a black key positioned between them are a half step apart in pitch.

Major Scales: There are seven different notes in a major scale. For the sake of simplicity, let's first focus on the major scale in the key of C, which has no sharps or flats in its *key signature*. The key signature is the presence or absence of sharps or flats that follows the time signature, (which is explained in Chapter 6) on a standard sheet music staff. The notes in the C major scale are C–D–E–F–G–A–B (and the octave C). (The "eighth" note of a major scale is simply the root of the scale an octave higher.) Going from notes 1–2 (C–D), 2–3 (D–E), 4–5 (F–G), 5–6 (G–A), and 6–7 (A–B) are all whole steps. Going from notes 3–4 (E–F) and 7–8 (B–C) are half steps. The same holds true for any major scale key. The 1st, 3rd, and 5th of a C major chord are C, E, and G.

The key signature for G major has one sharp, F♯. The notes in that scale are G–A–B–C–D–E–F♯–(G) with half steps going from notes 3–4 (B–C) and 7–8 (F♯–G). The 1st, 3rd, and 5th of a G major chord are G, B, and D.

The key of D major has two sharps, F♯ and C♯. The notes in that scale are D–E–F♯–G–A–B–C♯–(D) with half steps going from F♯ to G and C♯ to D. The 1st, 3rd, and 5th of a D major chord are D, F♯, and A.

I've described the scales for the keys of G, C, and D and the composition of the major chords G, C, and D for two reasons: 1) The three primary tunings for Scruggs-style banjo are G, C, and D. 2) G tuning is the most often used tuning in my music, and the three most used chords when playing in the key of G major are the major chords G, C, and D.

Notice in the G scale that C is the 4th note in the scale, and D is the 5th note in that scale. *The three most often used chords in any major key are the major chords built upon the 1st, 4th, and 5th notes of the key's scale.* So when you're playing in the key of C, for example, expect to play a lot of C, F, and G chords.

Minor Scales: There are also seven different notes in a minor scale. There are three kinds of minor scales: natural, melodic, and harmonic—only natural minor scales are discussed here.

Let's first focus on the natural A minor scale, which has no sharps or flats in its key signature. The notes in that scale are A–B–C–D–E–F–G–(A). Unlike major scales, the two half steps that occur in any natural minor scale are between the notes 2 and 3 and the notes 5 and 6.

The key of A minor is called the *relative minor* to the key of C major because both keys share the same key signature. To determine the relative minor of any major key, count up to the 6th note of the major scale. E is the 6th note in the G major scale, so E minor is the relative minor to G major. Since the key of E minor shares the same key signature as G major, the eight notes in the E minor scale are E–F♯–G–A–B–C–D–(E) with half steps going from notes 2–3 (F♯–G) and 5–6 (B–C).

THE FIFTH STRING

The fifth string is known as a *drone string* because it is rarely fretted in Scruggs-style banjo, thereby sounding only the note to which it's tuned. It is also sometimes called the *thumb string* because the index and middle fingers rarely pick it.

When you are learning to pick lead and play backup, keep in mind that the open fifth string should not be played along with all chords because it clashes with the harmony of many chords.

The open fifth string in G tuning works harmoniously in the chords G, E♭, C, G minor, E minor, and C minor, as it is either the 1st, 3rd, or 5th in those chords. It can also serve as a 7th to an A chord and as a 6th to a B♭ chord.

Let's now summarize what makes up the four different kinds of chords seen in the tablatures of this book:

1. **Major Chord:** A major chord consists of the 1st, 3rd, and 5th notes of the major scale for which the chord is named.

   In the example below, the 1st, 3rd, and 5th of the G chord are the notes G, B, and D.

   Major chords are commonly called whatever the 1st, or root note, happens to be. In other words, it isn't necessary to say "G major." Simply saying "G" is understood to mean G major.

   Major chords, as with all kinds of chords, can have more than three notes in the chord. If the notes added to a G chord, for example, are octaves to the 1st, 3rd, and 5th, it is still called a G chord.

G Major Chord

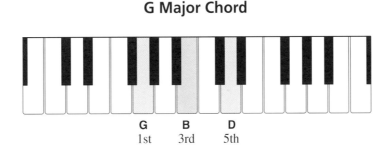

2. **Minor Chord:** A minor chord consists of the 1st, 3rd, and 5th notes of the minor scale for which the chord is named.

   In the example below, the 1st, 3rd, and 5th of the G minor chord are the notes G, B♭, and D.

   As mentioned before, E minor is the relative minor of G major since those two keys share the same key signature. G minor is called the *parallel minor* of G major because their scales both start on the note G.

   An easy way to think of minor chords is to know that they differ from their parallel major chords only in that the 3rd of a minor chord is one half step lower than the 3rd of its parallel major chord.

   Minor chords are often abbreviated with the letter "m" or a minus sign (-). For example, G minor can be written as Gm or G -.

G Minor Chord

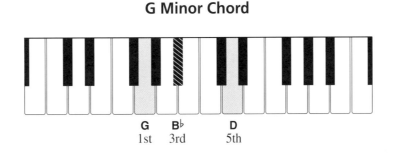

3. Sixth Chord: A sixth chord differs from a major chord in that the 6th note of the scale is added to the major chord. "Sixth" is commonly shortened to "6." A G sixth chord is often written as G6.

G Sixth Chord

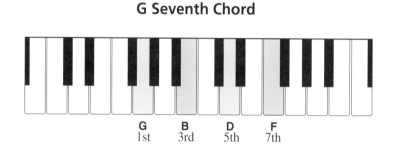

4. Seventh Chord: A seventh chord differs from a major chord in that the flatted, or flattened, 7th note of the scale is added to the chord. F# is the seventh note in a G scale; F is the flatted 7th. "Seventh" is commonly shortened to "7." A G seventh chord is often written as G7.

G Seventh Chord

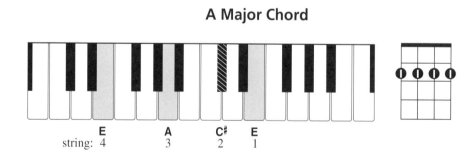

Now apply what you know about chords to the banjo. In G tuning, a barred A major chord made on the four long strings at the second fret of a banjo is compared below to an A chord played on a piano. The key of A has three sharps in its key signature, and the notes in that scale are A–B–C#–D–E–F#–G#–(A). The 1st of a chord is not always the lowest sounding note in a chord. Sometimes the voicing of a chord has the 3rd or the 5th of the chord as the lowest sounding note. A lower E note is shaded on the keyboard since that note is played on the fourth string of the banjo at the second fret. Make the barred A major chord with your index finger and make each note of the chord ring clearly as you brush down on the four long strings with your right thumb:

A Major Chord

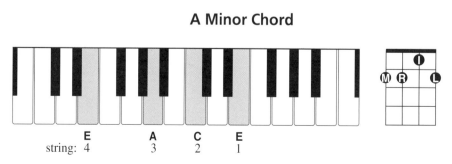

The following fingering box shows one of three ways seen in this chapter to fret a full, or closed, minor chord. Form the chord shape and again brush down on the four long strings while making each note ring clearly:

A Minor Chord

Play an A6 chord by barring at the second fret and fretting the first string at the fourth fret with your little finger. Fretting the first string at the fourth fret sounds the note F♯, which is the 6th note in the A major scale:

A Sixth Chord

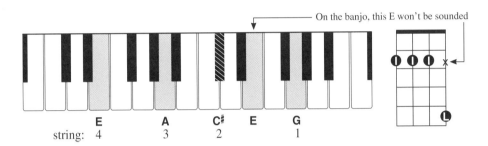

string: E   A   C♯   E   F♯
         4   3   2   1

Now make an A7 chord by barring at the second fret and fretting the first string at the fifth fret with your little finger. When played, the fretted first string will sound the note G, which is the flatted 7th in the key of A:

A Seventh Chord

string: E   A   C♯   E   G
         4   3   2   1

There are many other kinds of chords not found in the tablatures of this book such as suspended, diminished, and augmented chords. At some point in time you might want to study other types of chords, but for now stay focused on learning the major, minor, sixth, and seventh chords that are used in this book.

As mentioned earlier, the three most commonly used chords in major keys are the three major chords built upon the 1st, 4th, and 5th notes in any particular key's scale. The most commonly used minor chord in songs played in a major key is the relative minor of that key. For the key of G major, those four chords are G, C, D, and E minor.

In G tuning, practice making all of those chords common to the key of G and then practice changing from one chord to another until you can make those chord changes smoothly. Learn both the full chord positions and the opened chord positions at the lower frets. Then add other chords that are used fairly often in the key of G such as A, A7, and A minor.

G tuning is not limited to the key of G or using a capo when playing in certain other keys. When you are comfortable making those G related chords and chord changes, practice changing chords in other keys as well, such as D, E, and F while in G tuning.

Below in the first, second, and third diagrams are three ways of fretting closed minor chords at the first fret. As with the closed major chord positions in the chart on page 25, moving the three closed minor chord positions up one fret raises the chord name one half step. A simple way of making an opened E minor chord at the second fret is shown in the fourth diagram:

A Minor
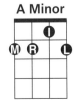

C♯ Minor
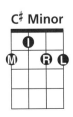

F Minor
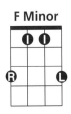

E Minor
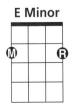

G, C, D, F, and A are often-used major chords in the music I play when in G tuning. The following chart includes the three full major chord fingerings shown on page 24. The unfretted open G chord and an open C chord position at the first fret are also shown.

The first D chord shown with the fingering starting at the second fret can also be made with the first or fourth string unfretted for an open D chord.

Learn and feel comfortable with making all the fingering positions. When playing rhythmic chords as backup to others, you normally don't want to be jumping all over the neck when making chord changes. For example, if you're playing a G chord at the seventh fret, practice going to the C chord made at the nearby eighth fret.

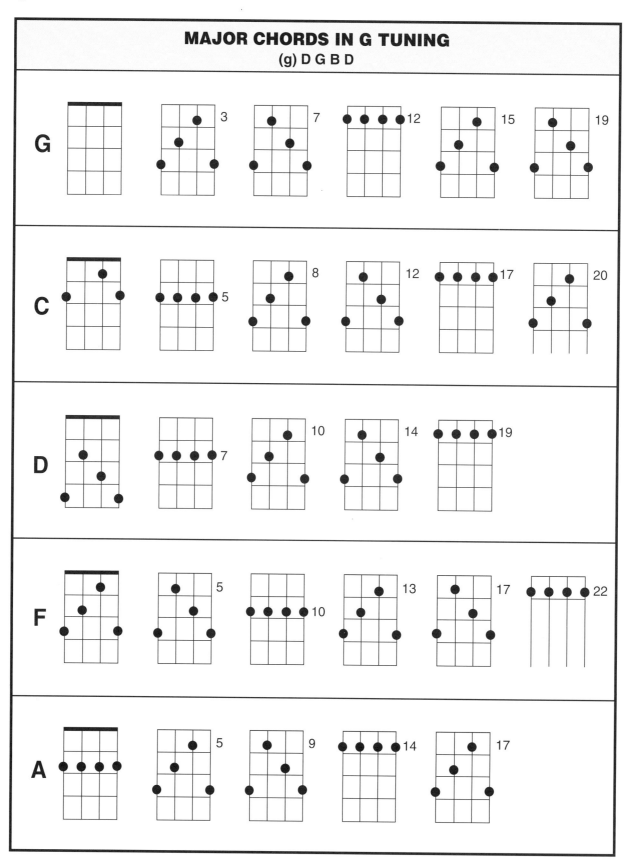

MAJOR CHORDS IN G TUNING
(g) D G B D

THE NASHVILLE NUMBER SYSTEM

It isn't necessary that you learn what has become known as the "Nashville number system" for the purposes of this book—I've included this section only for those of you who might find it of interest. Nashville studio musicians devised the number system in the late 1950s, and it evolved somewhat over the years.

Studio musicians in Nashville are also known as "session players." They are professional musicians that perform most of the music recorded there. More often than not, those session players arrive at a recording studio ready to play songs that they have never before heard.

The record producer or recording artist will play the song about to be recorded for the musicians to hear and will often give them a chord chart that guides the players through the chord changes in the song. If the chord chart has not been prepared in advance, the musicians will write their own charts as the song is being played for them. The chord charts are usually in the form of the (Nashville) number system.

Instead of the chords' letter names, numbers are used to show the musicians what chords are played during every measure of music about to be recorded.

Let's look at the G major scale as an example to show how the number system works. The first seven notes in that scale are G–A–B–C–D–E–F$\sharp$. A major chord can be built upon each of those notes. In the number system, those seven major chords, G, A, B, C, D, E, and F$\sharp$, are called 1, 2, 3, 4, 5, 6, and 7, respectively. The 7 chord (F$\sharp$ in this example) is rarely used. The more often-used seven-flat chord (F in this example) is written as 7b. As other examples in the key of G, E minor is written as 6-, or 6m, and the chord A7 is written as 2^7.

The instrumental "Flint Hill Special," which I play in the key of G, has what I call "verse" sections that are sixteen measures long. It also has eight-measure tuning sections in it where I use my second-string and third-string tuners to bend certain notes. A chord chart showing the names of those chords in those sections is written as:

(Verse section):	G	G	C	C		G	G	D	D
	G	G	C	C		G	D	G	G
(Tuning section):	D	D	D	G		D	D	D	G

A chord chart using the number system for those two sections is written as:

(Verse section):	1	1	4	4		1	1	5	5
	1	1	4	4		1	5	1	1
(Tuning section):	5	5	5	1		5	5	5	1

The advantage of the number system over chord charts using the names of chords is that a numbered chart works for any key in which a song may be played.

Sometimes a recording artist will go into a recording session thinking, for example, that the key of C is the key in which he or she will sing a certain song. If the artist suddenly decides that the key of C is too high or too low for his or her voice and chooses another key, the musicians don't have to waste expensive studio time by writing out a new chart using the new chord names. Instead, they think of their chart numbers as representing the chords in the new key.

For example, if when in the key of C the first four chords of a numbered chart are 1–4–5–1, those numbers represent the chords C–F–G–C. If the key of C were to be changed to the key of D, those numbers would then represent the chords D–G–A–D. Most Nashville session players call that 1–4–5–1 chord sequence "fourteen fifty-one." As another example of that verbal shorthand, the chord sequence 1–1–4–4 is called "eleven forty-four."

Sometimes measures, or bars, in a song have more than one chord. They are called "split bars." If, for example, a measure is equally divided with a 1 and a 5 chord, that measure is referred to as "one split five" and written as 15 or 1/5 in the number system.

Other musical symbols and terms described in the next chapter, "How to Read Tablature," are also used in the number system for arrangement purposes.

 # HOW TO READ TABLATURE

You don't have to know how to read music in order to learn how to play the material in the Song Section since all the tunes are written in a simpler form of music notation called *tablature*. Standard sheet music and tablature do have certain things in common, such as *measures*, *time signatures*, and *timing indicators*, which are explained in the next chapter, "Timing."

Tablature, also known as *tab*, is a system of musical notation that uses letters, numbers, and symbols to indicate left-hand fingerings and fingering techniques. And with banjo tablature the work of the right hand is also shown. Tablature can be written in different formats. This chapter describes the format used in this book.

A standard sheet music staff has five horizontal lines divided into measures where individual notes are placed upon, above, under, and between certain staff lines depending on the note played. Five-string banjo tablature also has a staff of five lines divided into measures, but those lines represent the five strings. From top to bottom, the lines represent the first, second, third, fourth, and fifth strings respectively. A number placed upon a line indicates the fret at which that string is to be fretted by the left hand. A zero indicates the string is not fretted, but played open. An "x" indicates a picked string is only dampened by a fretting finger and not fretted.

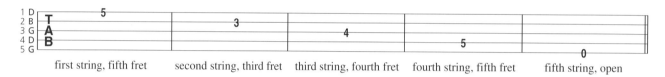

first string, fifth fret	second string, third fret	third string, fourth fret	fourth string, fifth fret	fifth string, open

An open C chord in G tuning is shown in the chord chart on page 30. The left index finger frets the second string, the middle finger frets the fourth string, and the ring finger frets the first string. When played, the resulting notes from the first string to the fifth string are E–C–G–E–G. Tablature shows it as:

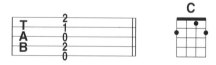

The work of the right hand is shown below the staff lines. Letters placed below the fret numbers on the staff lines tell you which fingers of the right hand are picking the strings:

T = thumb   I = index finger   M = middle finger

Let's take a look at the two-measure tablature below written for banjo in G tuning. The vertical lines directly below the fret numbers are timing indicators that tell you those notes are each *quarter* notes, so each of those notes have equal time value. The tab shows one possible way of playing a D major scale that starts on the fourth string while picking each note with the thumb of the right hand.

The fretted notes could be fretted with any of your left-hand fingers, but when picking, always look for a quick and easy way to fret the strings. One way to play the scale is by fretting the second-fret notes E, A, and C♯ with your index finger, the fourth-fret notes F♯ and B with your ring finger, and the third fret D note with your middle finger. By fretting the strings as described in this particular example, your left hand will stay in one area around the neck and fingerboard.

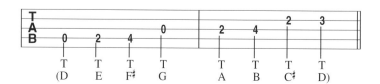

Sometimes the right hand picks more than one string at the same time. When that occurs, the right-hand letters "T," "I," and "M" are stacked under the fret numbers of the strings being picked. The thumb always picks downward on the strings, and the index and middle fingers always pick upward on the strings. When the thumb and the middle and/or index fingers pick at the same time, that action is called a *pinch*. When just the middle and index fingers pick strings at the same time, that action is called a *clench*, or a *spank*. Four examples are shown in the tablature below.

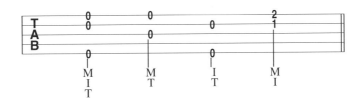

The right-hand thumb occasionally performs a technique called a *thumb brush*. A brush involves dragging the thumb down across all or several strings in one rapid motion. An example of a brush is shown as:

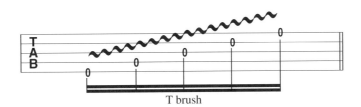

T brush

Additional information is sometimes placed above the fret numbers telling you that the left-hand fingers are doing more than merely fretting the strings. How to play left-hand techniques, such as *hammer-ons, slides, chokes, pull-offs,* and *push-offs,* is explained in Chapter 9.

Examples of how hammer-ons and pull-offs or push-offs are written in tablature are shown below:

There are two ways of sliding indicated by a diagonal line. You can slide up or down. An arc tying together two fret numbers indicates that only the first note is plucked. If a slide's fret numbers are not tied by an arc, then both notes are plucked and "T," "I," or "M" is placed below the second note of the slide.

Choking is a technique that bends the pitch of a note upward. The change in pitch can vary. The two kinds of chokes seen most often in this book are half-step chokes and whole-step chokes:

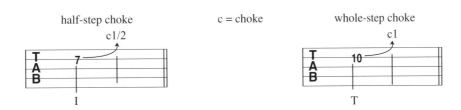

If a choked note is sustained and then lowered to its original pitch, a downward arrow shows at what point in musical time that note is lowered:

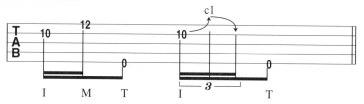

When tuners are used, upward and downward arrows indicate a string being tuned up or tuned down. The word "full" placed over an arrow means the note changes a whole step. "1/2" over an arrow indicates the note changes a half step in pitch.

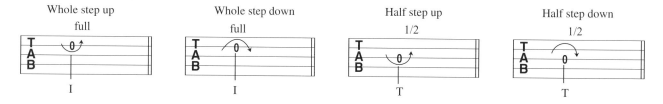

Chord names are placed above certain measures in the Song Section that show the chord changes an accompanist would play while backing up the banjo. If, for example, a chord is to be played for two measures, the chord name is placed above the first of those two measures as shown in the six-measure tab below:

G	C	D	G
TAB	TAB	TAB	TAB	TAB	TAB

The vertical lines that divide a staff into measures of time are called *bar lines.*

A double bar is placed at the end of a song and is also used to signify sections within a song. For example, the second solo in the Flatt & Scruggs 1949 recording of "Foggy Mountain Breakdown" has four sixteen-measure sections. A double bar is placed at the end of each of those sections: (▱)

Other standard music symbols and terms are used in a song's tablature that direct you to other sections within that song.

Two dots in front of a double bar (▱) tell you to go back to the beginning of the song or to the previous double bar that has two dots following that first double bar (▱).

Sometimes a repeated section of music has a first and second ending. When that occurs, play the first ending only the first time you play the section and play the second ending only the second time the section is played:

Another type of repeat involves what is known as a *coda* and *the sign.* When you are playing a section of music and see "D.S. al Coda" written over a measure, complete that measure and then go back to the sign (𝄋) and play from there until you finish the measure labeled "*To Coda* ⊕." From there, skip to the section labeled "⊕ Coda."

𝄋   *To Coda* ⊕   **D.S. al Coda**   ⊕ *Coda*

Sometimes a song's tempo will gradually slow down, particularly during the ending of a song as happens in "Flint Hill Special." When that happens, the slowing down of the tempo is called a *ritard*. The abbreviation for ritard is *rit*.

The symbol (⁒) placed within a measure tells you to repeat the previous measure. If there is a number over it, the number tells you to repeat the previous measure that number of times.

The symbol (¢) indicates *cut time*. In cut time, each note's time value is to be cut in half. In other words, the music is to be played twice as fast as it is written. The time values of different kinds of notes are taught in the following chapter, "Timing."

A *fermata* lets you know that the tempo of a tune stops. The symbol for a fermata (𝄐) is sometimes called the "bird's eye." If the bird's eye is over the last note or last chord of a tune, the note or chord sustains after being played.

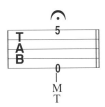

An advantage of tablature over standard sheet music notation is that tablature shows not only the note to be played, but how and where on the fingerboard the note is to be played. To illustrate this point, one D sixteenth note written in standard music form appears as:

There are many different ways that D note can be played on the banjo. You can see twenty-six possibilities in the illustration below where the arrows point to the same D note that would be written on standard sheet music staff lines.

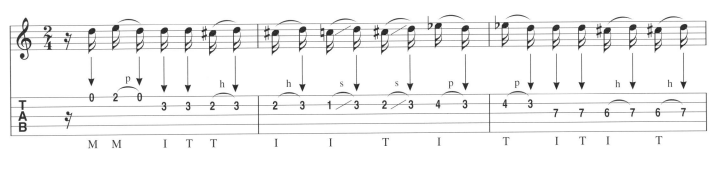

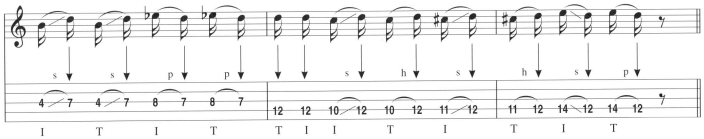

This diagram shows the names of notes sounded when the strings are fretted up the neck while in G tuning.

The notes seen on the standard sheet music staff lines correspond to the open and fretted notes on the tab lines directly below those sheet music lines. *Ledger lines* are the small horizontal lines placed above standard music staff lines as the notes get higher in pitch.

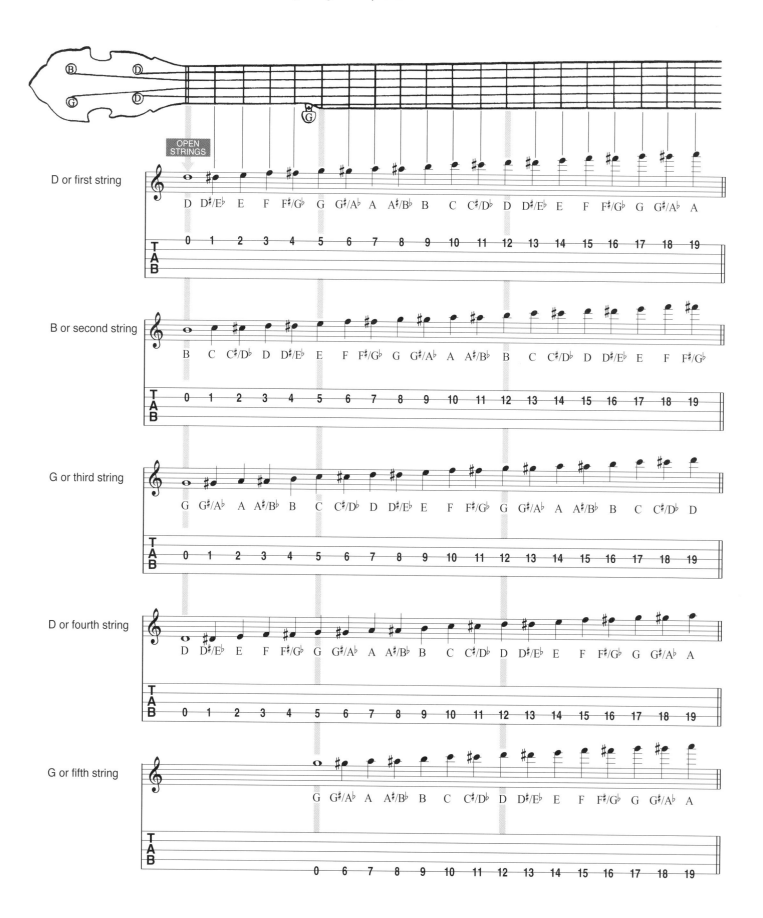

TIMING

When we were growing up, my oldest brother, Junie, and oldest sister, Eula Mae, were real sticklers when it came to keeping time. Sometimes they would begin playing a tune together on the front porch and then while still playing, walk in opposite directions around the house until they met in the back yard. If they were still playing the tune together, they would be satisfied their timing was perfect. To this day, I still don't know how in the world they could tell whose timing was off if they came around the house out of sync with one another!

Timing is indeed very important, especially when playing with other musicians. If a band is playing a song and a member of the band is playing too slow, or behind the beat, that member is said to be "dragging." If another member is playing too fast, or ahead of the beat, that member is said to be "rushing." Neither dragging nor rushing is good. The ideal is to play "in the pocket."

Playing in the pocket does not mean to play with machine-like precision—the late Waylon Jennings used to say of his recordings, "If you get it perfect, nobody's going to like it." I believe Waylon knew what he was talking about. Timing in a band situation is all about "feel" and musical interaction.

Playing methodically on the beat can become boring and predictable to the ear. Sometimes it's better to add excitement to the music by playing "on top of the beat," which will *drive* the music. Sometimes it's better to relax the music's intensity by *laying back*, which involves playing on the "backside" of the beat. Whether driving the music or laying back, always be aware of the pulse of the beat and stay within it.

Tablature staff lines are divided into *measures* by vertical lines, which are called *bar lines*. Measures are also known as *bars*. Each measure is equal in time value unless the *time signature* changes within a song.

There are two numbers to be aware of in a time signature, which is shown before the first measure of tablature notation. The upper number tells how many beats there are to a measure. The lower number tells what kind of note equals one beat of music. A *quarter note* equals one beat in the tablatures of this book. A *whole note* (𝅝) is the longest note in a 4/4 measure and is equal to four beats of music. Most of the tunes in this book have two beats per measure, so the time signature to be most concerned about at this point is called "two-four" and written as 2/4 with the 2 placed over the 4 on the tablature's first staff:

A *timing indicator* is a symbol placed below a left-hand fret number that tells you the time value of that note. A vertical line known as a *stem* is the timing indicator that tells you the note is a quarter note and that the time value for the note is equal to one beat of music. The following tablature consists of two measures with two quarter notes in each of those measures:

The longest note in a 2/4 measure is a *half note* and is equal to two beats. Two quarter notes are tied together to represent a half note. Since the two notes are tied together, only the first note is picked:

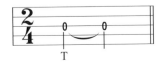

An *eighth note* has the time value of one half-beat of music. A timing indicator called a *flag* is attached to a note's stem to signify that the note is an eighth note:

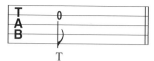

Two eighth notes are equal to one beat of music in 2/4 time. Two consecutive eighth notes beginning or ending a measure are *beamed* together to show you that their combined time value is one beat:

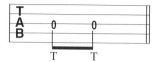

Four consecutive eighth notes within a 2/4 measure are beamed in two sets of two notes in order to show you the two separate beats within that measure:

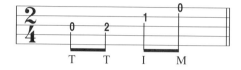

The first and third eighth notes shown in the tablature above fall on the *downbeats* of the measure. The second and fourth eighth notes fall on the *offbeats* of the measure.

A *sixteenth note* equals one quarter-beat of time value, so two sixteenth notes equal the time value of one eighth note. Two flags are attached to the stem of a sixteenth note. Four consecutive sixteenth notes that begin or end a 2/4 measure are double-beamed and equal one beat of music. When eight consecutive sixteenth notes are played in a measure, the notes are double-beamed in two sets of four, showing you where the two beats of music fall within that measure. The downbeats fall on the first and fifth sixteenth notes:

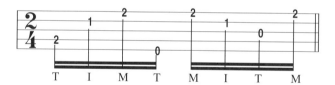

A *thirty-second note* equals one eighth of a beat in time value and has three flags attached to its stem. Two thirty-second notes have the same time value as one sixteenth note. Thirty-second notes are triple-beamed when played in series:

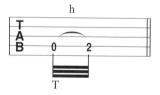

Sometimes a beat of music involves different kinds of notes. In the following tablature, the first beat starts with an eighth note followed by two sixteenth notes. The second beat begins with two sixteenth notes, followed by an eighth note. The three notes in each beat are beamed together:

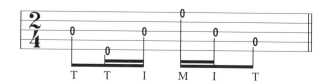

A *dot* placed right after a note increases that note's time value by one half, so a *dotted* quarter note, for example, has a time value of one and one-half beats:

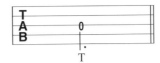

A *grace note* is a note played very quickly and has no real time value of its own. A grace note and the linked note that follows it occupies the time value of the linked note. Most grace notes seen in this book occur when playing a slide, especially if the slide is made very quickly. Also, grace notes are sometimes used following notes to indicate notes within left-hand fretting shapes. A grace note is flagged with a diagonal line drawn through the stem and flag(s) of the note:

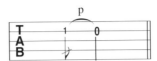

Sometimes there are no sounds heard during a measure of music. A *rest* sign signifies where those moments of silence occur. Rests, as do notes, also have different time values:

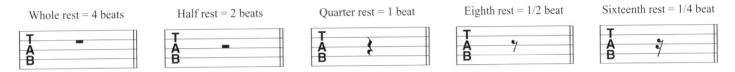

| Whole rest = 4 beats | Half rest = 2 beats | Quarter rest = 1 beat | Eighth rest = 1/2 beat | Sixteenth rest = 1/4 beat |

All the 4/4 measures of tablature below have four beats in them. Use your arithmetic to verify that statement. (*Hint:* Don't add up what appear to be fractions over the staff—they are shorthand for half, quarter, eighth, sixteenth, and thirty-second notes and rests.):

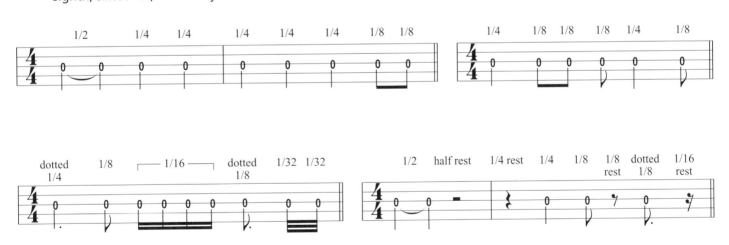

Remember to not confuse notes with beats. It's important to know that the time value of a quarter note, for example, is one beat of music and not one-quarter beat of music.

Playing along with recordings is another good way of improving your sense of rhythm and timing abilities. Picking with friends who have a good sense of timing is a great way of improving your abilities—you can benefit from the exchange of musical ideas and also know the good feeling that comes when everyone is playing in the pocket.

A metronome can be a useful tool to have when practicing alone. Many of them have built-in drum sounds and rhythmic patterns to play to, and precise tempos can be set. Some of those metronomes have a button that you can tap in time with recordings in order to determine the tempo used in those recordings.

RIGHT-HAND ROLLS AND LEFT-HAND TECHNIQUES

THE RIGHT HAND

Long ago someone told me that he had recently begun learning to play three-finger style 5-string banjo. He played a tune for me, and I was very much surprised to see that he was using his thumb, index, middle, and ring fingers to pick. When I complimented him on his "four-finger" approach to playing, he in turn was surprised to find out that the term "three-finger style" is not to be taken literally.

Three-finger style picking, of course, involves the thumb, the index finger, and the middle finger of the right hand picking the strings.

The thumb always picks down on the strings and is responsible for the notes played on the fifth string. The thumb also picks many of the melody notes on the second, third, and fourth strings. Only rarely do I use my thumb on the first string, such as in the Flatt & Scruggs recording of "Pike County Breakdown." I like to play as much of the melody as I can with my thumb since the thumb can pick stronger than the index and middle fingers.

The index finger shares that melodic responsibility primarily on the second and third strings. The index finger always picks upward on the strings.

The lion's share of work for the middle finger is picking upward on the first string.

When I was young and learning to pick with my thumb and index and middle fingers, the few three-finger banjo pickers that I had an opportunity to hear played virtually nothing but what is called the *forward roll*. As I grew older, I came to believe that melody notes should stand out from all the other notes surrounding them. I suppose, for that reason, I developed different rolls and timing patterns that helped to bring out the syncopated and accented melody lines that are so tied to the rhythm and the meter of the words being sung in a song.

My family and I at that time were fairly isolated on our farm, and the opportunities that I had to hear other banjo players pick were limited. Looking back, I think that may have been a blessing as far as the development of Scruggs-style picking is concerned. Had I often been around other pickers that had been playing three-finger banjo longer than me, I may have ended up simply mimicking their styles or being told that I was "doing it all wrong" when I ventured beyond the forward roll.

The forward roll and four other fundamental rolls that I use are taught in Chapter 9, "Exercises in Picking." When it comes time to practice those rolls, practice them diligently and at your own pace and speed until you can play them all smoothly and with ease.

~

Let's now take a look at examples of the five basic rolls that you will be learning in different sections of Chapter 9. Refer back to this chapter when you are studying Chapter 9 if you want to see those five rolls grouped together.

Let's start with the forward roll.

Forward Roll

The forward roll involves the thumb, index, and middle fingers picking in sequence and shown as "T I M T I M," as in the following two measures of tablature:

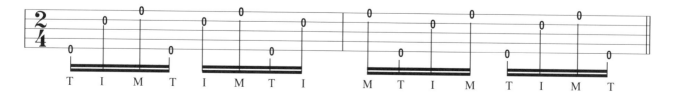

40

Backward Roll

The picking sequence "M I T M I T" (middle, index, thumb) is called a *backward roll:*

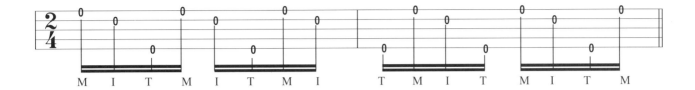

Reverse Roll

Sometimes a measure or passage within a song will start with a forward roll and end with a backward roll. The combination of those two rolls played back to back is called a *reverse roll*. Notice in the following example of tablature that T I M T is then followed by M I T M:

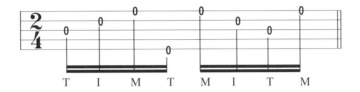

Alternating Thumb Pattern

In measures and passages where every other note is picked by the thumb and then alternately followed by the index and middle fingers, the roll is called an *alternating thumb pattern* or *alternating thumb roll*. Right-hand notation shows the sequence as "T I T M T I T M":

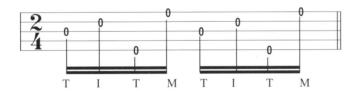

Foggy Mountain Roll

The following roll and variations of it are used in "Foggy Mountain Breakdown" (I M T M T I M T):

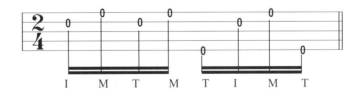

There are many variations of the five basic rolls that involve different right-hand timing patterns. Using those various timing patterns can add a lot to the drive and syncopation of your playing. They, too, are taught in the chapter, "Exercises in Picking." Three examples are seen in the tablatures below:

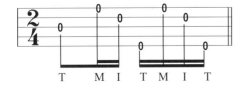 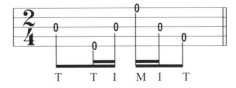 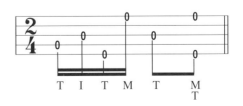

THE LEFT HAND

Another beginning banjo player told me many years ago that he had figured out the key to Scruggs-style picking. I asked him what that key might be, and he answered, "It's all in the timing of the right hand."

He was no doubt sincere in his belief, but I believe there's a lot more to it than just the right hand picking three-finger rolls. The old saying, "Don't let your left hand know what your right hand is doing" flies right out the window when it comes to playing any stringed instrument.

To me, the left hand is just as important as the right hand in my style of picking. In fact, the left hand is not limited to merely fretting strings, making chord positions, and twisting D tuners.

For example, let's take a look at a measure of music heard in the 1949 recording of "Foggy Mountain Breakdown" that involves two left-hand techniques known as *hammer-ons* and *pull-offs,* which are taught in Chapter 9. The right-hand tablature below shows that the right hand makes eight plucks during that measure: I M T M T I M T. Yet, if you listen closely to the recording, you'll hear more than eight notes being played in that measure. That's because the left hand is busy with "picking" two hammer-ons and one pull-off in that measure as shown in the tab:

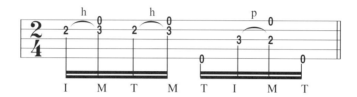

When playing any tune, try to position your left hand on the neck so that you can utilize your stronger left-hand fingers to execute left-hand maneuvers. I make most slides and hammers, for example, with the middle finger of my left hand.

In terms of volume, the right hand has an advantage over the left hand because of the right-hand thumb pick and finger picks. So when practicing the left-hand techniques described in Chapter 9, keep in mind that the left-hand fingers must play notes aggressively and with authority in order to compete with the volume produced by the right hand.

Also, it's very important that you learn all the fingering positions for making chords and can make them effortlessly. By doing so you can make quick and smooth chord changes while playing backup chords and rhythm patterns regardless of where your left hand is positioned on the neck.

Be aware of and focus on both your right and left hands when practicing the lessons in the "Exercises in Picking" chapter and the tunes in the "Song Section" chapter.

It's all right at times to pay more attention to one hand over the other when first practicing certain lessons, but I urge you to remember that both hands are equally important if you want to become a complete banjo player.

PLAYING THE BANJO—BASIC TIPS

Before playing a show, I like to spend a little time warming up by picking a simple song or two such as "Fireball Mail" and the old fiddle and banjo tune "Katy Hill." By doing so, my hands and fingers will feel loose and limber when it's time to go on stage. If you're a beginner, playing a few simple chords is a good way to loosen up your fingers before practicing.

In G tuning, try making the simple chords shown in the diagrams below. The circled letters indicate which fingers fret the strings to make the chords. The G chord is played open with no strings fretted. With your left hand, make the low fret position C and D chords:

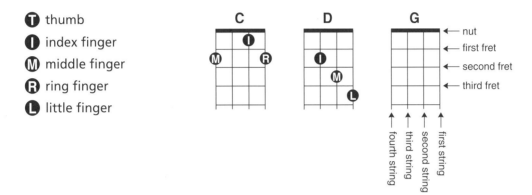

Let's review a few points mentioned in Chapter 4, "Chords." Your fingertips should come down perpendicular to the strings. Fret the strings firmly, not directly on the frets, but in the fretboard areas just in front of the frets. For example, in the C chord diagram the middle finger frets the fourth string at the second fret. The middle finger should fret the string closer to the second fret than the first, and not directly in the middle area between those frets.

Make sure that only one string is touched by each of your fingertips. If another string is only slightly touched by a fretting finger, the string can buzz or not ring as loud and as true as it should sound. Clip your fingernails shorter if they interfere with your fretting of the strings.

Start with the C chord. After forming the chord shape with your left hand, brush down with your right thumb across the four long strings. If your left hand is fretting the chord correctly, each string will sound clearly and distinctly. When you can play the C chord cleanly, repeat the process with the D chord.

When you can easily play the C and D chords, practice going from each chord to the other chords at any speed you desire until you can make all those moves cleanly and without hesitation. When going from one fretted chord to another, do not lift your fingertips high above the strings. Think of economy of movement and stay as close to the strings as you can. Try playing the different chord changes below:

G	C	G	C	G (play many times)	G	D	G	D	G (play many times)
C	D	C	D	C (play many times)	D	C	D	C	D (play many times)

When you can make the chord changes easily, try strumming the chords along with the lyrics to "My Cabin in Caroline" as shown on the next page. When doing so, play the chords in tempo. If you want to add the open fifth string, remember that the fifth-string G note is part of the G and C chords, but not the D chord.

For each measure, count "one two" either out loud or to yourself while giving equal time value to beat 1 and beat 2. If you have never played a stringed instrument before and don't know how to strum, simply brush down on the strings with your right thumb on the counts of one. When you can play the chord changes smoothly on the counts of one, try brushing down with your thumb on both beats 1 and 2.

This early exercise is to get you accustomed to working with both hands at the same time and *in* time. Again, play at any tempo that you desire. Focus on staying in time with both your left and your right hands:

My Cabin in Caroline

By LESTER FLATT
and EARL SCRUGGS

Verse:
      G   G   C   G
There's a cabin in the pines in the hills of Caroline

      G   G   D   D
And a blue-eyed girl is waiting there for me

      G   G   C   G
I'll be going back some day, and from her I'll never stray

      G   D   G   G
And the cabin in the hills of Caroline

Chorus:
      C   C   G   G
Oh, the cabin in the shadow of the pines

      G   G   D   D
And the blue-eyed girl way down in Caroline

      G   G   C   G
Someday she'll be my wife, and we'll live a happy life

      G   D   G   G
In the cabin in the hills of Caroline

When practicing the lessons in Chapter 9, wear your picks as shown in the picture below.

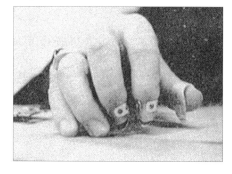

When picking, I anchor my right hand with my ring finger and little finger touching the banjo head with only enough pressure to give my hand stability. Many players use the same anchoring technique. Many others prefer to anchor only one finger. I anchor both my ring and little fingers because my hand feels nearly twice as stable as it does when only one finger is anchored. It also feels natural to me. Try anchoring with both fingers when you start out practicing. If you then feel that method is not working for you, you can experiment with anchoring only one finger.

Avoid anchoring too heavily. If you apply too much pressure, the banjo head will not vibrate enough and your sound will be dampened. Clip your ring and little fingernails short enough to prevent them from scratching through your banjo head.

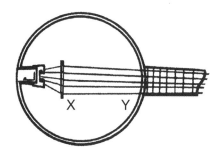

Where your hand is positioned on the head affects the tone. You will get a brighter and more cutting tone when picking close to the bridge at the X position shown in the diagram; that's where I play most lead breaks.

A banjo is by nature a bright sounding instrument—when playing up the neck, it can sound too bright to the point of sounding tinny and brittle. An effective way to take that unwanted edge off the tone is to play at the Y position where a deeper, mellower sound is produced. I often play at position Y when playing backup on slower songs.

There are other "sweet" spots between the X and Y positions that produce tones not as bright as when played at the X position and not as mellow as when played at the Y position. Try different anchoring locations to find the tones that sound best to you when playing certain passages in a song.

44

I occasionally play at position Y for a couple of measures or so when picking at the lower and middle fret positions in order to get contrasting tones within a passage of a tune.

If you have the Flatt & Scruggs *Foggy Mountain Jamboree* album or *The Essential Earl Scruggs* CD, listen to the first three measures in the twelve-bar B section of the instrumental "Shuckin' The Corn" to hear the tonal differences within that section of the tune. Those measures sound mellower than the other measures of the B section because I moved my right hand closer to the Y position.

Another example of that picking technique is on the Flatt & Scruggs album, *Foggy Mountain Banjo*. If you have that recording, listen to the first sixteen-bar B section of "Ground Speed." In that section, I picked closer to the Y position during the 1st & 2nd, 5th & 6th, and 9th & 10th measures. In all the other measures in that section, I moved my right hand back toward the X position of the banjo head.

As one more example of that right-hand technique, listen to "Reuben" if you have *Foggy Mountain Banjo* or *The Essential Earl Scruggs*. I played the first sixteen bars of the first break with my hand close to the X position. There are several left-hand chokes in the last sixteen measures of the first break. I moved my right hand a bit closer to position Y for measures seventeen through twenty-four. For the next few measures, I not only moved my hand even closer to position Y, I played those notes softer in volume. For the last few measures of the break, I increased the volume as my right hand moved back toward the X position.

When positions X and Y are mentioned in Chapter 9, do not think of them as being confined to two specific points on your banjo head. Think of them as general locations and remember that there are many sweet spots between the two.

A photograph showing my hand anchored close to the Y position, but not at the extreme Y position, is on the second page of the Table of Contents. Also notice how my ring and little fingers are anchored, or "planted," on the banjo head in that photograph.

As mentioned in Chapter 1, I round off the point of my thumb pick in order to get a fuller tone. What you do with your finger picks will also affect the tone. Pick so that your finger picks strike as flat as possible against the strings for a fuller tone.

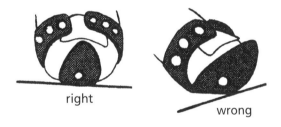

right   wrong

A REVIEW—FACTORS THAT AFFECT BANJO TONE AND VOLUME

Certain parts of your banjo directly affect its tone and volume as discussed in Chapter 1. The tone ring, the resonator, the tightness of the head, and the gauge and condition of your strings are just a few of the contributing factors to overall tone and volume.

Keep in mind it isn't just your banjo's tone and volume that you and others will notice and judge—it's also *your* tone and *your* volume. How hard you pick the strings, where you choose to anchor your hand on the head, and the amount of pressure you apply when anchoring figure into the equation.

Picks have a great deal to do with tone and volume. I recommend that you begin learning to play with picks even though they might feel awkward to you at first. After trying that, if you think the picks are holding you back, then sidetrack them for awhile until you feel more comfortable with your picking. I learned to play without picks, and it did take a while to get used to the difference once I started playing with them.

If you are a beginner, once your playing skills have advanced to the intermediate level and beyond, don't be shy about experimenting with your own ideas. That's what makes the musical world go around!

EXERCISES IN PICKING

Before moving on to the practice exercises, it is important that you have learned to read tablature, learned the timing values of notes and measures of music, and know how to form the chord shapes taught in Chapter 4. Learn each lesson in the exercises before moving on to the next one. If it's only learning how to make a few simple chord changes at first, practice making those changes over and over until you can do them easily.

The exercises are designed to teach you right-hand roll patterns and left-hand techniques that I use. After learning a few of those rolls and techniques, we will advance to picking a tune called "Cripple Creek" as well as sections from other tunes.

Do not be overly concerned with fast breakdown tempos at first. The beauty of picking lies in the smoothness, clarity, and tone of individual notes and not how fast you can play them. Start out playing with tempos that are comfortable to you and gradually build up your picking speed with time and practice.

Practice picking both loudly and softly in order to add to the dynamics of your playing. It will make your picking style far more interesting to others.

If you have the instructional recording that corresponds to certain lessons in this chapter, it will help you to hear and better understand the lessons as you practice them. Audio icons with track numbers are placed next to the lessons heard on the recording. If you have the "book-only" edition of this book and wish to order the instructional recording, you can do so by going to the Merchandise section of my website (earlscruggs.com).

TRACK 1

Go through each lesson in the exercises slowly and patiently before proceeding to the next one. If you've never played a stringed instrument before, the fingertips of your fretting hand might feel tender at first from fretting the strings. Your fingertips will soon toughen with more practice. If the joints in your fretting hand and fingers begin to feel sore from practicing, chances are that you are exerting too much pressure on the strings when fretting them. Press the strings down with only enough pressure so that each string will ring clearly when plucked.

TRACK 2

We'll start out in G tuning, so if you have the recording listen to Track 2 to tune with my banjo starting with the fourth string, D.

EXERCISE I: Basic Rhythm

The first exercise teaches you a simple way to play chords rhythmically. Even though it is a very basic rhythm, it's one that is often used by advanced players when playing backup chords up the neck.

Three-finger style banjo chords are made by *pinches*. Pinching involves picking down with the thumb on a string while at the same time picking upward on other strings with the index finger and/or middle finger.

The following tablature is in 2/4 time with two beats per measure. The measures consist of eighth notes, which have the time value of one half-beat of music. If you are a beginner, start out playing the tablature while counting "1 and 2 and" for each measure with the downbeats falling on counts 1 and 2 and the offbeats falling on the word "and." Count out loud while you are playing if counting out loud helps you.

Anchor your right hand on the banjo head and play the basic rhythm with just your right hand playing only the first measure of tablature over and over. Find a tempo that's comfortable for you (it can be as slow as you want) and count "1 and 2 and" in a steady cadence for every measure you play (+ = "and" in the text).

(1) The thumb plucks down on the third string on the first downbeat of the measure.

(+) Pinch—the thumb picks down on the fifth string, the middle finger picks up on the first string, and the index finger picks up on the second string, all at the same time on the first offbeat of the measure.

(2) The thumb picks down on the 4th string on the second downbeat of the measure.

(+) Pinch again on the second offbeat of the measure.

Now study the rest of the tablature below and note that the right hand picks the same pattern and the same strings in both the G chord and C chord measures. Also notice that there's no first-, second-, and fifth-string pinch on the offbeats in the D7 measures. That's because the open fifth-string G note is not a part of a D7 chord. The notes played by the thumb on the downbeats of those D7 measures sustain as the index and middle fingers continue to pick on the offbeats. Practice playing the D7 pattern over and over until it becomes easy to play.

Now try the basic rhythm with just your right hand playing the G chord. Then add the fretted C and D7 chords as shown in the tablature below:

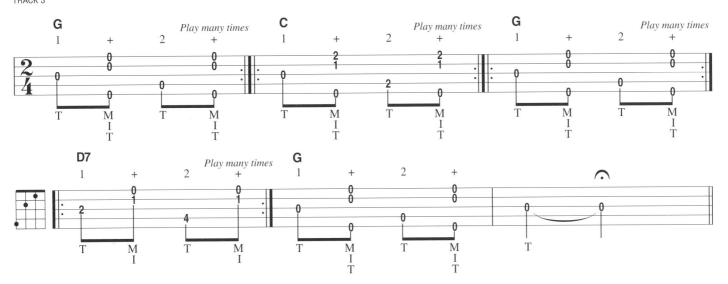

EXERCISE II: Working with the Thumb

Now practice the basic *forward roll* (T I M T I M). Play it over and over until you can pick it smoothly and evenly. Again, picking speed is not important at this time. Be more concerned with the smoothness of your roll as you gradually build up speed while playing the T I M sequence. In the example below:

T = The thumb picks down on the fifth string.

I = The index finger picks up on the second string.

M = The middle finger picks up on the first string.

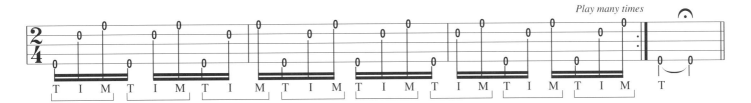

I cannot over-emphasize the importance of the thumb in Scruggs-style picking. Study the tablature below of the *alternating thumb pattern* T I T M T I T M. Notice that the thumb, which plays many melody notes in Scruggs-style, works back and forth between the fourth, fifth, and third strings. When playing the alternating thumb pattern, the thumb picks every other note. The index and middle fingers alternate with the follow-up notes to the thumb. Try playing the pattern slowly at first and gradually build up speed:

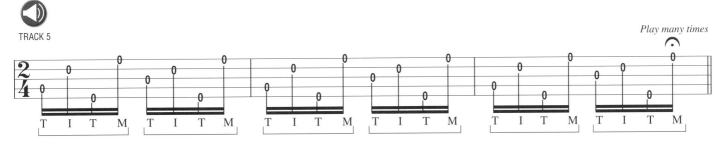

Now practice the alternating thumb pattern (T I T M T I T M) as in the previous tablature, but this time hold an open C chord shape as you play it. Fret the first string at the second fret with your ring finger, the second string at the first fret with your index finger, and the fourth string at the second fret with your middle finger.

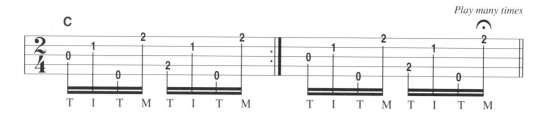

Now try mixing the basic rhythm with the alternating thumb pattern:

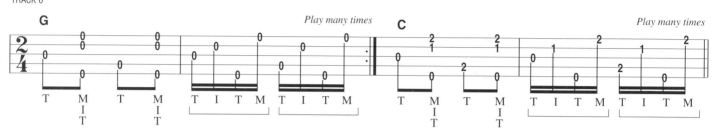

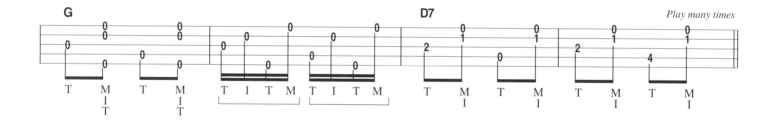

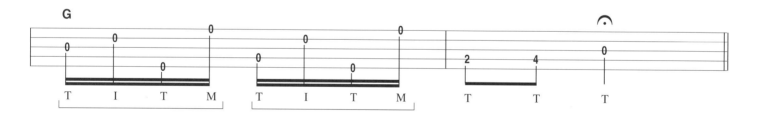

EXERCISE III: Sliding

Sliding is a simple left-hand technique that makes it possible to sound two notes with one pluck. A slide is sometimes used to open a tune, and it also enables you to play the melody of a song the way it is sung. I make most slides with the middle finger of my left hand because it is the strongest of the fretting fingers.

Fret the third string at the second fret with your left middle finger and pick the string with your right thumb. Then while the note is still sounding, slide your left middle finger up to the fourth fret to raise the pitch of the note one whole step. Make sure you keep the string pressed against the fretboard as you slide your finger from the second to the fourth fret. Try making the slides at different speeds:

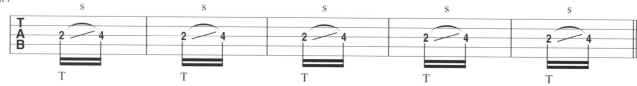

Now slide from the second fret to the fifth fret on the fourth string, again using your middle finger for the slide:

TRACK 8

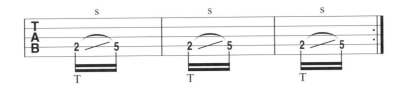

Now apply sliding to the basic rhythm you have learned:

TRACK 9

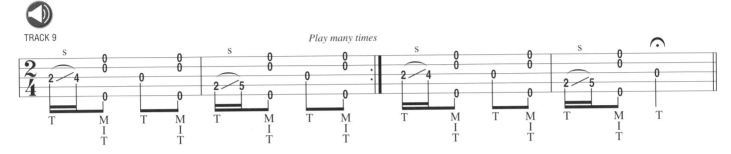

Next, try sliding while picking the alternating thumb pattern (T I T M):

TRACK 10

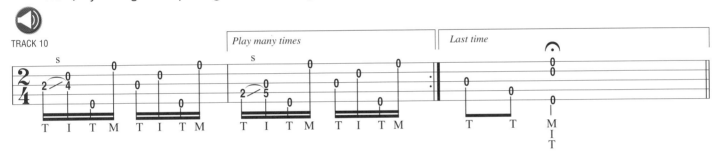

Next, mix the slides into both the basic rhythm and alternating thumb pattern:

TRACK 11

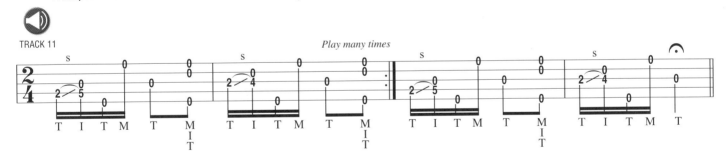

When you are confident you can play the previous lessons well, try playing a simplified version of the chorus of "Cripple Creek." Play it over and over until you can play it smoothly:

TRACK 12

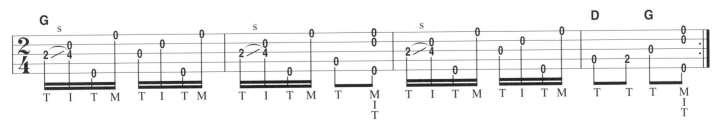

EXERCISE IV: Hammering On

Your fretting hand can sound notes when you're picking the banjo. *Hammering on* or *hammering* is a method of doing that by fretting a string hard enough to make it sound. The result is called a hammer-on or hammer.

In the example below, pick the open third string with your thumb and then quickly bring the middle finger of your left hand down on that third string at the second fret. Press down on the string firmly, closer to the second fret than the first fret. When hammering-on at first, bring your finger down upon the string from about 3/4-inch above the fingerboard. You can reduce that distance as you get more and more accustomed to hammering and have built up your playing speed:

TRACK 13

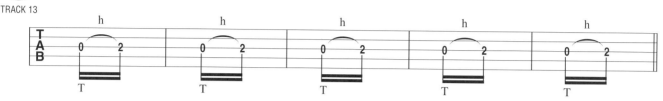

Hammers are not always made on an open string. For example, fret the second string at the second fret with your index finger and then hammer at the third fret with your middle finger after picking the string. Focus on giving equal time value to the fretted and hammered notes:

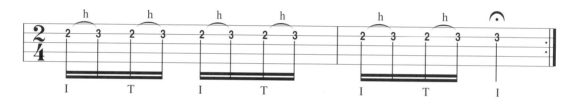

Now hammer into the basic rhythm:

TRACK 14

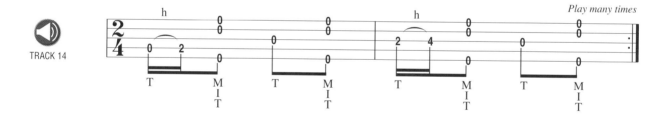

Now add the alternating thumb pattern (T I T M) while hammering on to the fourth string at the second fret:

TRACK 15

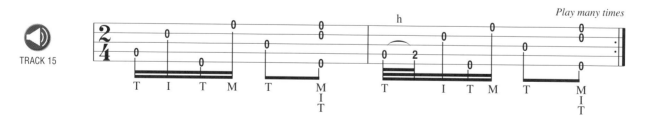

Try mixing hammering and sliding into the basic rhythm and alternating thumb pattern (T I T M):

TRACK 16

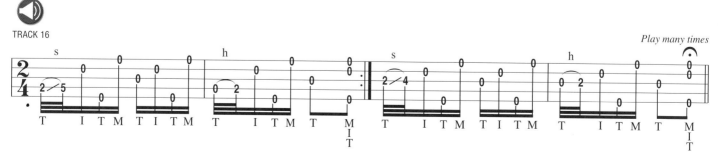

Before advancing to another left-hand technique, try a variation of the forward roll heard in the first section of Track 17. The first eighth note in each measure is picked by the index finger:

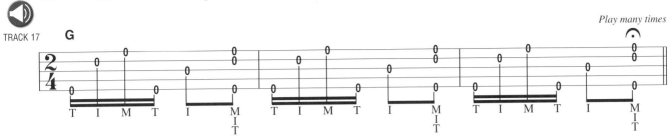

Now add a C chord as heard in the second section of Track 17.

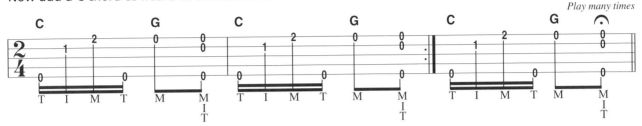

Now apply the techniques you have learned to "Cripple Creek." In this lesson, the opening slide is on the first string, and the tune begins with a thumb and middle finger pinch:

By EARL SCRUGGS

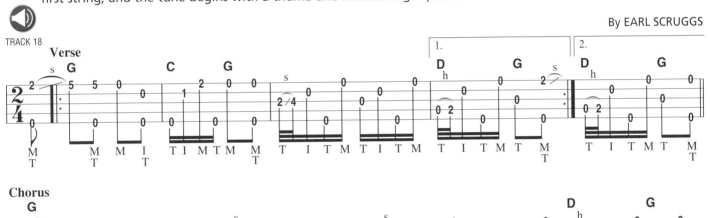

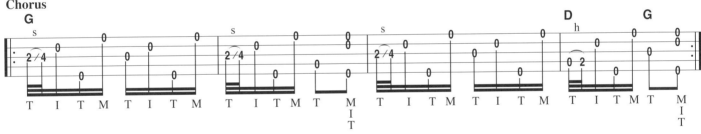

EXERCISE V: Pulling Off and Pushing Off

Pulling off is another left-hand technique that quickly brings out a different note from the string being picked.

With the following pull-off, fret the first string at the second fret with your middle finger. Pick the first string with the middle finger of your right hand and then pull your left middle finger off the string and toward your palm. Make the pull-off with enough force to make the string sound as if it has been picked again.

Work on making the volume created by the left hand equal to that of the right hand:

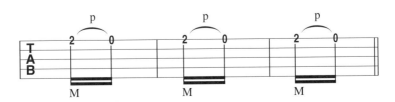

Pull-offs don't always result in an open string. In the following example, fret with your middle finger at the third fret and then make the pull-off with the string already having been fretted by your index finger at the second fret:

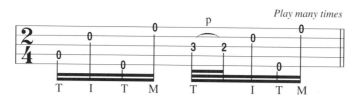

Without using your right hand, do a series of *hammer pull-offs* on the first string at the second fret. Hammer down with your middle finger and then make your pull-off, giving equal time value to both the hammered and pulled notes. Try making the hammer pull-offs at different speeds:

TRACK 20

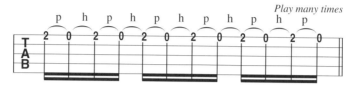

Next, add pull-offs to your basic rhythm:

TRACK 21

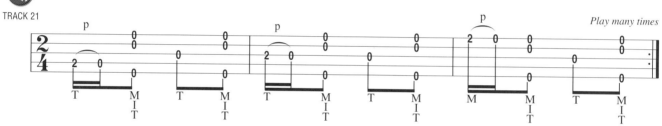

A pull-off involves the left hand plucking a string toward its palm. A *push-off* involves pushing the string away from the palm. Whether a pull-off or a push-off is made usually depends on the direction that the finger doing the technique should be traveling after the push or pull. In the following example the left-hand middle finger pushes off from the second fret of the third string and then frets the fourth string at the second fret:

TRACK 22

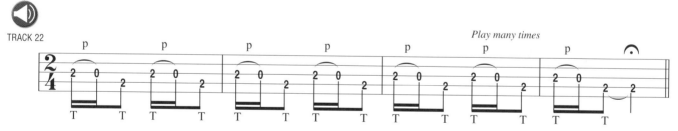

Now practice pushing off while playing an alternating thumb pattern. The push-off shown below out of open G can also be played out of the low fret C chord formation as was done in "Flint Hill Special" and "Silver Eagle." Both of those tunes are in the Song Section. Strive for clarity as you make your push-offs:

TRACK 23

Now try pulling-off and pushing-off along with sliding while playing the alternating thumb pattern. The first "p" represents a pull-off, and the second "p" represents a push-off:

TRACK 24

Play many times

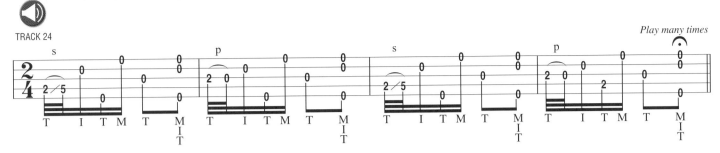

Now play "Cripple Creek" again and incorporate the new techniques you've learned into the tune:

TRACK 25 **Verse section**

Play many times

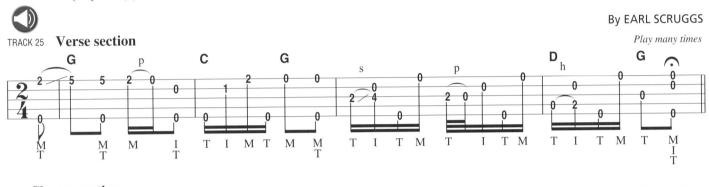

Chorus section

Play many times

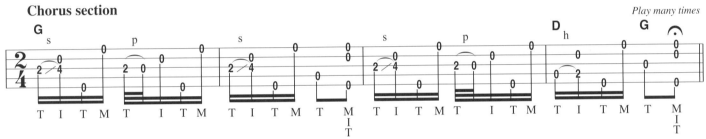

Try another variation of the forward roll:

TRACK 26

Play many times

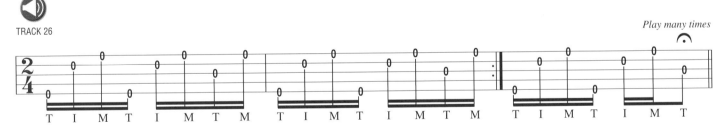

Now use this new variation of the forward roll in the chorus of "Cripple Creek:"

TRACK 27

Play many times

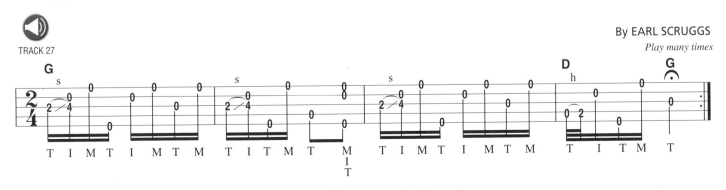

Now try playing the first and second banjo breaks heard in the Flatt & Scruggs version of "Cripple Creek." If you want to play along with the recording, capo at the second fret and hook your fifth string at the seventh fret as described in Chapter 2. When reading a tablature's fret numbers while capoed, always think of your capo as serving as the nut on your banjo neck—the fret numbers are relative to the capoed fret position.

CRIPPLE CREEK

Sound Sources—Flatt & Scruggs *Foggy Mountain Banjo* and *The Essential Earl Scruggs:*
First and second banjo breaks

(G tuning) Key of A: Capo at 2nd fret

By EARL SCRUGGS

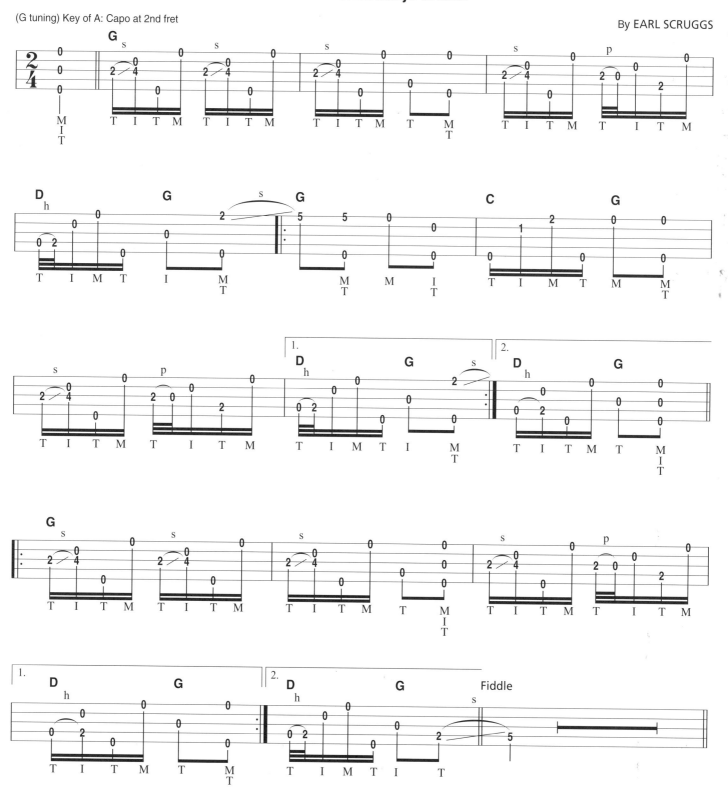

Second break

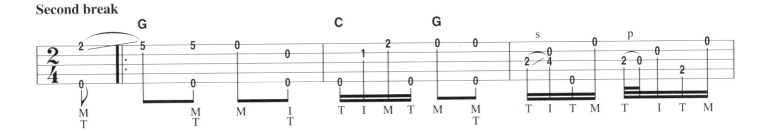

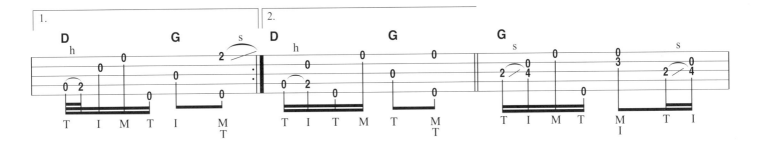

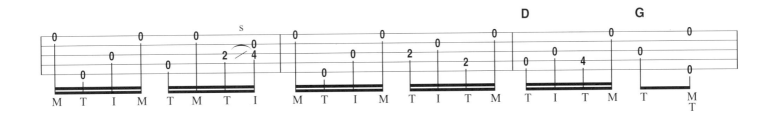

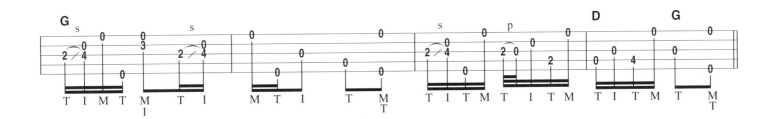

The late Paul Warren, born in Lyles, Tennessee in 1918, played fiddle on the *Foggy Mountain Banjo* recording of "Cripple Creek." He was a member of the Foggy Mountain Boys for many years, playing fiddle and singing the bass part in the group's harmony.

Paul knew many old-time tunes, and he and I almost always played at least one fiddle and banjo tune in concerts during the Flatt & Scruggs days.

One of his many musical credits was playing fiddle on Kitty Wells' classic recording of "It Wasn't God Who Made Honky Tonk Angels."

Paul used to say that his father, who played frailing-style banjo, and "Fiddlin'" Arthur Smith were his primary musical influences when he was growing up and learning to play fiddle.

EXERCISE VI: Forward Roll and Reverse Roll

There are many variations of how the forward roll (T I M) can be incorporated into a musical passage. Four of them are demonstrated in Track 28 and they are shown below.

The first two rolls differ in that there are two sixteenth-note pick-ups leading into the first downbeat of the measure in the first example and one eighth-note pick-up into the second. The third variation heard in Track 28 begins on the downbeat with the second string and with the T I M sequence entering on the offbeat of the first beat of the measure. The forward roll pattern for the first and fourth tablatures are both T I M T I M T M, but notice that the tabs differ in that the seventh sixteenth notes are played on different strings. Take the time to practice each of the variations over and over until you can pick them all smoothly. Then get your left hand involved by playing a C chord and E minor chord at times while repeating those rolls over and over. (A simple second-fret open fingering position for Em is shown on page 29.)

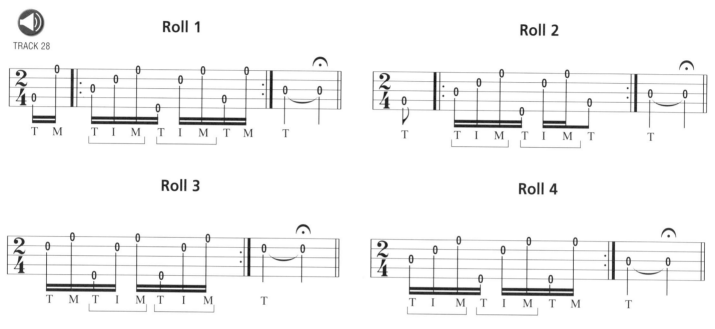

The patterns heard in Track 28 are often used in the Song Section of the book. The second one is a good pattern for working the thumb into the melody of a song. The third pattern is a good one to use when hammering on and is discussed in more detail in the Advanced Left-Hand Techniques section of this chapter.

As with any kind of roll, there are many variations of the forward roll when it comes to timing and which strings are picked during a roll. Below are two more examples of the forward roll within a measure:

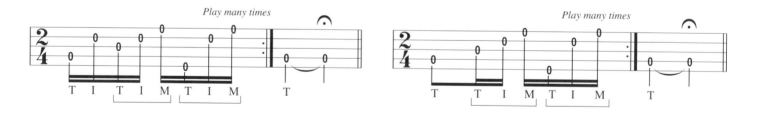

A *reverse roll* is a combination of forward and *backward* rolls. The backward roll, M I T M I T, is discussed in the next exercise section. Try picking a reverse roll where the picking sequence is T I M T followed by M I T M.

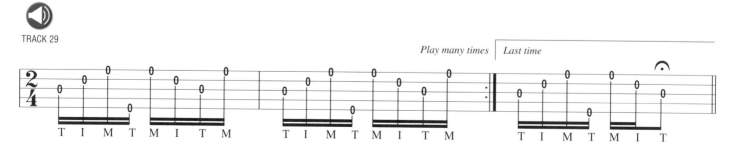

One way to kick off "Ballad of Jed Clampett" (the theme song for *The Beverly Hillbillies*) is to use the forward roll pattern heard in the fourth section of Track 28 (T̲ ̲I̲ ̲M̲ ̲T̲ ̲I̲ ̲M̲ ̲T̲ ̲M̲) along with the reverse roll (T̲ ̲I̲ ̲M̲ ̲T̲ ̲ ̲M̲ ̲I̲ ̲T̲ ̲M̲):

TRACK 30

By PAUL HENNING

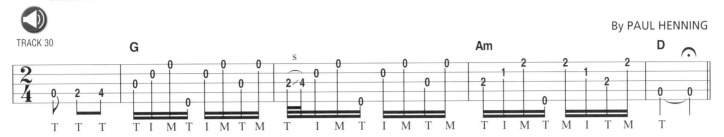

There are other ways to play the first break of "Jed." Try kicking off the tune using a combination of basic rhythm, the alternating thumb pattern, and the reverse roll:

TRACK 31

"BALLAD OF JED CLAMPETT"

By PAUL HENNING

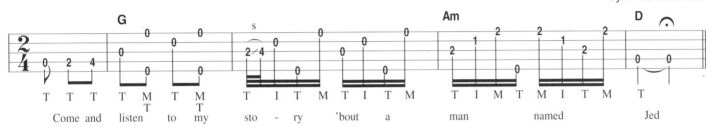

Flatt & Scruggs on the set of "The Beverly Hillbillies"
L–R: Buddy Ebsen, Irene Ryan, Donna Douglas, Lester, and Earl

Playing music is much more interesting to me when a tune is not played the same way time and time again. Keep in mind that the tablatures in the Song Section of the book merely reflect the way I played any particular song at one given time. By learning many different roll patterns and how to work them into a song, you'll have a variety of methods from which to choose when picking any tune.

EXERCISE VII: Backward Roll

The backward roll (M I T M I T) is another pattern I enjoy playing because it can add new elements of syncopation into a song. Practice the roll over and over until you can play it smoothly.

TRACK 32

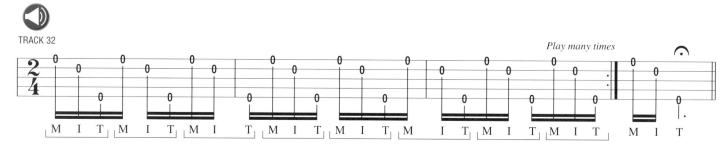

Let's work now with another tuning. Tune your fourth string D down a whole step to C so that you'll be in C tuning. Try playing the backward roll used in the opening line of "Home Sweet Home," a tune on the *Foggy Mountain Banjo* album. Use the partial chord shapes shown in the fingering boxes as you play a simplified version of that opening line:

TRACK 33

By EARL SCRUGGS

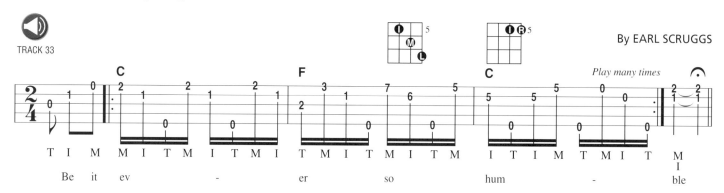

There are many backward rolls played in "Home Sweet Home," which is included in the Song Section chapter. The instrumental "Ground Speed," which is on the *Foggy Mountain Banjo* album, also starts off with a backward roll. Tablature for "Ground Speed" is also in the Song Section.

"Foggy Mountain Banjo" album cover
– Painting by Thomas B. Allen

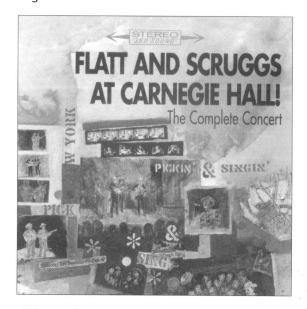

"Flatt and Scruggs at Carnegie Hall!" album cover
– Painting by Thomas B. Allen

EXERCISE VIII: Advanced Left-Hand Techniques

Put your banjo back into G tuning by raising the fourth string C up to the note D. Before moving on to some advanced left-hand techniques, try playing two variations of a reverse roll where the "M" of T I M immediately becomes the "M" of M I T.

TRACK 34

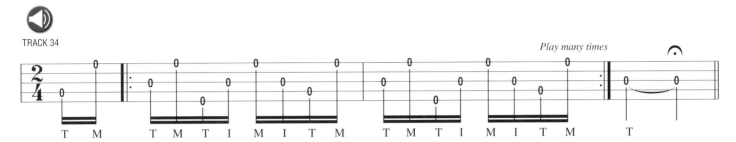

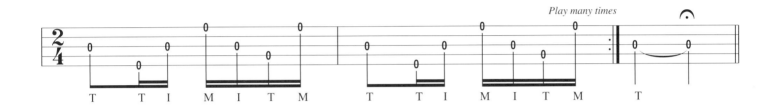

When you can play the above patterns smoothly, move on to the two patterns below and play them over and over until they become second nature to you.

The slide movement with the follow-up notes is an often-used *lick* or *riff* that can lead up to a break or fall at the end of breaks within a song. Note that as the left-hand middle finger finishes making the slide from the second fret to the fourth fret, the right-hand middle finger is simultaneously picking the first string:

TRACK 35

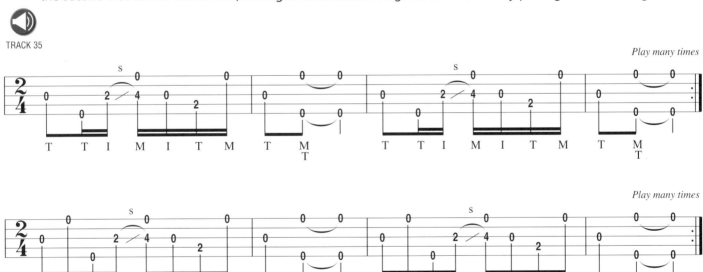

As a review, practice sliding while playing the alternating thumb pattern over and over:

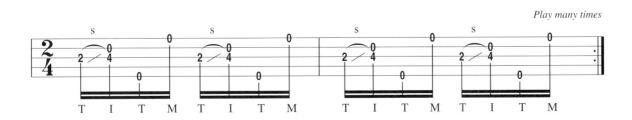

Now pick the third forward roll that you learned on Track 28 and emphasize the second string with your right-hand thumb:

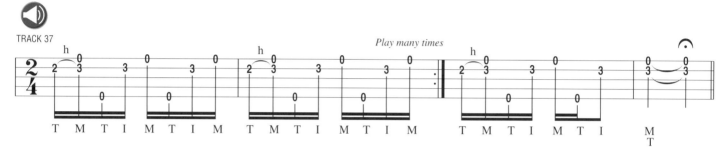

Now while playing the previous roll, add a hammer on the second string. Fret the second string with your index finger at the second fret and hammer at the third fret with your middle finger:

In Chapter 7, I talk about a roll pattern I use in the tune "Foggy Mountain Breakdown" (I M T M T I M T), which involves picking eight sixteenth notes. Let's work up to the double hammers heard often in that tune. First, while using only your right hand, try playing a simplified version of that roll (I T T I M T). The simplified version begins with two eighth notes followed by four sixteenth notes; pick the first eighth note with your index finger:

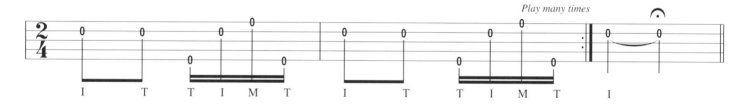

Now play another variation (I T M T I M T), that begins with one eighth note followed by six sixteenth notes:

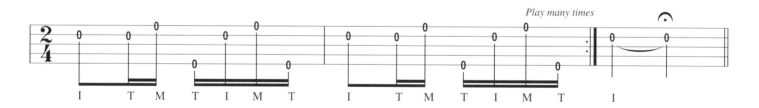

When you feel comfortable with playing the two previous variations, practice the eight-note Foggy Mountain roll (I M T M T I M T) over and over. As with any new roll pattern that you are learning, start with a tempo that is comfortable to you and then gradually build up your picking speed:

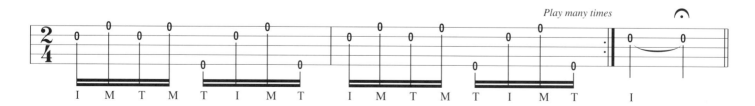

Now get your left hand involved with the rolls you have been practicing. "Foggy Mountain Breakdown" kicks off with a double hammer. Practice the double hammer in the first section of Track 38 by using the I T T I M T roll variation. As you have done before, fret the second string at the second fret with your index finger and hammer on the string at the third fret with your middle finger:

TRACK 38

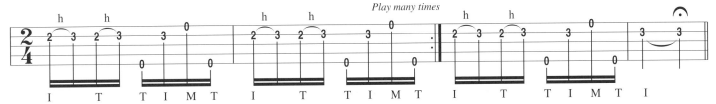

When you are satisfied that you are playing the previous lesson well, move on to the second section of Track 38 shown below. Practice the double hammer while picking the Foggy Mountain roll I M T M T I M T. Notice that the first string is added at the same time that the second-string hammers are completed. This makes for a fuller sound since the open first-string D is in unison with the hammered second string:

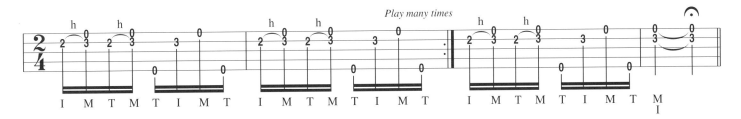

Now play an often-used reverse roll pattern while hammering and then making a pull-off. Hammer with your middle finger having already fretted the third string with your index finger. When making the pull-offs, fret the third string at the second fret with your index finger and at the third fret with your middle finger:

TRACK 39

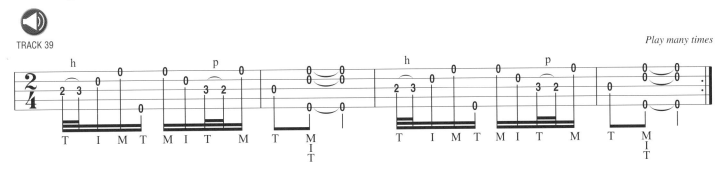

The following lesson is done exactly as the previous one, except the first string is fretted at the second fret with the index finger immediately following the hammers:

TRACK 40

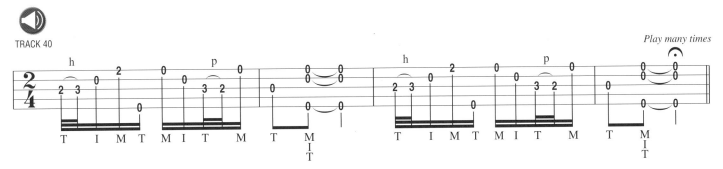

Tablature for "Flint Hill Special," a tune that uses several of the left-hand techniques described in this chapter, is in the Chapter 10 "Song Section." Try playing a few of the passages in the tune. Do not be concerned with the tuner sections of the song at this point. Scruggs tuners are discussed in Exercise XI.

EXERCISE IX: Fill-Ins, Lead-Ins & Kickoffs

When a banjo break has ended, there is often a measure or two before a vocalist or another instrumentalist comes in with a new section of a song. You can fill those spaces with a variety of musical licks called *fill-ins.*

A simple fill-in lick to practice occurs after the opening banjo break in "Hot Corn, Cold Corn" on the *Flatt and Scruggs at Carnegie Hall!* album. A variation of that fill-in happens after the opening break in "Blue Ridge Cabin Home" heard on the Flatt & Scruggs (F&S) *Foggy Mountain Jamboree* album. Both of those songs are included in the Song Section. Try playing the fill-in heard in the "Hot Corn, Cold Corn" recording:

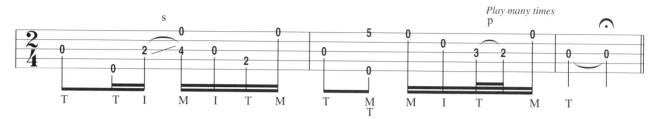

The two-bar fill-in after the first banjo break in "Yonder Stands Little Maggie" on the F&S *Carnegie Hall* album can repeat as many times as needed until someone else takes the lead:

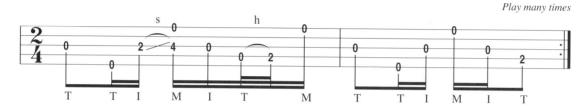

The lick played at the end of the opening banjo break in "Salty Dog Blues" on the *Carnegie Hall* album can also be repeated over and over:

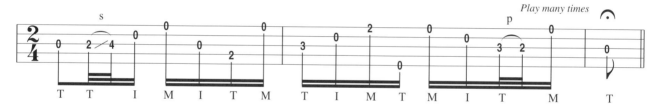

Now try playing the fill-in that I picked at the end of the second banjo break in "Salty Dog Blues:"

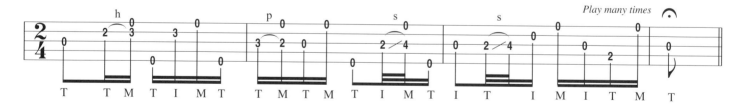

Shuffle Feel

If you have the *Carnegie Hall* album, listen to "Footprints in the Snow" and "I Wonder Where You Are Tonight." Those mid-tempo songs are played with a bouncy *shuffle feel,* or *triplet feel,* where the time value of the first of two sixteenth notes in this book's tablature is slightly longer than the second note. Eight consecutive sixteenth notes played in a shuffle might be "sung" as "*dah*-da-*dah*-da-*dah*-da-*dah*-da" where:

Many early rock 'n' roll classics such as Bill Haley & the Comets' "Rock Around the Clock" have a strong shuffle feel. Another example is the Earl Scruggs Revue's "Carolina Boogie" on the *Live at Kansas State* album. Tracks 48, 49, 52, and 58 are also examples of shuffle-feel banjo picking.

I played backup to Paul Warren's opening fiddle break in "Footprints in the Snow." The fill-in heard at the end of that fiddle break is shown in the following tablature. Play each of the seven-note fill-in licks with a shuffle feel:

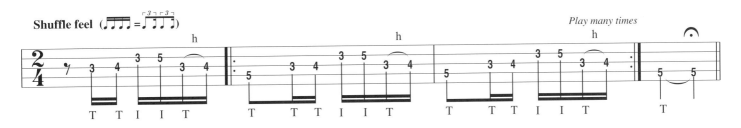

Now get your right middle finger involved with the picking by adding the first string to the more accentuated notes in the previous fill-in lick:

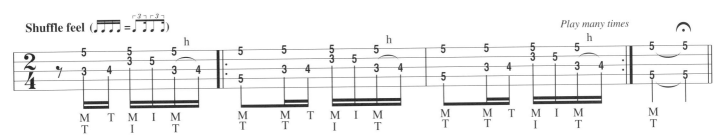

Fill-in licks at the end of the banjo break in "My Cabin in Caroline" on the F&S *Country Music* album are:

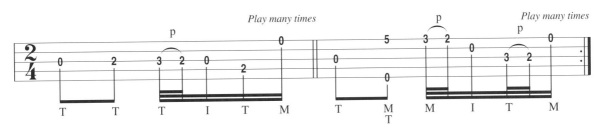

Another often-used fill-in to practice is:

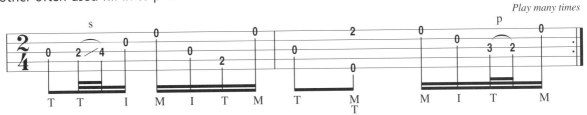

A fill-in heard in the Flatt & Scruggs versions of "Doin' My Time" and "Down the Road" is:

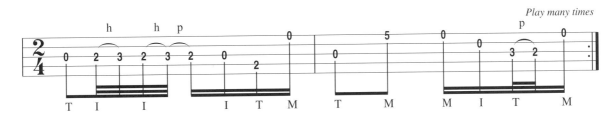

Now practice a bluesy sounding fill-in I sometimes use that involves a double hammer, pull-offs, and a slide:

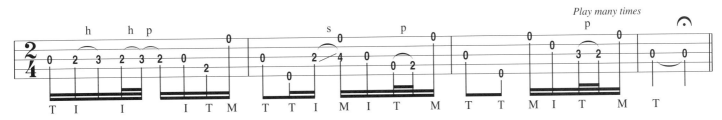

Lead-ins and Kickoffs

There are certain licks called *lead-ins* that work well in leading into other instrumental breaks and vocals. The lead-in to the second verse of "Ballad of Jed Clampett" is a simple *walkup* played on the third and fourth strings:

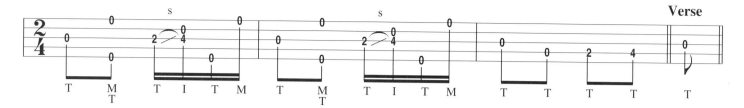

A more syncopated variation of the walkup played at the end of the previous tablature is:

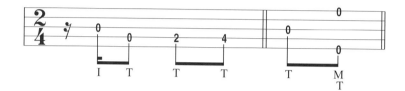

The two-bar walkup lick shown in the above tablature also works as a good kickoff lick to start a song.

Three sets of two eighth notes serve to kickoff "The Wreck of the Old '97" on the *Hard Travelin'* album after the fiddle mimics a lonesome sounding train whistle and is shown in the following tablature:

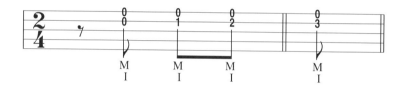

A hammer-on serves as part of the kickoff leading into "Earl's Breakdown" as heard on the *Foggy Mountain Jamboree* album:

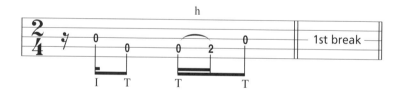

Kickoffs sound best to my ear when the range of the notes played lead in to the range of the notes played in the melody of a tune. The downbeat of the first section of "Ground Speed" on the *Foggy Mountain Banjo* album is played on the twelfth fret of the first string as shown in the tab below. The kickoff to "Ground Speed" begins on the eighth and ninth frets:

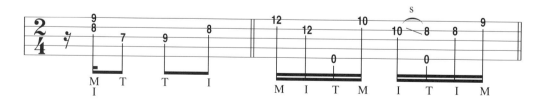

Kickoffs are often very simple licks, but do not underestimate their importance—when playing with a band, they establish the tempo of songs for all to follow. Learn to play them with confidence and authority.

EXERCISE X: Waltz Rhythm (Three-Four Time)

Songs in *waltz* or *three-four time* can be a fun change of pace. 3/4 time is also called *three-quarter time*, where each measure has three beats with one quarter note equaling one beat. Try playing the basic and rolling waltz rhythms. If counting out loud helps you, count "1 2 3" for each bar of the basic waltz rhythm and "1 and 2 and 3 and" for each bar of the rolling waltz rhythm. Start with the basic rhythm:

Basic waltz rhythm

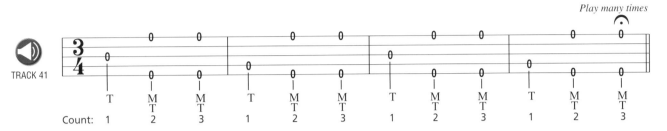

Now play a simple rolling waltz rhythm heard in the second part of Track 41 using a forward roll (T I M T I M):

Rolling waltz rhythm

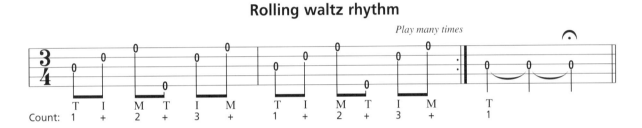

Now mix the basic waltz rhythm with the rolling waltz rhythm:

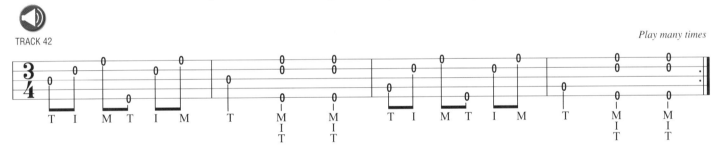

Now add a slide as heard in the second section of Track 42:

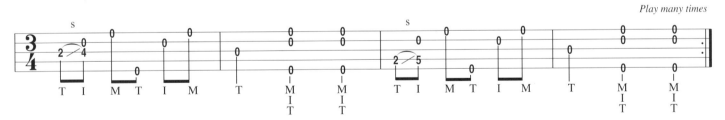

Next, practice a hammer and then a pull-off in three-four time:

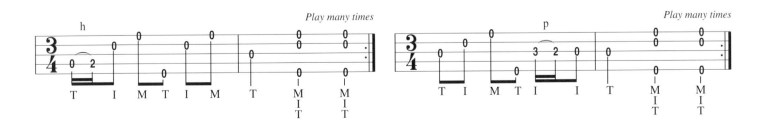

When you feel comfortable playing all of the previous waltz time lessons, play the opening break of "Good Times are Past and Gone" as heard on the F&S album *Folk Songs of Our Land*. As with the tablature for "Cripple Creek" on pages 54–55, capo at the second fret and hook your fifth string at the seventh fret if you want to play along with the recording. When capoed, remember that tablature fret numbers are relative to the capoed fret. (The capoed fret is "0" in the tab.)

GOOD TIMES ARE PAST AND GONE

Sound source—Flatt & Scruggs *Folk Songs of Our Land*: Opening banjo break

By LESTER FLATT and EARL SCRUGGS

(G tuning) Key of A: Capo at 2nd fret

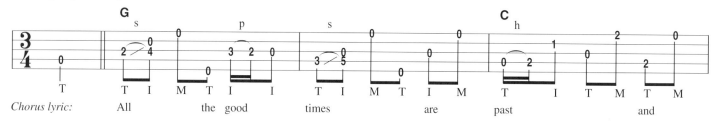

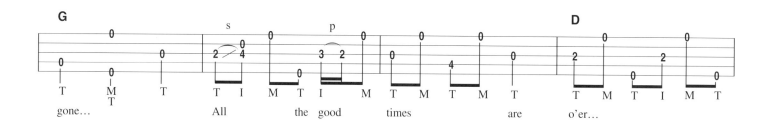

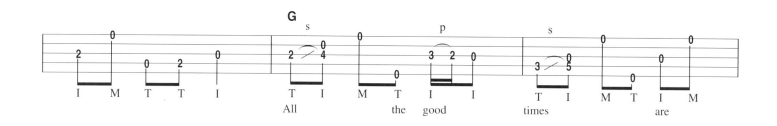

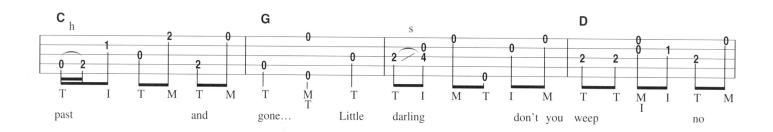

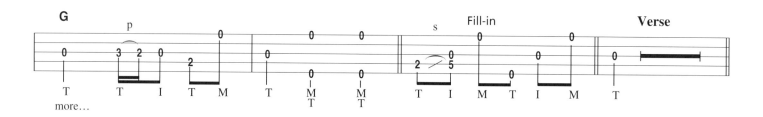

EXERCISE XI: Scruggs Tuners

Let's review some of what is discussed on page 19. I usually set my tuners so that when tuned down in G tuning, the second-string tuner stops on the note A, and the third-string tuner stops on F♯. When tuned back up, the second-string tuner stops on the note B, and the third-string tuner stops on the note G. Those notes provide a quick and easy way to go from G tuning to D tuning and then back again to G tuning on the four long strings.

TRACK 43

If your banjo has second- and third-string tuners, first set them at the high position in G tuning. Set your second-string tuner for the note B and then your third-string tuner for the note G. Then set your B-string tuner to stop a whole step lower for the note A and the G-string tuner to stop a half step lower for the note F♯ in the low position. Then swing the tuners back up to the high position.

Now play the opening of "Flint Hill Special," as heard in the last section of Track 43 and shown in the next tablature. ("Flint Hill Special" is on the F&S *Foggy Mountain Jamboree* album.) The "full" over an arrow tells you the tuner changes the note a whole step; the "1/2" over an arrow tells you it's a half step tuning. Practice it many times, slowly at first and then build up speed, as your left hand becomes more accustomed to twisting the pegs in time with the music:

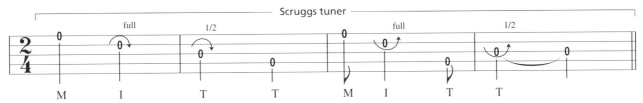

The tuner breaks throughout the rest of "Flint Hill Special" differ by one note, having an eighth note set up the initial tuning maneuver as in the third measure of the opening tuning section heard on Track 43. The additional eighth-note setup puts the accent of the first tuner move on the offbeat, which adds more syncopation to the tuning passage. Practice it over and over until the tuning maneuvers become easy for you to play:

TRACK 44

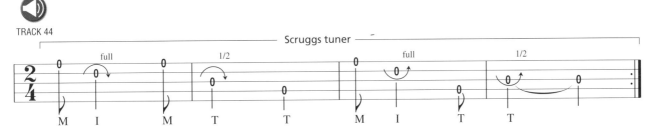

The second-string tuning in "Earl's Breakdown" (on the *Foggy Mountain Jamboree* album) involves picking the string and then de-tuning and then re-tuning in one continuous slur. Listen to the recording if you have it to hear the cadence and feel of the tuner at work:

TRACK 45

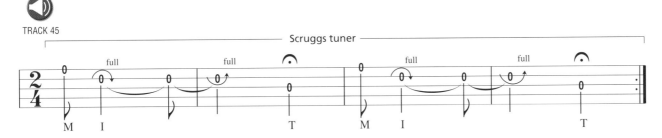

EXERCISE XII: Harmonic Chimes

You can make pretty sounds called *chimes* on your banjo. Chimes are also known as *harmonics*. If you have the *Foggy Mountain Banjo* album, listen to "Bugle Call Rag" and "Reuben" to hear examples of harmonic chimes being played. There are also many chimes in the tune "Foggy Mountain Chimes" which is on the *Foggy Mountain Jamboree* album. Tablature for "Foggy Mountain Chimes" is in the Song Section.

Try chiming some notes by resting your left ring finger very *lightly* on the long strings directly over the twelfth fret. Without pressing down on those strings, pluck each of those strings one at a time with your right hand. For a clearer chime, lift your left ring finger after picking each string. Using the ring or little finger of your left hand leaves you in good fingering position to move on to other frets after playing harmonic chimes within a tune. Remember to always rest your left finger very lightly on the strings when chiming a note.

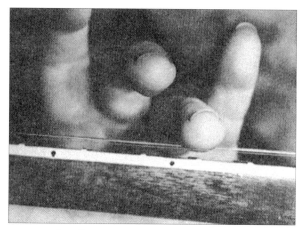

Ring finger positioned to make chimes

When playing a series of chimed notes in an up-tempo tune such as "Bugle Call Rag," you will not have time to lift your finger from the strings after chiming each individual note. You might find that making each note chime clearly at fast tempos to be difficult at first but, as with everything else you have been learning, a lot of practice will pay off.

With your banjo in G tuning, try playing a chimed bugle call on the four long strings over the twelfth fret. Notice that the chimed notes are an octave above the open-string notes. Play the bugle call over and over with the goal being to hear each chimed note distinctly and clearly as you gradually increase your playing speed:

TRACK 46

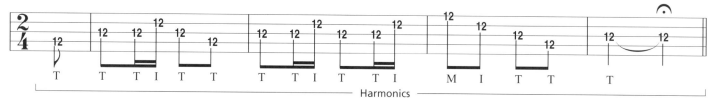

Occasionally, harmonics make a nice simple ending for a song. Chime the first, second, and third strings over the fifth fret by making a right-hand pinch as heard in the second section of Track 46. Those chimed notes are two octaves above the notes sounded on those strings when played open. Then make the pinch over the twelfth fret:

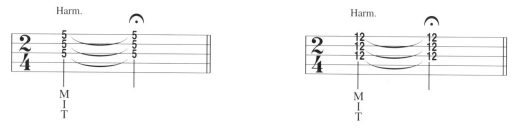

Notes chimed over the seventh and nineteenth frets are a 5th interval higher than the notes sounded when chimed over the twelfth fret. (Remember what is stated in Chapter 4, "Chords:" The 5th note in a G major scale is D, and the D chord is the 5 chord in the key of G.) Now play the bugle call pattern over the seventh fret and notice that those chimed notes are notes that are in a D chord, which are D, F♯, and A. Again, play the pattern over and over until you feel comfortable playing it and can hear all the chimed notes clearly:

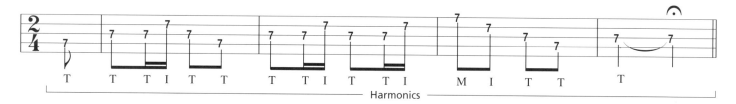

When you pluck a string, it vibrates and produces what are known as *overtones*. Because of the nature of sound waves and the overtones they can produce, harmonic chimes can not be made over every fret. I play chimes on the four long strings at the fifth, seventh, twelfth, and nineteenth frets.

EXERCISE XIII: Advanced Rhythm and Backup

As important as picking lead breaks are when playing with a band, never underestimate the importance of your backup work in support of others when it's their turn to sing or take their own instrumental breaks. A great rhythm section is an important asset to any lead player and singer, so remember that when you hand off your lead breaks to others, you become part of *their* rhythm section.

As I mention in the Preface of this book, I've heard some musicians that constantly pick as if they were forever playing lead when playing in a group—even when its someone else's turn to take the lead. To me, that approach to playing becomes very boring very quickly; and it compares with two people talking at once—it makes it difficult to understand what either person is trying to communicate to the listener.

When playing backup to other instrumentalists, I listen not only to what they are playing but where they are playing on their instruments as well. When someone is playing high notes up the neck, I want to play lower backup notes and chord positions so that their notes stand out from mine. So of course when they are playing in a lower range, I prefer to play notes and chord positions at the middle and higher frets of the neck.

Three closed chord positions used to make major chords while in G tuning are shown in Chapter 4, "Chords." Remember that a closed or full chord position is one in which all four long strings of your banjo are fretted. When playing rhythm up the neck, you will be playing closed chords, which are used in the next few lessons. So take the time to learn how to make those three closed chord positions if you haven't done so already. I encourage you to not be tempted to rely on the simple barred-chord position—I rarely use it. The more complicated fingering positions have a definite advantage over barred chords in that the fretting fingers are better positioned to add color to the backup with the addition of hammer-ons, slides, and pull-offs.

Take advantage of the X and Y positions on your banjo head (described on page 44) in order to achieve different tonal qualities in your backup playing. And don't limit yourself to only those two extreme positions—there are many points in between the two that can add to the dynamics of your rhythm and backup.

Let's now look at a couple of techniques that I use when playing backup.

Vamping

When playing certain backups, I like to shorten the sustained length of fretted notes and at times even totally mute certain fretted strings so that they have no sustaining power or "ring" at all. I refer to both those techniques as *vamping*. I usually play vamped rhythm patterns with my right hand anchored on the banjo head closer to the Y position than position X.

I shorten the length of those notes by releasing the fretted pressure on the strings immediately after they have been picked so that the strings are still touching my fingertips but not quite touching the fretboard.

For a fully muted effect, I make a full chord fingering position without pressing the strings against the fingerboard. My fretting fingers then press down about halfway to the fingerboard while I'm picking the strings. The result is a percussive effect where the notes played have little or no true tonal value as far as pitch is concerned.

In G tuning, try both vamping techniques described above. Use the full chord position as shown in the fingering boxes for the G, C, and D chords. The numbers to the right of the boxes represent fret positions:

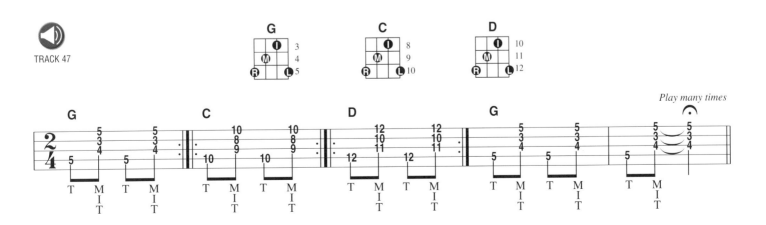

Now practice vamping a mid-tempo rhythm pattern played with a shuffle feel. First, vamp each string by fully pressing the strings to the fretboard when fretting the chords and then releasing the strings to a half-fretted position after the strings are plucked. Then play the pattern using the fully muted vamp technique:

TRACK 48

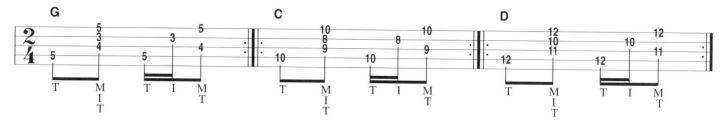

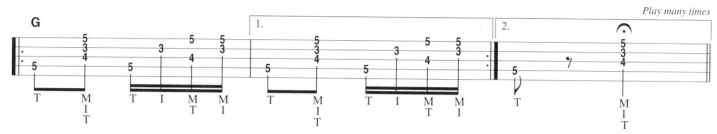

When you feel comfortable with playing the previous vamping lessons, try a more advanced approach to playing vamped rhythm heard in Track 49. Play each chord using two different fingering positions.

Use the chord position shown in the box on the left for the first beat of the measures. For the second beat of each measure use the chord position shown in the box on the right.

TRACK 49

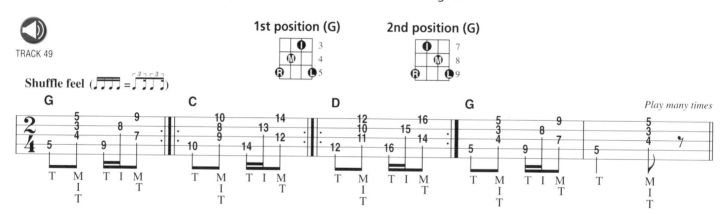

Next, try another rhythm pattern while using the vamping technique of releasing the strings to a half-fretted position after picking them:

TRACK 50

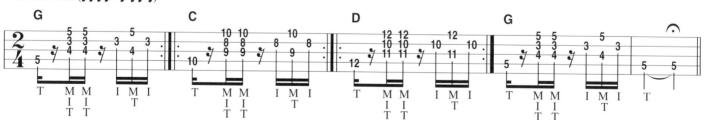

Examples of the vamping method that you have been practicing can be heard on the F&S *Carnegie Hall* album during the fiddle breaks in "Flint Hill Special" and "Footprints in the Snow."

TRACK 51

Now combine the vamping techniques of shortening the length of a note played while fully muting other strings. Play the pattern shown in the above tablature while holding the first, second, and third strings with only enough pressure to mute the strings. Fret the fourth string only long enough to get a sound and then quickly release it to about a one-half fretted position after the string is plucked.

An example of muted vamping can be heard as Josh Graves comes in for a Dobro break on "When I Left East Virginia," a track from the Flatt & Scruggs album *Hard Travelin'—The Ballad of Jed Clampett*. Other examples are heard in the Earl Scruggs Revue's version of "Lonesome Ruben," which is on the *Dueling Banjos* album.

In the next tablature, notice the long slide played on the third string leading into the C chord. I sometimes anticipate a chord change by sliding up or down on a string into the next chord instead of completely letting go of a chord before fretting the next one. By using that technique, chord changes are more fluid, especially in faster paced tunes. Now add a hammer into your vamping pattern:

TRACK 52

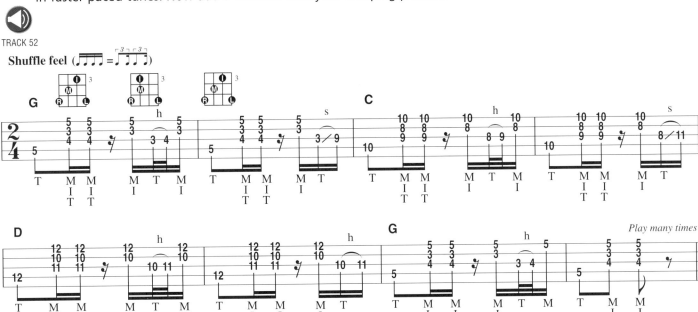

Now try vamping while connecting the chord changes with fourth-string bass runs:

TRACK 53

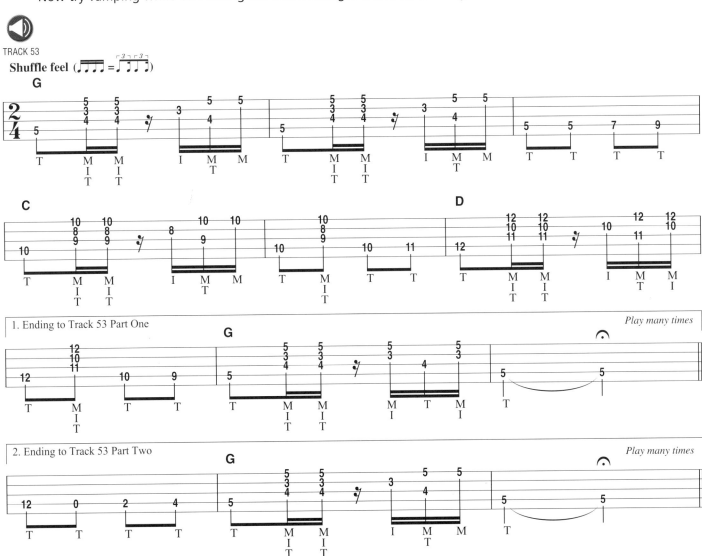

71

Vamping can serve as an ending to a tune such as in "Flint Hill Special." Play the following tablature and use the vamping technique of lifting the fretted notes to a half-fretted position after playing them:

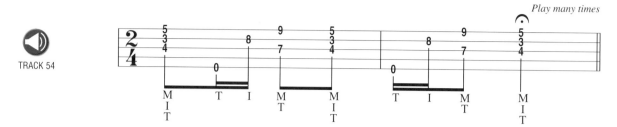

More Backup Techniques

If you have the *Foggy Mountain Banjo* album, listen to the backup I played during the fiddle breaks in "Cripple Creek" and "Cumberland Gap." It's a mixture of vamping and picking certain melody lines played closer to the Y position area of the banjo head to contrast with the lead breaks played closer to the bridge. The first eight bars of backup heard during the second fiddle break in "Cripple Creek" are shown in the following tablature:

By EARL SCRUGGS

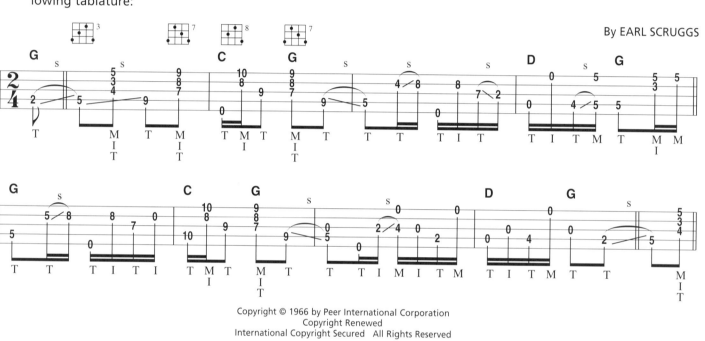

When picking melodic lines as backup, try to avoid playing the melody sung or played by others. In the first verse of "When I Left East Virginia" on the *Hard Travelin'* album, I played notes that contrasted to the melody that Lester sang. When the notes he sang went higher in pitch, the notes I played went lower and vice versa:

By LESTER FLATT and EARL SCRUGGS

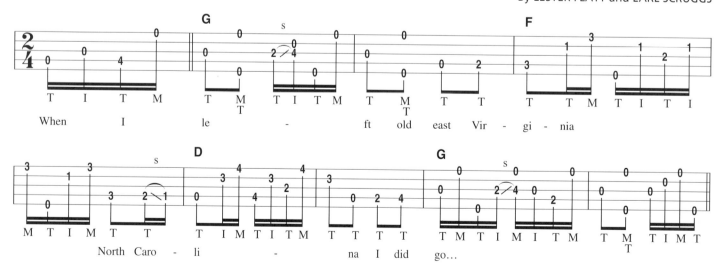

Other examples of how picking can serve as backup can be heard in "The Wreck of the Old '97" on the Flatt & Scruggs *Hard Travelin'* album and in "T for Texas" on the Earl Scruggs Revue *Live at Kansas State* album. Again as in the previous tablature, the notes played are different than the melodies sung in those songs.

When playing chords up the neck, I sometimes fret the fifth string with my thumb to add a 6th or a 7th interval to a closed chord. Playing those chords with different roll patterns can add new colors to your backup work. A C6 chord is shown in the picture with the thumb fretting the fifth string at the seventh fret. Fret the fifth string at the eighth fret to make a C7 chord.

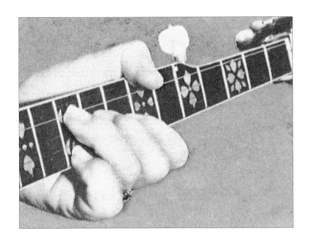
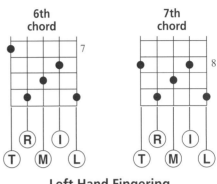

Left Hand Fingering

If you have the sound sources, listen for 6th and 7th chords played during certain backup passages. For examples, listen to "Blue Ridge Cabin Home," which is on the *Foggy Mountain Jamboree* album, the "You Bake Right with Martha White" heard on the *Carnegie Hall* album and the *Hard Travelin'* track "Dixie Home."

Practice playing the 6th and 7th chord positions using different roll patterns as you move the chords up the neck and then back down again.

Let's start with a forward roll. While holding a C6 chord, play a forward roll starting on the fifth string:

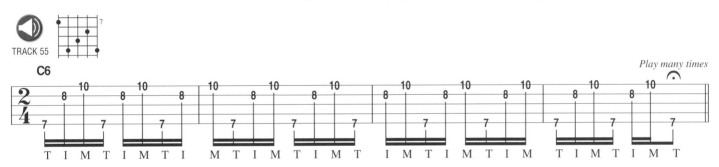

Now pick the C6 chord using other roll patterns as heard in the second section of Track 55. Of course many variations are possible:

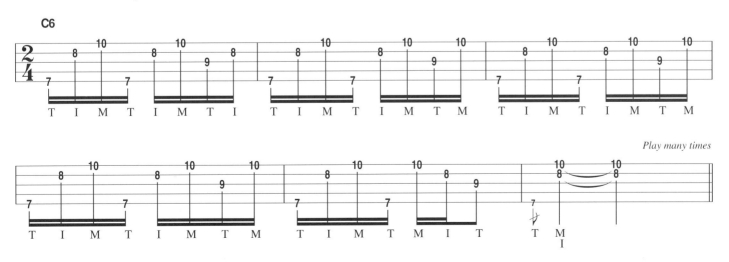

A backup lick picked in "Blue Ridge Cabin Home" on the *Foggy Mountain Jamboree* album is shown in the next tab. A *half choke* is used in the lick. Chokes are made by pushing up or pulling down on a fretted string while keeping the string pressed against the fretboard for a slurred or bent effect. Push up on the second string at the eleventh fret, raising the note a half step from B♭ to B. (Choking is discussed in more detail in Exercise XIV.)

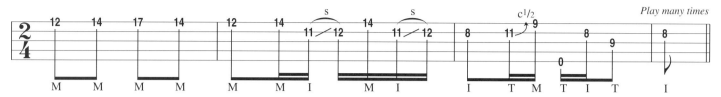

A catchy backup lick is played in "My Cabin in Caroline" on *The Original Sound of Flatt and Scruggs* album:

TRACK 56

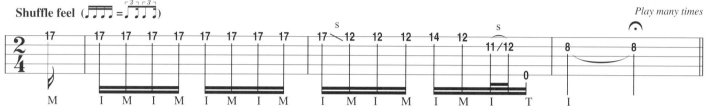

Boogie-woogie style backup can be fun to play. Examples can be heard on the *Carnegie Hall* track, "Footprints in the Snow" and in "Carolina Boogie," which is on the Revue album *Live at Kansas State*. Try picking the following boogie-woogie lick:

TRACK 57

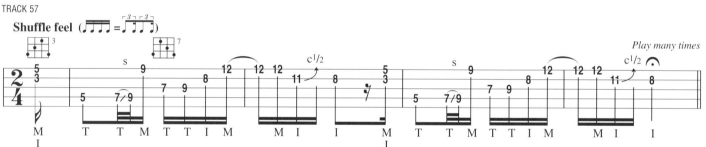

Now play a boogie-woogie rhythm as played in the second section of Track 57. Make a G6 by fretting the first string at the ninth fret with your ring finger; fret the second string at the eighth fret with your index finger; fret the third string at the ninth fret with your middle finger:

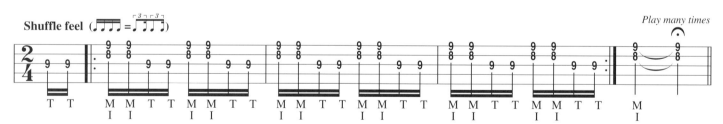

The following backup pattern works well in slow and mid-tempo songs and is played on the first and second strings. Only the index and middle fingers of the right hand are used to play the lick. Mute the other strings by resting your right thumb over the fourth and fifth strings with the tip of your thumb touching the third string:

TRACK 58

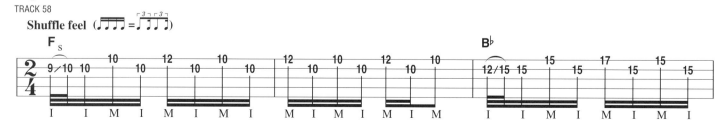

74

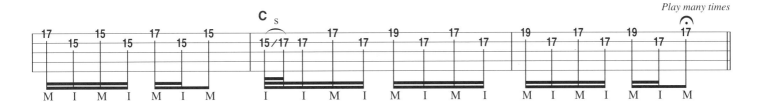

Similar backup licks to the one above also work well for songs in 3/4 time. Examples can be heard in "Good Times are Past and Gone," "Rambling 'Round Your City" on the Earl Scruggs Revue's *Live at Kansas State* album, and "Bummin' an Old Freight Train" from the album *The Fabulous Sound of Flatt and Scruggs.*

Another type of backup that I occasionally use on slower songs involves hammering. It was inspired by the late Floyd Cramer's piano style that often mimicked the pedal effect used on steel guitars:

TRACK 59

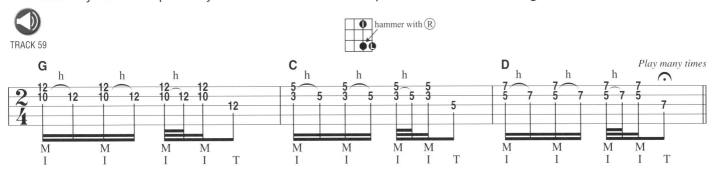

Backup work doesn't have to be limited to playing rhythm and picking melody lines and licks. On the *Hard Travelin'* album I used my second-string tuner in response to some of the lyrics in "Bound to Ride." I sometimes use harmonic chimes while playing backup such as in the recordings of "Cora Is Gone" and "Doin' My Time," which are on the album *The Original Sound of Flatt and Scruggs.*

"Doin' My Time" is also a bonus track on a more recent recording that my Family & Friends band and I played for the live CD *The Three Pickers* in December 2002. In the band that night were Brad Davis on acoustic guitar, Rob Ickes on Dobro, John Jorgenson on electric guitar and mandolin, Glen Duncan on fiddle, Martin Parker on drums, and my son Gary on bass. The "Three Pickers" are Doc Watson, Ricky Skaggs, and myself. Alison Krauss was our special guest that night. The concert is also on DVD.

Several of the backup techniques described in this section are heard in the "Foggy Mountain Rock/Foggy Mountain Special" banjo & guitar medley that I recorded with Marty Stuart for the 2001 *Earl Scruggs and Friends* CD. If you have the audio, listen to the vamping and picking techniques where I play backup to Marty's lead guitar parts. Also listen to Marty's rhythm techniques when he plays backup to me. Listen not only to the notes and rhythm patterns we played but also listen for the dynamics heard and felt in the recording.

Add dynamics to your picking by playing at different volumes. Some musicians tend to drag the beat when playing softly. Others tend to rush when playing loud. Practice a few songs where you start out playing full volume and then begin to play softer and softer as if you were fading out on a record. Then do the opposite. Whether picking full volume or softly, learn to stay in the pocket as discussed at the beginning of Chapter 6.

EXERCISE XIV: Choking and Playing Up the Neck

Choking is a left-hand technique used to slur, or bend, a note upward in pitch for a blues-like effect. Make a choke by pushing up or pulling down on a plucked fretted string while keeping the string fully pressed against the fretboard.

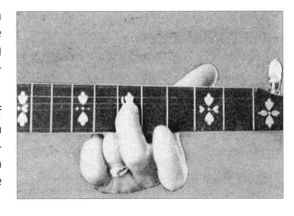

Always make a choke within one given fretboard area—if you start a choke at the tenth fret, for example, stay within the tenth fret area while making the choke. In Scruggs-style, chokes begin the instant the string is picked. I often make a choke by pushing up on a string with my middle finger as shown in the picture.

Notes can be choked a half step or a whole step up in pitch—and even more, or less, if you wish. But for now, be more concerned with half chokes and whole chokes, for they are the ones seen most often in this book.

Most Scruggs-style banjo chokes are made quickly—as soon as the fretting finger completes the choke, the finger moves on to another string or fret position. However, there are times when I choke a string and then hold the raised note for a semi-beat or more before releasing the choked string to its original fretted position. I like using that technique because it creates another bluesy effect as the choked note drops in pitch.

Sometimes when that technique of sustaining a choked note is used, a downward arrow indicates at what point in a measure the choked note is lowered as shown in the following tablature.

The tablature shows four whole-step chokes heard in "Lonesome Road Blues" on the *Foggy Mountain Banjo* album. Choke the B string at the tenth fret and raise the note A to the note B, which is the same note you hear when you pick the B string fretted at the twelfth fret. Hold the last choke and then release it back to its original fretted position at the tenth fret as heard in the first example in Track 60.

TRACK 60

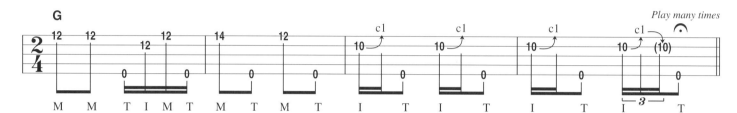

The number "3" under the set of three sixteenth notes before the last note played in the previous tablature tells you those three notes are timed as *triplets*, which means they have the timing value of two sixteenth notes in that measure. (Remember that earlier in this chapter you counted two beats of music as "one and two and" with all four syllables having equal time value. If two beats of music are played as triplets, you count "one-and-a two-and-a" with all six syllables having equal time value.) The triplet feel of that last choke dropping in pitch adds to the syncopation of the passage. The "10" surrounded by parentheses "(10)" on the second string after the choked note is slackened tells you that picking that string again at the tenth fret is optional. A *pre-choke* occurs when the choking finger chokes the string before it is picked.

Now practice the half-step choke played in the second section of Track 60:

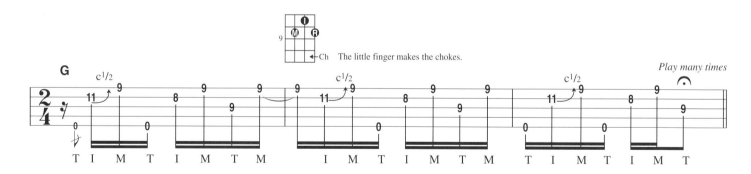

The third section of Track 60 is a variation of the previous tablature:

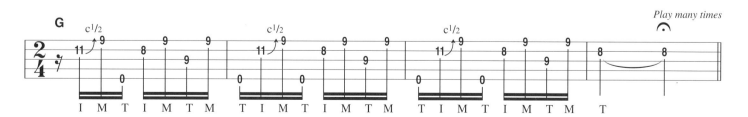

As with the previous lesson, use your little finger to play the half-step choke heard at the end of "Earl's Breakdown" on the *Foggy Mountain Jamboree* album:

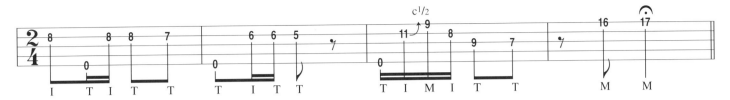

Another way to indicate a sustained choke and its release is by using a single arrow that shows the direction, timing, and duration of the choke. The following tab shows examples of that method found in the 17th and 18th measures of the first section of "Reuben," in D tuning. Play the Foggy Mountain Roll in the first measure:

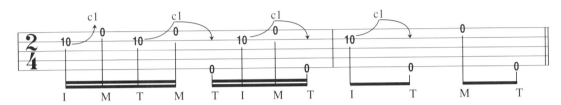

Making chokes at the higher fret positions is easier than making them down around the nut since the strings become more flexible the higher up the neck you go. And only rarely do I choke a string by pulling it toward my palm. The tablature below is from the *Carnegie Hall* recording of "Dig a Hole in the Meadow" and shows a rare example of a pulled choke at a lower fret. I made that choke by pulling the fourth string down toward my palm for a good reason—pushing up on the fourth string for that choke runs the risk of sending the string off the fretboard! "Dig a Hole in the Meadow" is a mid-tempo song played in C tuning, so tune your fourth string down from D to C and practice making a fourth-string pulled choke at the second fret:

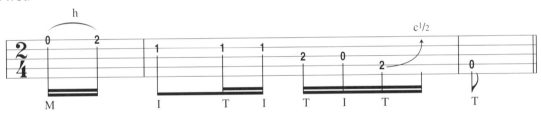

You can get some nice effects using chokes while picking close to the neck. For example, in "Mama's Blues," played in D tuning on the *Carnegie Hall* album, I made the banjo "talk" by using many chokes while picking closer to the neck. In G tuning try mimicking a train whistle by making two half-note chokes at the same time:

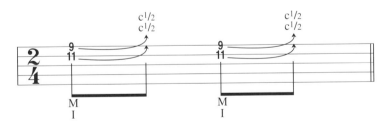

Finally, play the traditional "shave-and-a-haircut—two bits!" ending lick that occurs in "Cripple Creek" on the *Foggy Mountain Banjo* album. (In case you don't know, "two bits" is an old term meaning twenty-five cents.)

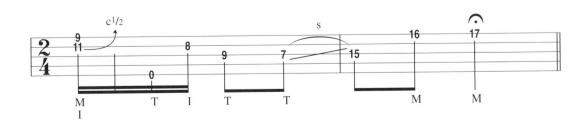

Playing Up the Neck

Playing lead breaks up the neck can be more of a challenge at first than playing down around the nut position in that the four long strings are rarely played open when picking lead up the neck. To simplify matters when first learning to play up the neck, focus on the melody of a song.

In G tuning, for example, many melody notes will be found within the three full chord positions you have learned. That is not to say you will be making full chords when playing leads up the neck—many times you will be making partial chord shapes on two or three of the long strings. (Playing lead also involves playing *passing notes,* which are notes not found in a particular chord.) Examples of partial chord shapes are seen in certain tablatures of the Song Section including "Home Sweet Home," "Sally Ann," and "Sally Goodwin."

Always know where you are on the neck. If you're playing at the twelfth fret, for example, know that the notes played there are an octave above the notes heard when the strings are played open. As another example, notes played at the seventeenth fret are an octave above the notes heard when played at the fifth fret.

Now that you have learned all the rolls and techniques described in this chapter, try playing the songs in the Song Section. And keep in mind that there are other tools besides tablature to help you with your picking.

- Listen to recordings that feature banjo and play along with them (and with other recordings as well) when the mood strikes you.

- Go to shows to see and hear other banjo players perform live. If you have the chance, attend music festivals that feature acoustic music. Many of those festivals have "parking lot" jams going on where both professional and amateur musicians bring their instruments and gather together to have their own unannounced and casual jam sessions going on.

- One-on-one private lessons with a good banjo instructor can be very helpful. Some instructors conduct banjo workshops open to groups of banjo students.

I've been a musician for many years and have been involved in many concerts and recordings along with many other shows on radio and television. I've always tried to not consider those occasions to be "working." It's all about "playing."

Have fun with your picking!

Earl in concert with his Family & Friends band
– Photo by Louise Scruggs

10 SONG SECTION

ablatures in the Song Section reflect the way I played one particular song at one particular point in time. For example, I originally recorded "Foggy Mountain Breakdown" in 1949. Considering the number of concerts, rehearsals, jam sessions, and radio and television shows that I've been involved with, I'm sure I've played that tune several thousand times over the years. If someone had been following me around and transcribing all of those occasions to tablature, there would probably be several thousand different tab versions of how I have picked that tune.

Part of the fun of playing music for me is knowing I'm not locked in to picking a song the same way every time I play it. Playing songs as the mood strikes me helps to keep those songs sounding fresh and new to me. I encourage you to think of tablature as a tool for learning how a tune can be played one certain way and not as a written-in-stone formula that you must use every time you play it—"there's more than one way to skin a cat," as the old saying goes.

The sound source from which each tablature is taken is noted below the song titles. Listen to those recordings if you have them so that you can hear and better understand certain elements in a recording that tablature does not capture, such as the dynamics of drive, feel, volume, and tempo.

Many of my recordings appear on re-issues such as Columbia Records' *The Essential Earl Scruggs*. In most cases the sound source listed is the album on which the songs originally appeared.

In addition to those album sources mentioned, Mercury Records has released "The Complete Mercury Sessions" by Flatt & Scruggs on CD which contains the twenty-eight tracks that we recorded while with Mercury from 1948 to 1950. Those tracks were originally issued as singles. Mercury would later reissue the tracks in three long-playing albums.

Some of the Earl Scruggs Revue recordings have been re-issued in CD format. The all-instrumental album *Dueling Banjos* and the Revue's *Live at Kansas State* have been released together on one CD titled *Dueling Banjos / Live at Kansas State.*

Another Revue CD is titled *Artist's Choice: The Best Tracks, 1970–1980*, which is a compilation of twenty-two Revue recordings. A British label

released the CD and there were a few errors as to which recorded versions of certain songs were to be used. The CD actually has twenty-three songs on it—in one instance, the Flatt & Scruggs version of "I Still Miss Someone" was somehow included in the collection instead of the version that my sons, Gary and Randy, and I recorded with Johnny Cash for the Revue's *Volume II* album!

Two tunes in the Song Section have no sound source listed because I have never recorded them. "Pretty Polly" is a song that Dave "Stringbean" Akeman used to sing and play frailing style on his banjo. "String" and I often played it when we had a chance to get together and pick. "Ground Hog" is a song I used to play on stage shows in the earlier days of Flatt & Scruggs.

Speaking of those earlier Flatt & Scruggs days, for several years we tuned up a half step in pitch over standard tuning. The reason for doing so was that Lester's voice was higher back in those days and two of his favorite keys to sing in were $G^\sharp$ and $B^\flat$. By tuning a half step sharp I avoided having to often capo at the first fret for G-tuning songs played in $G^\sharp$. I could simply pick those songs as if I were playing in the key of G. Lester could play his guitar in G position for songs in $G^\sharp$ and in A position for songs in $B^\flat$ without having to capo. Tuning up a half step higher made it easier for the fiddle player and everyone else as well.

In later Flatt & Scruggs years, Lester's voice lowered somewhat. We then began to tune to standard pitch in order to compensate for the change in his vocal range.

I'm telling you all of this because eight of the tunes in the Song Section were recorded in $G^\sharp$ even though the tablature is written for the key of G—the reason being that we played those songs as if we were in the key of G while using no capos.

If you want to play along with those early F&S recordings, you can tune up to open $G^\sharp$ tuning as I did back then with strings five through one tuned to $G^\sharp$–$D^\sharp$–$G^\sharp$–$B^\sharp$–$D^\sharp$ ($B^\sharp$ = C). As another option, you can capo at the first fret in G tuning and then tune your fifth string up a half step from G to $G^\sharp$.

Some of the tunes included in the Song Section were recorded while using a capo. For example, I recorded "Ballad of Jed Clampett" in the key of A while capoed at the second fret in G tuning. I do not recommend tuning your banjo up from G tuning to open A tuning if you play along with that recording for a couple of reasons. A whole step up can put too much stress on the banjo's neck, and the fifth string is subject to break when trying to tune it up that high. Simply hook the fifth string after capoing.

Remember, when reading tablature fret numbers while using a capo, the numbers are relative to the capoed fret position, not the banjo's nut. Think of the capo as a movable nut.

Chord changes shown in the tabs are the chords a rhythm accompanist would play as backup to you. Use those chord changes as a guide for what chords you would play as backup to other players.

The tablatures are very detailed. If you are a beginner or an intermediate-level player, do not expect to jump right in and play them all note for note. Set realistic goals for yourself. For example, when learning a new tune, if you feel that attempts to duplicate certain grace notes are unsuccessful and hindering your progress to a considerable degree, simply ignore them until you have become proficient with the more basic aspects of that tune.

I again encourage you to be open to your own creativity as your picking ability advances with all you are learning. If you "hear" a great idea in your head, then by all means try to incorporate it into your own bag of musical licks and tricks.

Song Index*

* Songs are played in G tuning (gDGBD) unless footnoted otherwise. Two songs appear in Chapter 9.
[1] This song is played in C tuning (gCGBD).
[2] This song is played in D tuning (f♯DF♯AD).
[3] This song is played in D minor tuning (aDFAD).
[4] This song is played in G modal tuning (gDGCD).
[5] This song is played in G tuning but with the 5th string hooked at the 7th fret for the key of D (aDGBD).
[#] This song was recorded in the key of G♯ with the banjo tuned up to open G♯ tuning (g♯D♯G♯B♯D♯: B♯ = C).

BALLAD OF JED CLAMPETT

Sound sources—Flatt & Scruggs *Hard Travelin' – The Ballad of Jed Clampett* and
The Essential Earl Scruggs: Opening break

By PAUL HENNING

(G tuning)
Key of A: Capo at 2nd fret and hook the 5th string

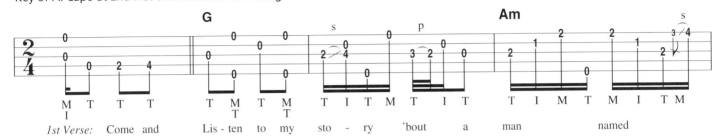

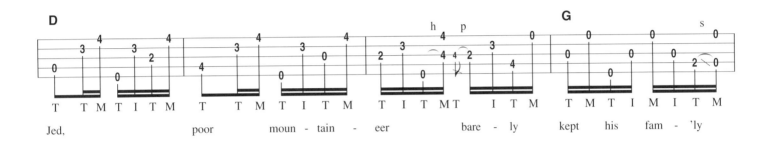

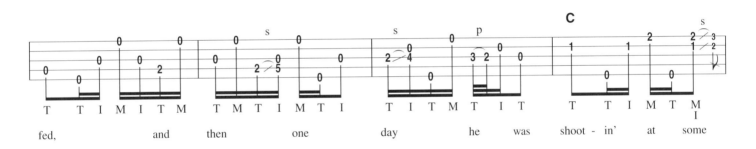

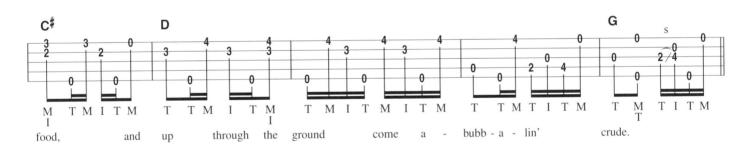

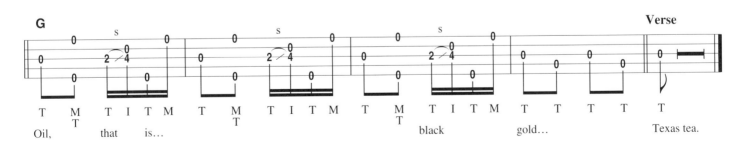

NOTE: Another version of "Ballad of Jed Clampett" appears on *Flatt and Scruggs at Carnegie Hall!*

CUMBERLAND GAP

Sound source—Flatt & Scruggs *Foggy Mountain Banjo:* Opening break

By EARL SCRUGGS

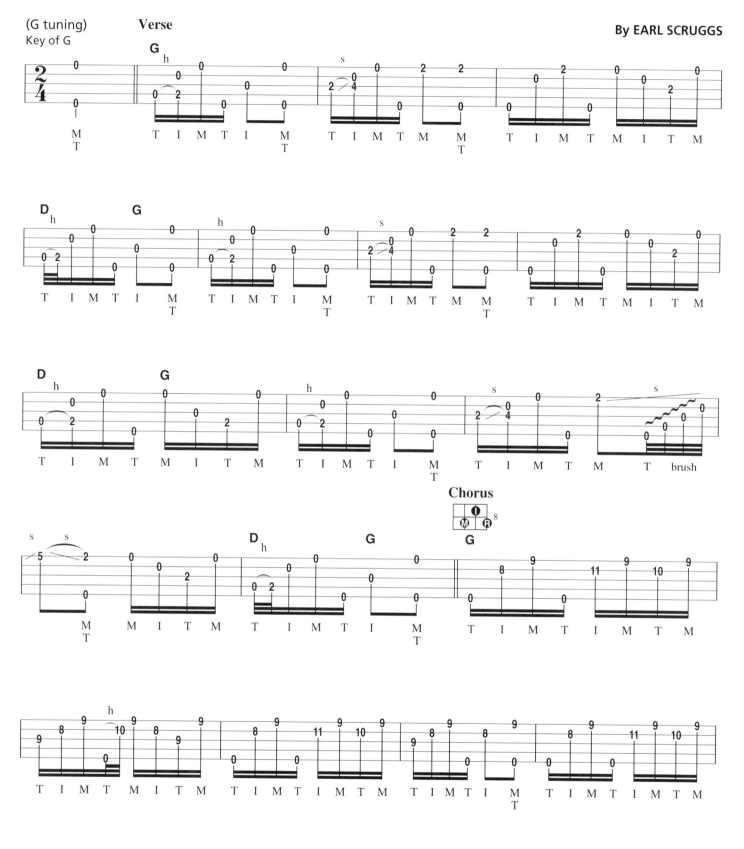

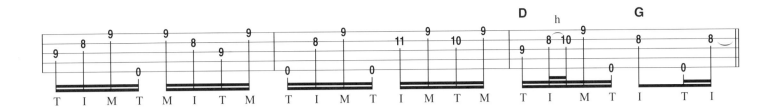

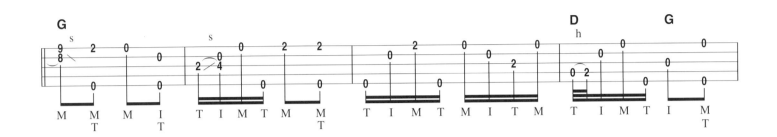

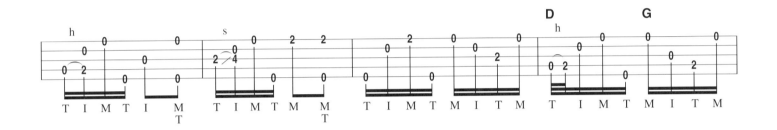

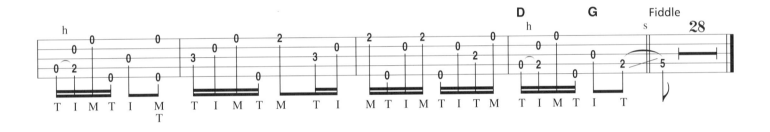

Variation for 2nd section in 2nd break

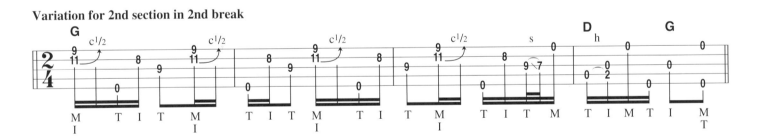

Ending

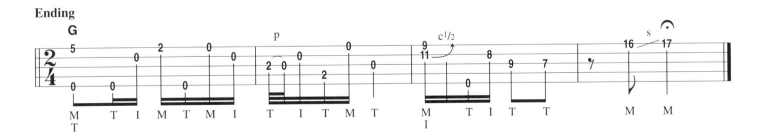

NOTE: Another version by Earl (accompanied by Hylo Brown and the Timberliners at the 1959 Newport Folk Festival) appears on *The Essential Earl Scruggs.*

PICK ALONG

Sound source—Flatt & Scruggs with Doc Watson: *Strictly Instrumental:* **Opening break**

(G tuning)
Key of G

By EARL SCRUGGS

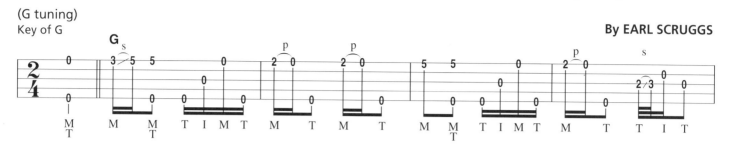

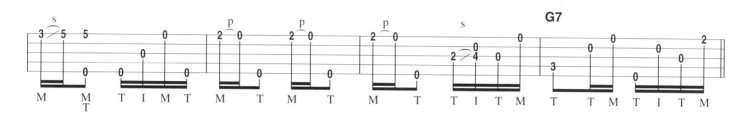

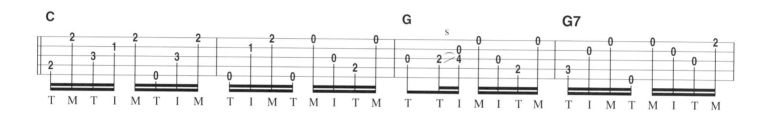

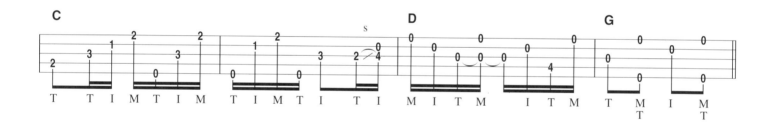

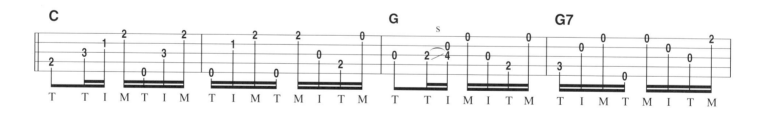

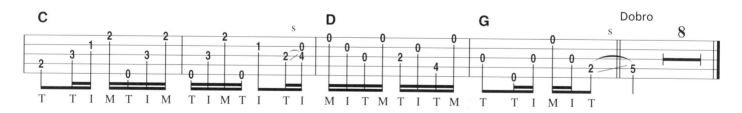

NOTE: Another version by the Earl Scruggs Revue appears on *Strike Anywhere*. Another version by Earl with Doc Watson and Ricky Skaggs appears on the Scruggs, Watson, & Skaggs *The Three Pickers* CD and DVD.

HOT CORN, COLD CORN

Sound source—*Flatt & Scruggs at Carnegie Hall!:* Opening break

By AKEMAN, CIRTAIN and STACEY

(G tuning) Key of G

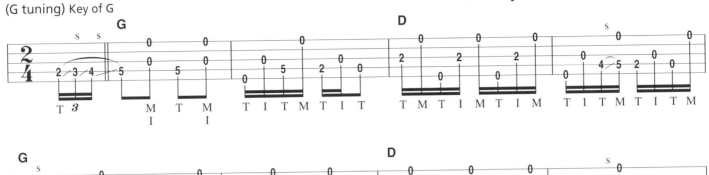

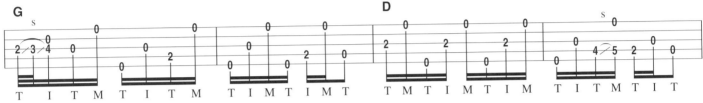

Chorus

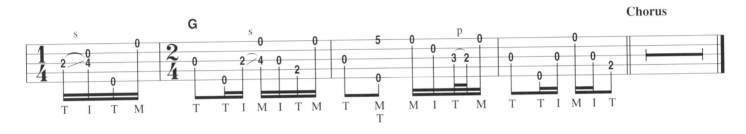

Earl Scruggs Signature Model "Standard"

The 1934 *circa* Gibson Granada that I've been playing since 1949 originally had gold-plated hardware. Except for the original tone ring, it now has nickel-plated hardware. I also replaced the original neck. Gibson introduced the Standard in 1984, and it replicates the appearance of my Granada as it looks today.

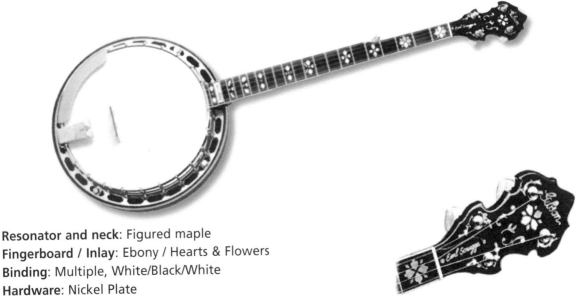

Resonator and neck: Figured maple
Fingerboard / Inlay: Ebony / Hearts & Flowers
Binding: Multiple, White/Black/White
Hardware: Nickel Plate
Tuners: Vintage 2-band
Finish: Exact Replica, Amber Brown
Case: Shaped Hardshell*

*Specifications provided by Gibson

"Standard" peghead

SILVER EAGLE

Sound source—Earl Scruggs Revue *Rockin' 'Cross the Country:* Opening break

(G tuning)
Key of G

By EARL SCRUGGS

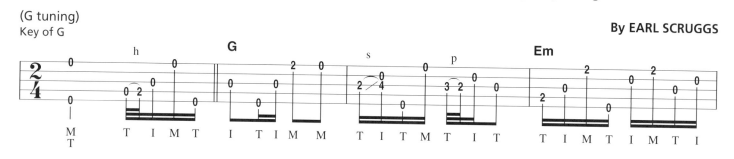

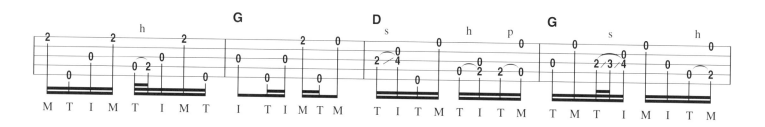

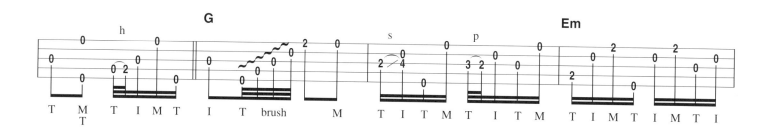

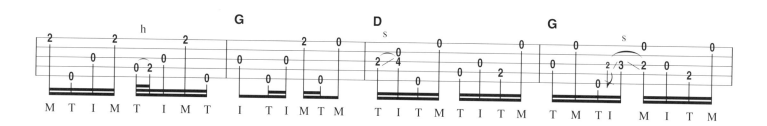

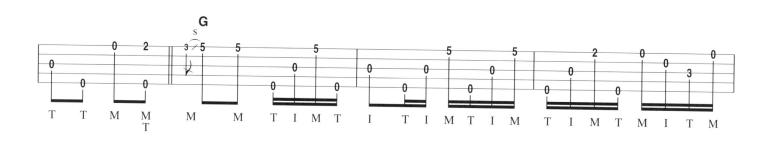

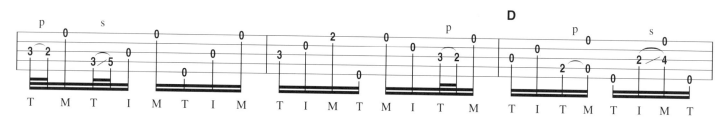

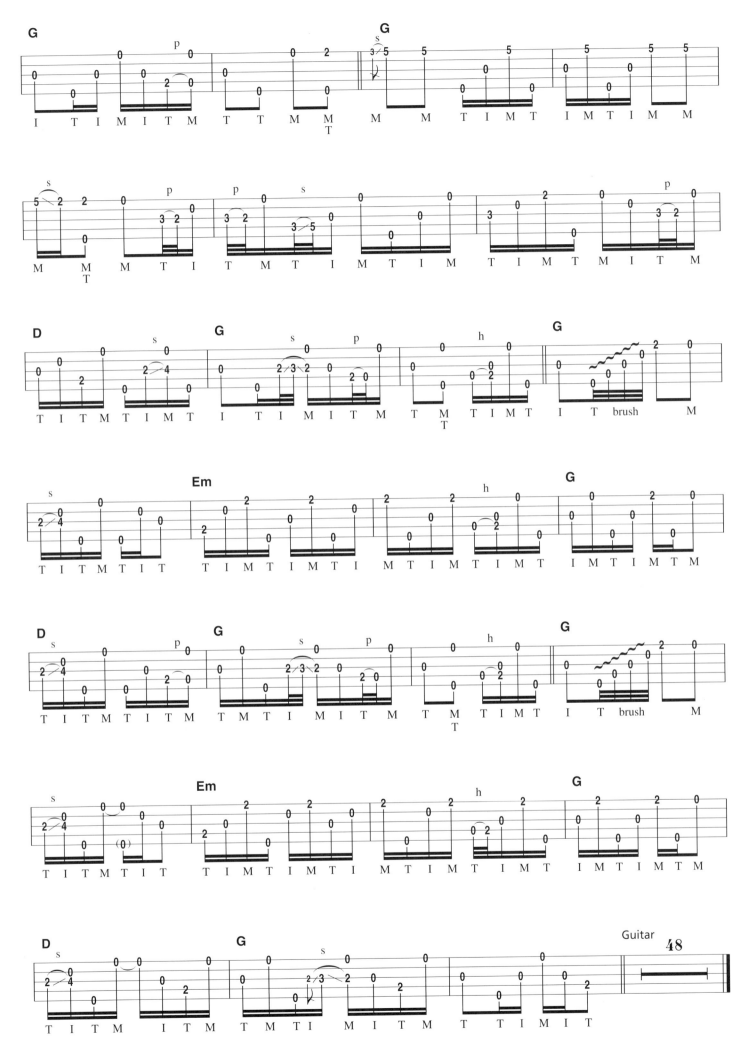

LITTLE DARLING PAL OF MINE

Sound source—Flatt & Scruggs *Foggy Mountain Banjo:* First and second breaks

By A. P. CARTER

(G tuning)
Key of G

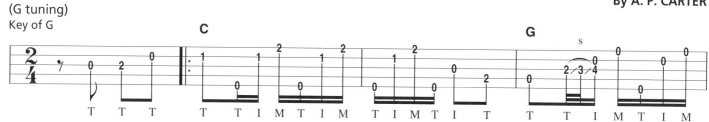

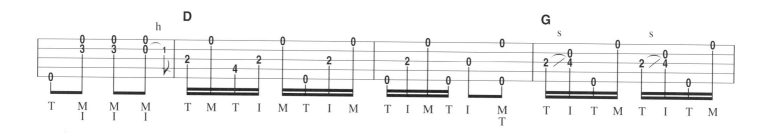

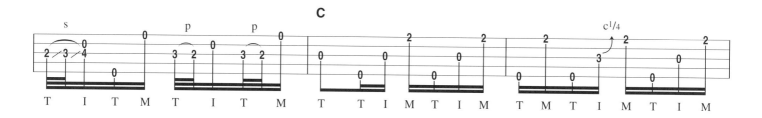

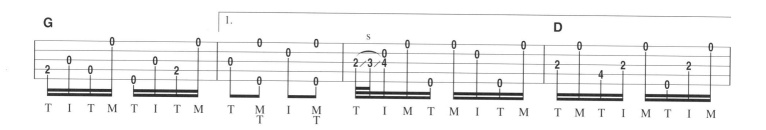

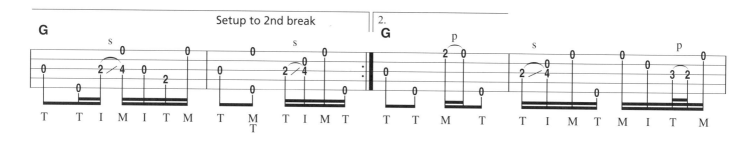

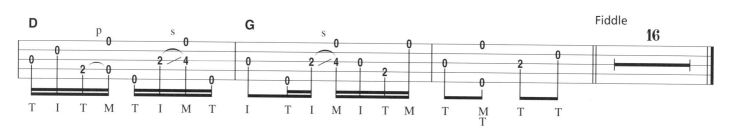

YOU BAKE RIGHT WITH MARTHA WHITE

Sound source—*Flatt & Scruggs at Carnegie Hall!*: First banjo break

By MARTHA WHITE MILLS, INC.

(G tuning)
Key of C

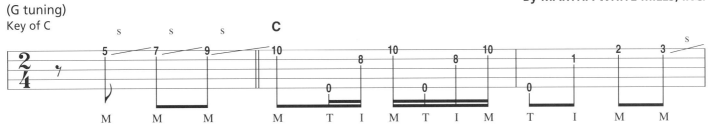

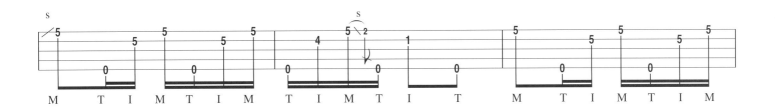

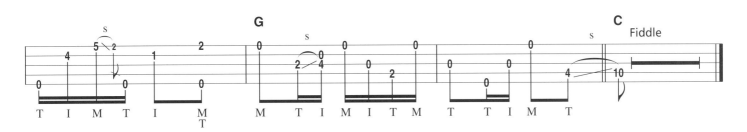

Earl featured on a Limited Edition package of Martha White Mills' corn meal mix in 2001

SALLY GOODWIN

Sound sources—Flatt & Scruggs *Foggy Mountain Banjo* **and**
The Essential Earl Scruggs: **Opening break**

By EARL SCRUGGS

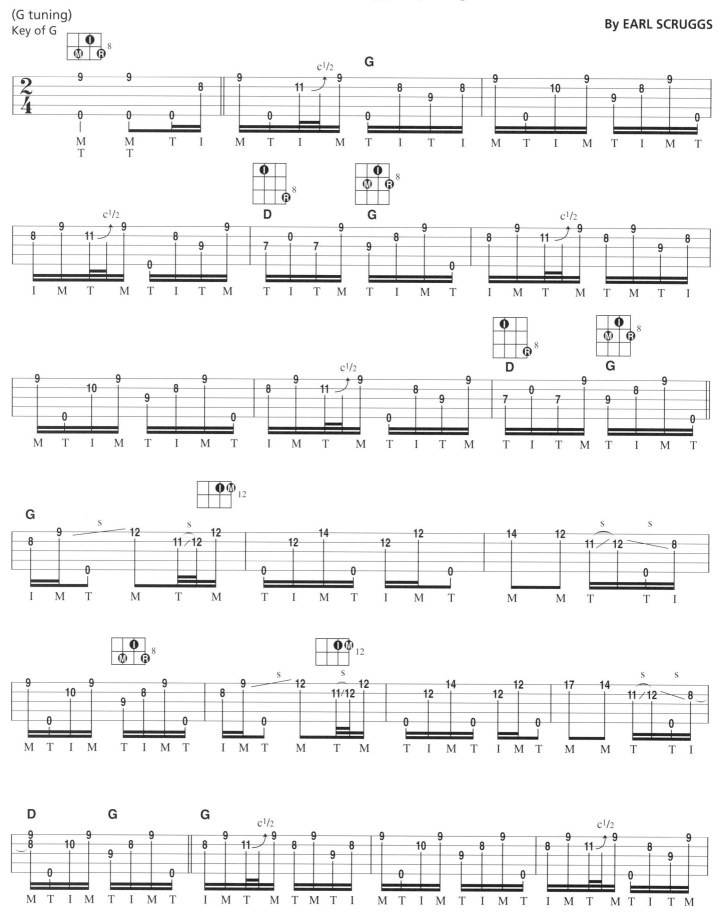

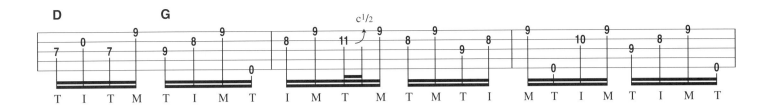
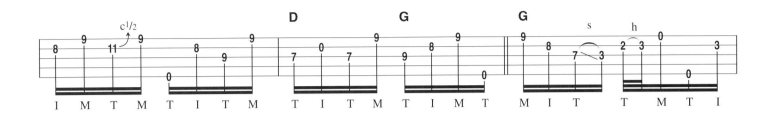
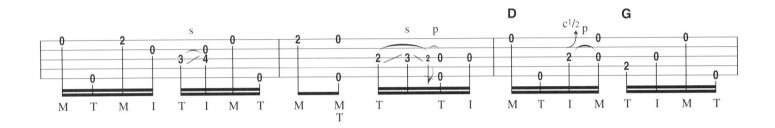
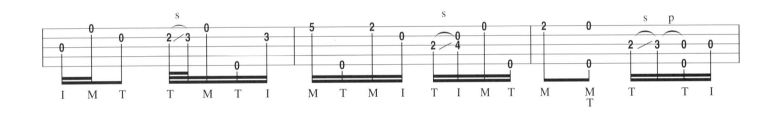
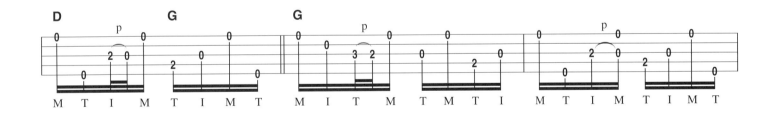
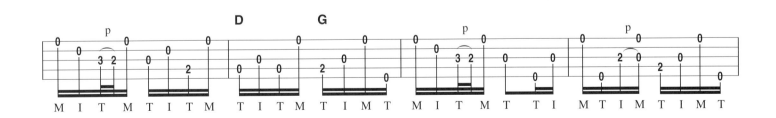
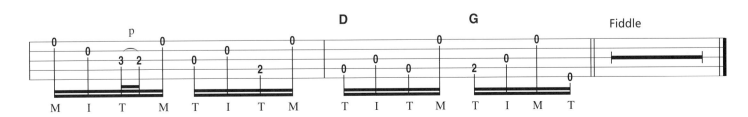

YONDER STANDS LITTLE MAGGIE

Sound source—*Flatt & Scruggs at Carnegie Hall!:* First and last breaks

(G tuning)
Key of A: Capo at 2nd fret and hook the 5th string

By L. CIRTAIN and G. STACEY

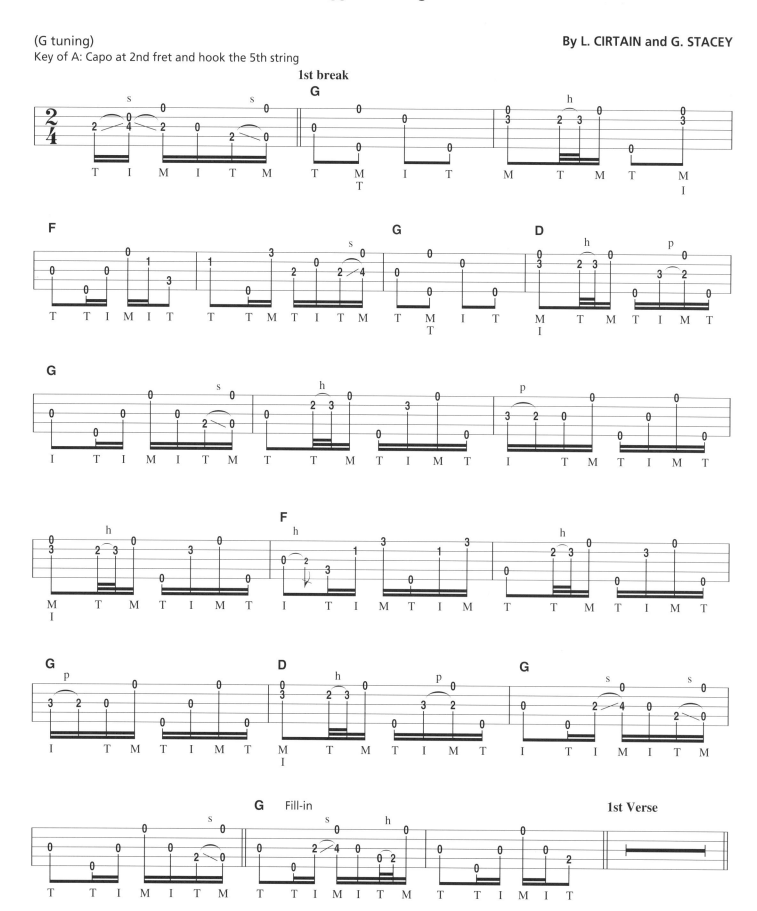

Setup bar

Last break

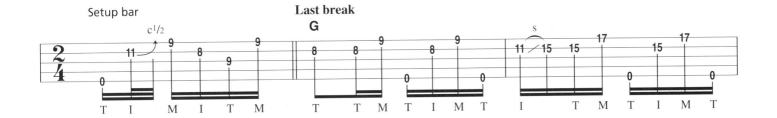

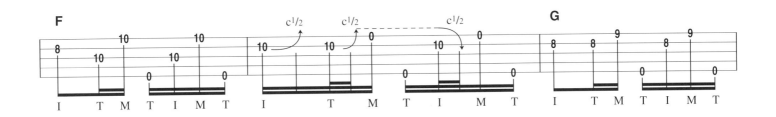

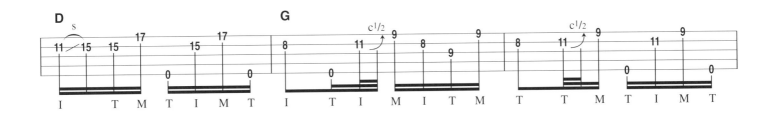

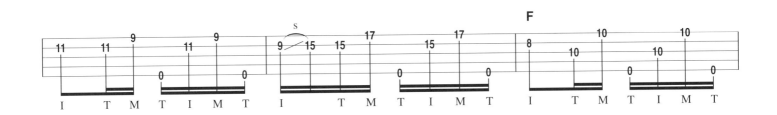

Fill-in

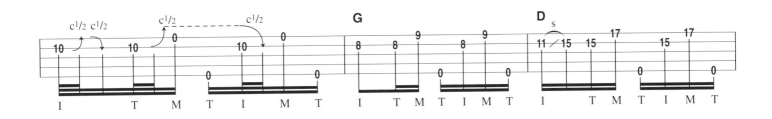

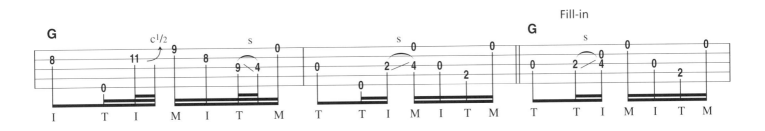

4th Verse

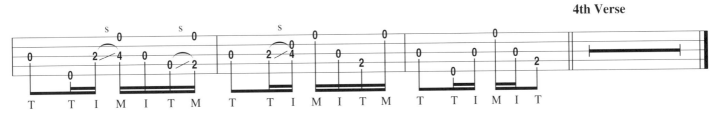

BLUE RIDGE CABIN HOME

Sound source—Flatt & Scruggs *Foggy Mountain Jamboree:* Opening break

(G tuning)
Key of B♭: Capo at 3rd fret and hook the 5th string.
Earl recorded this song in G♯ tuning, capoed at the 2nd fret.

By CIRTAIN and STACEY

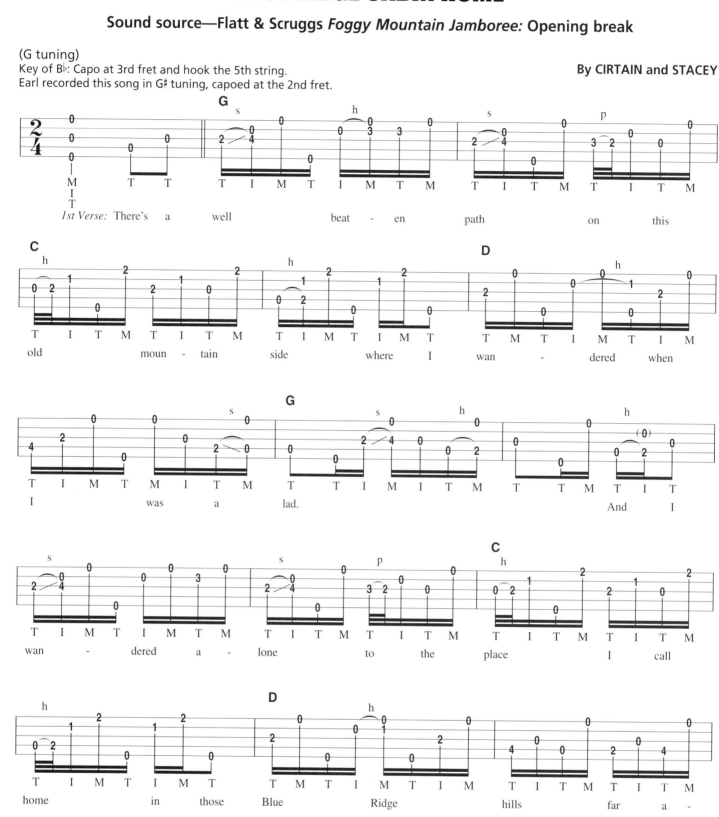

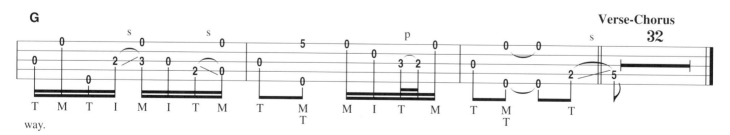

YOUR LOVE IS LIKE A FLOWER

Sound source—Flatt & Scruggs *Foggy Mountain Jamboree:* Opening break

By E. LILLY, L. FLATT and E. SCRUGGS

(G tuning)
Key of B♭: Capo at 3rd fret and hook the 5th string.
Earl recorded this song in G♯ tuning, capoed at the 2nd fret.

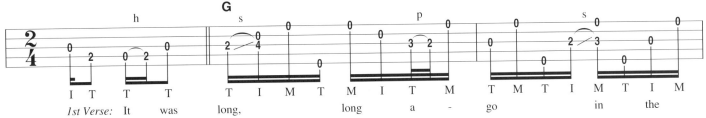

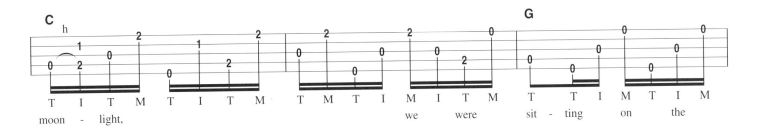

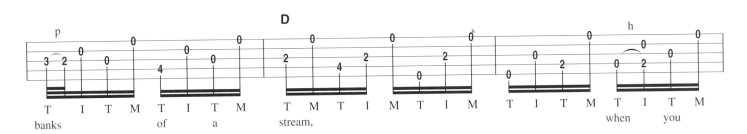

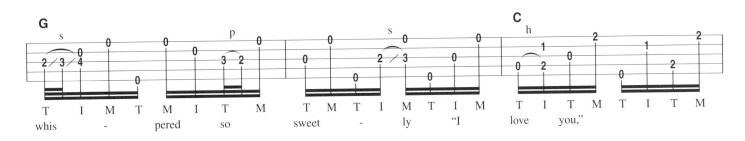

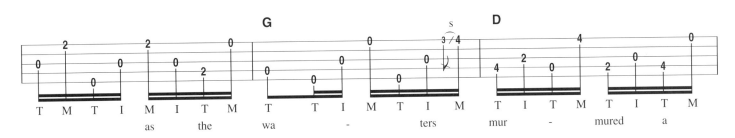

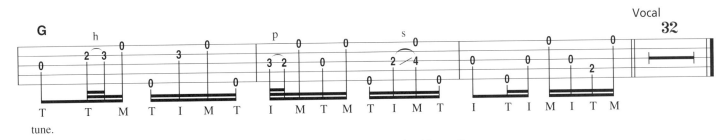

DEAR OLD DIXIE

Sound sources—Flatt & Scruggs *Lester Flatt & Earl Scruggs* and
The Essential Earl Scruggs: Intro and first section of opening break

By LESTER FLATT and EARL SCRUGGS

(G tuning)
Key of G (Recorded in G♯)

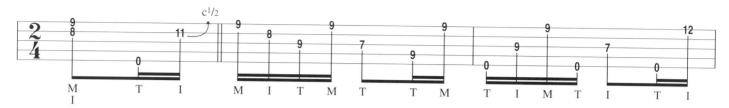

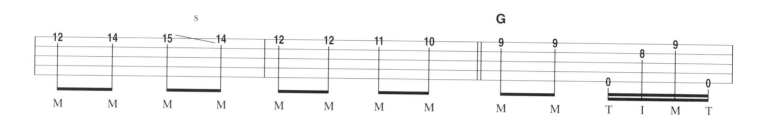

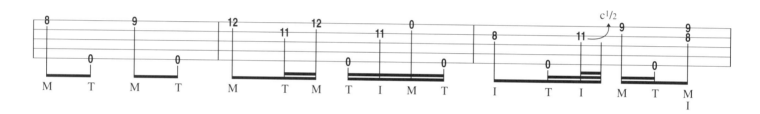

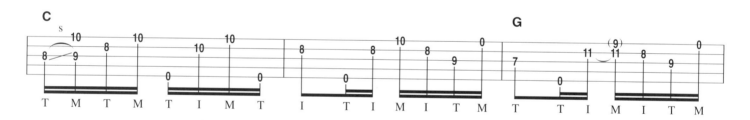

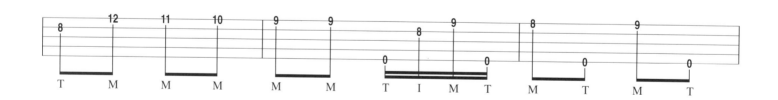

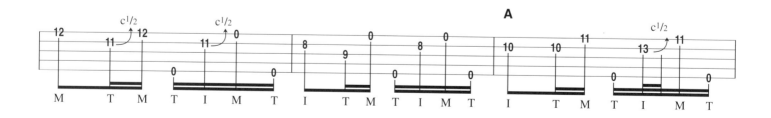

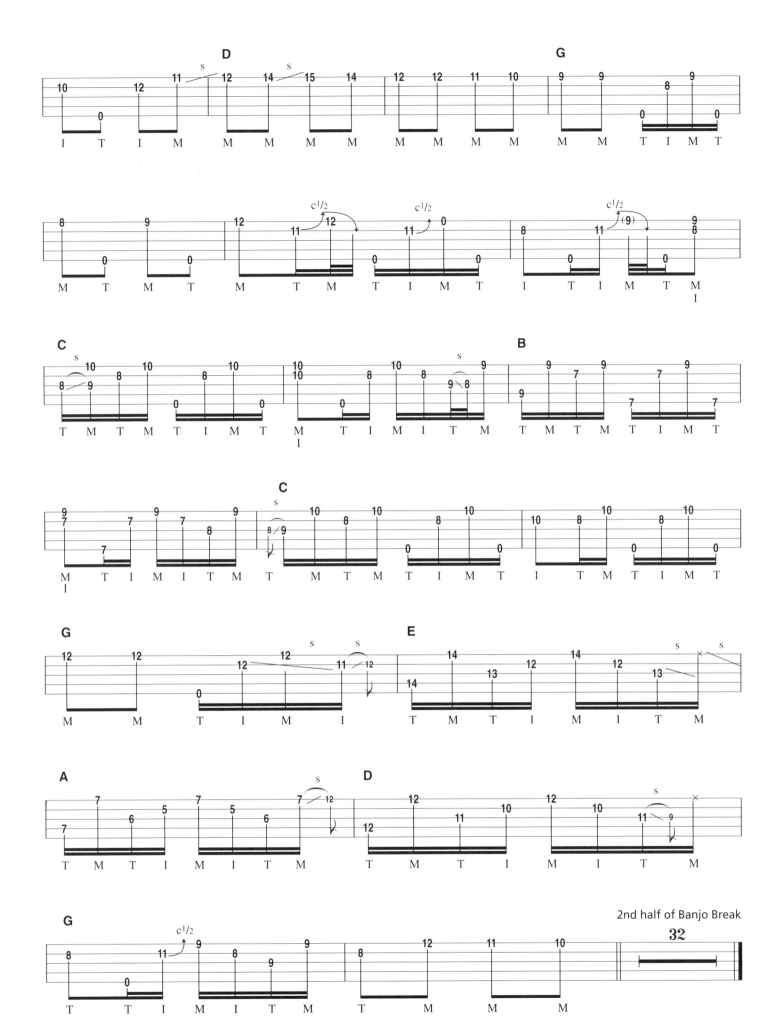

NOTE: This version is also on the Flatt & Scruggs *Kings of Bluegrass.*

EARL'S BREAKDOWN

Sound sources—Flatt & Scruggs *Foggy Mountain Jamboree* and
The Essential Earl Scruggs: All banjo breaks

By EARL SCRUGGS

(G tuning)
Key of G (Recorded in G♯)

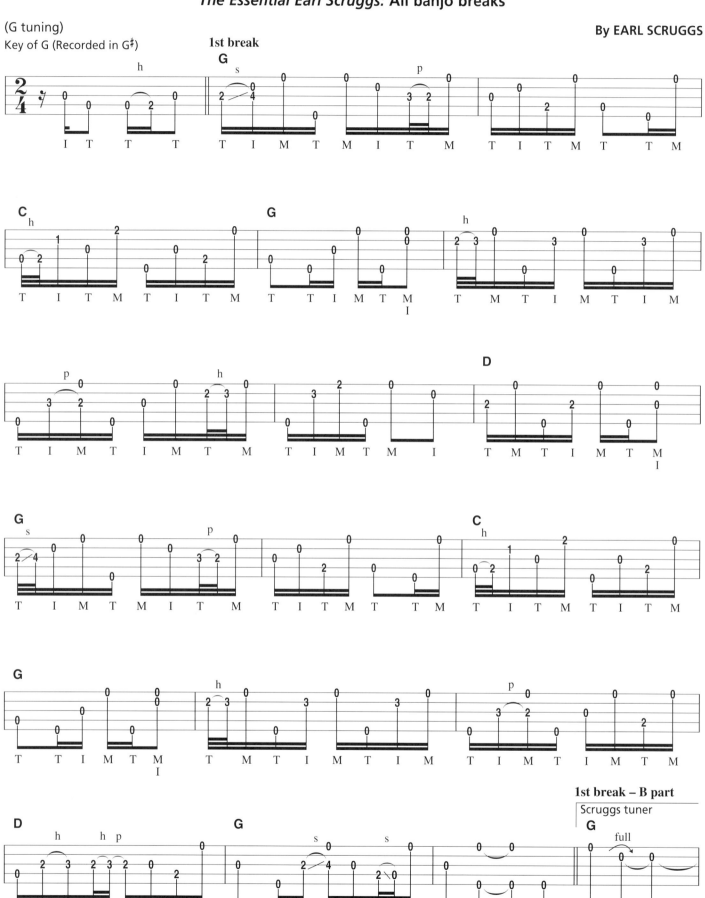

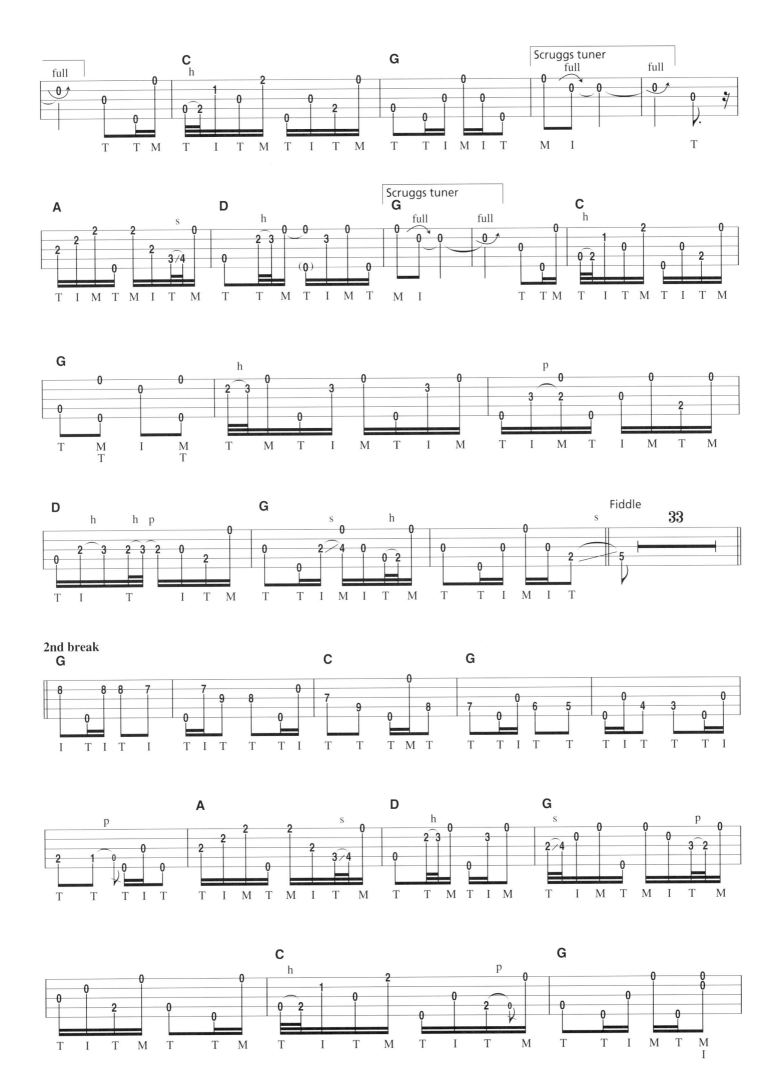

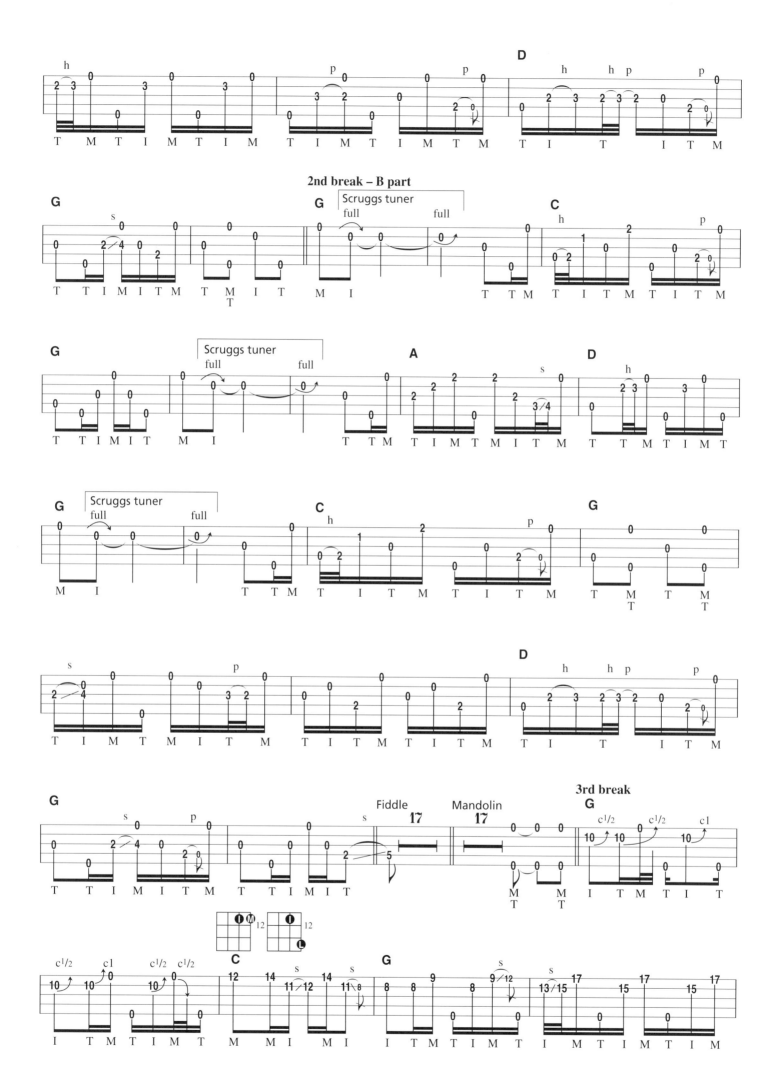

2nd break – B part

Scruggs tuner

Scruggs tuner

Scruggs tuner

3rd break

Fiddle   Mandolin

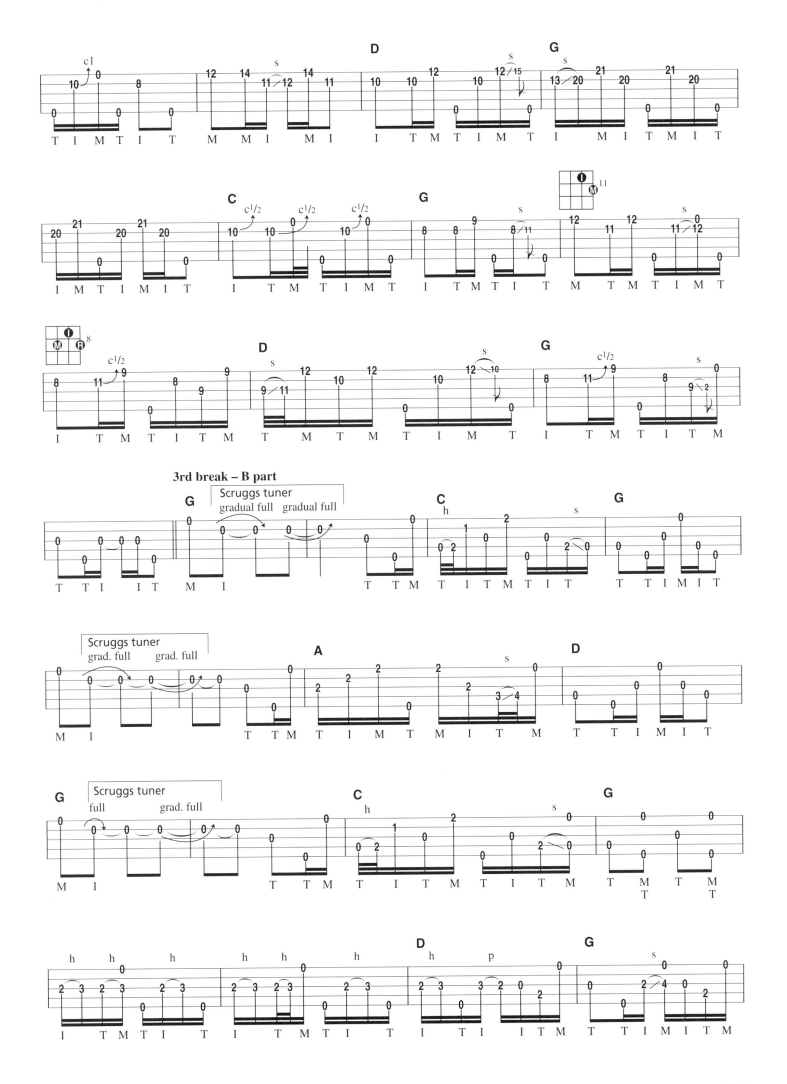

3rd break – B part

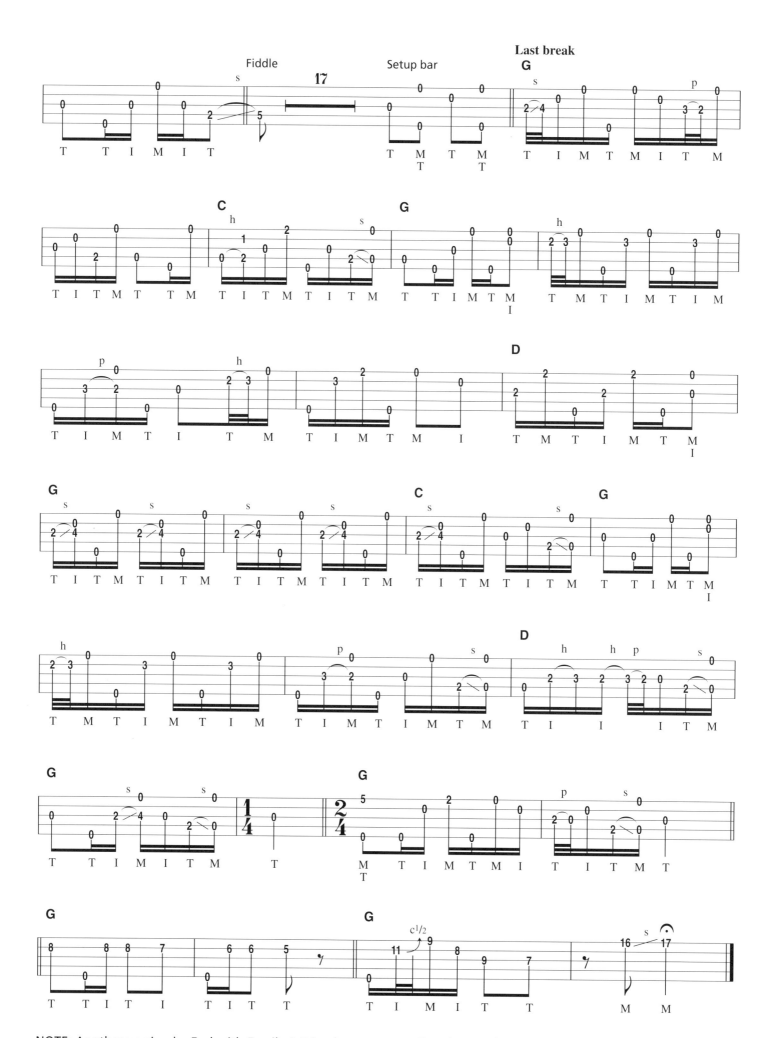

NOTE: Another version by Earl with Family & Friends appears on *The Three Pickers* CD and DVD. Another version by Earl with the Nitty Gritty Dirt Band appears on NGDB *Will the Circle Be Unbroken*.

MY CABIN IN CAROLINE

Sound source—Flatt & Scruggs *Country Music:* **Banjo break after the first chorus**

By LESTER FLATT and EARL SCRUGGS

(G tuning)
Key of G (Recorded in G♯)

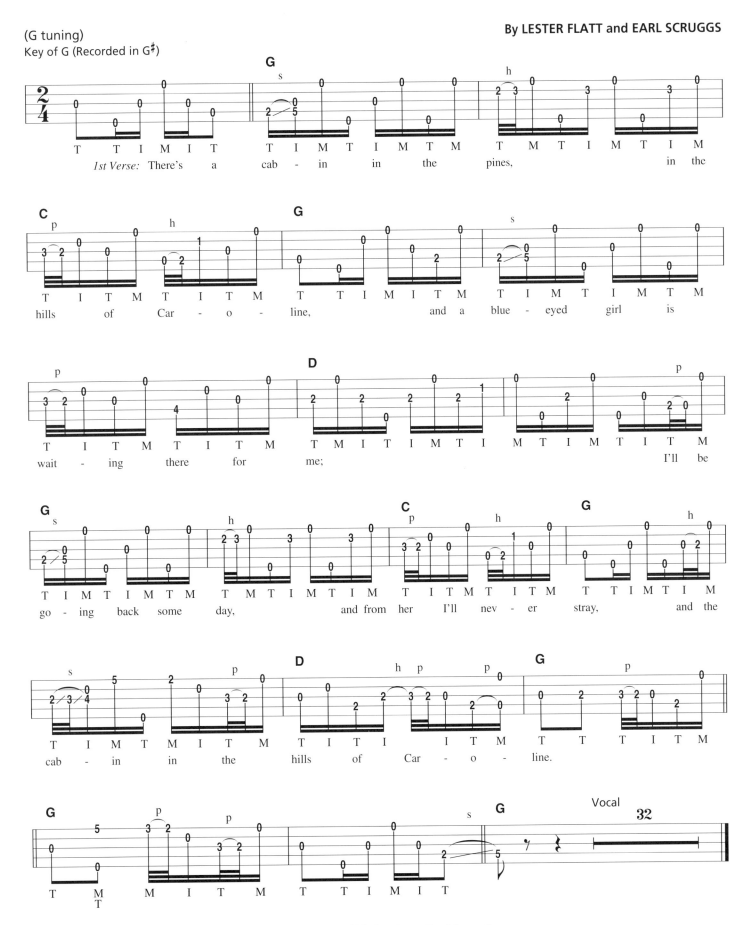

FLINT HILL SPECIAL

Sound sources—Flatt & Scruggs *Foggy Mountain Jamboree* **and** *The Essential Earl Scruggs:*
1st and 2nd breaks + last 8 bars of the last break and ending

(G tuning)
Key of G (Recorded in G#)

By EARL SCRUGGS

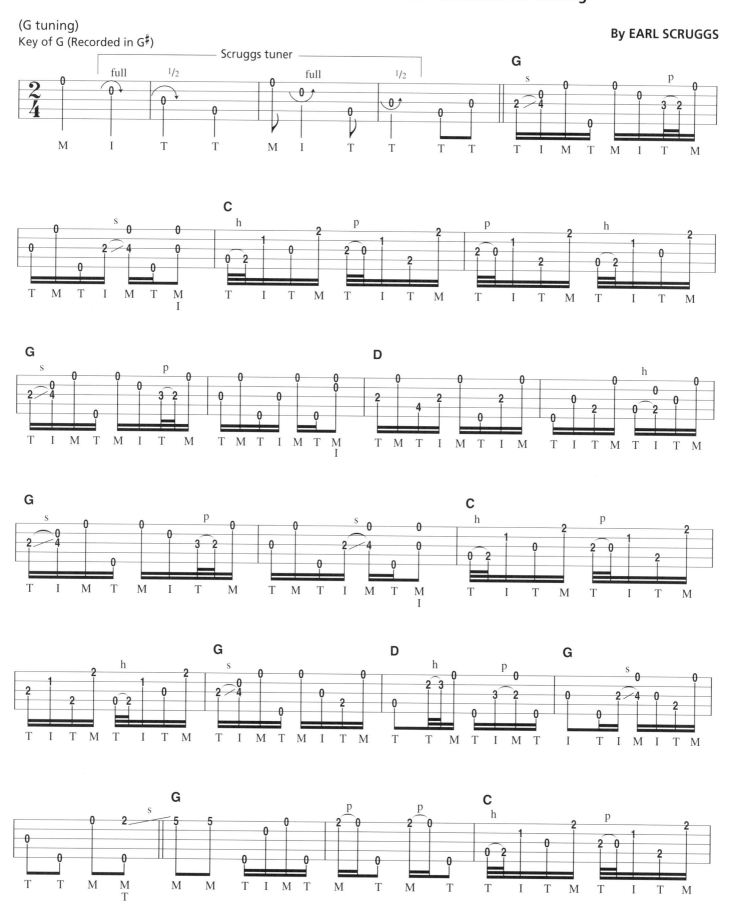

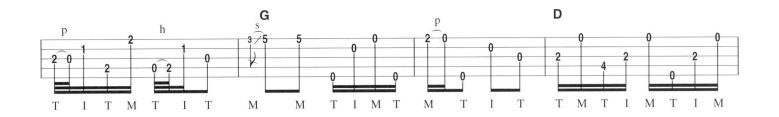

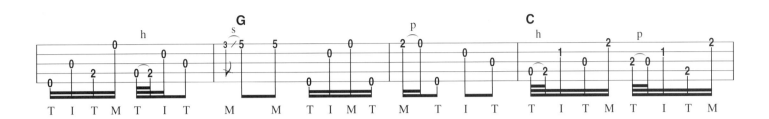

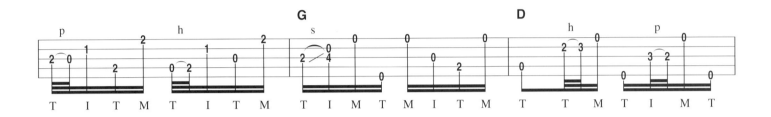

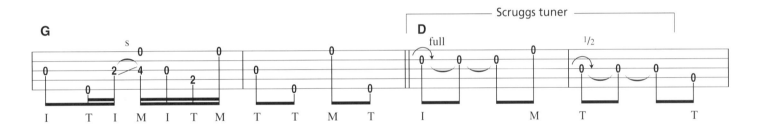

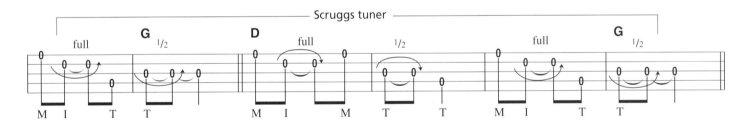

Fiddle Setup bar to 2nd break **2nd break**

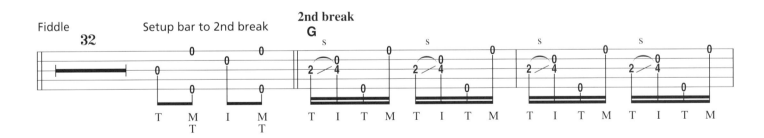

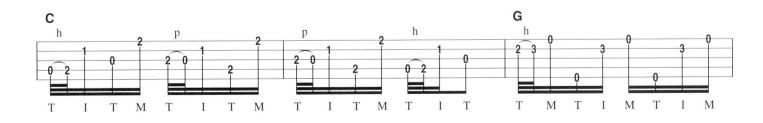

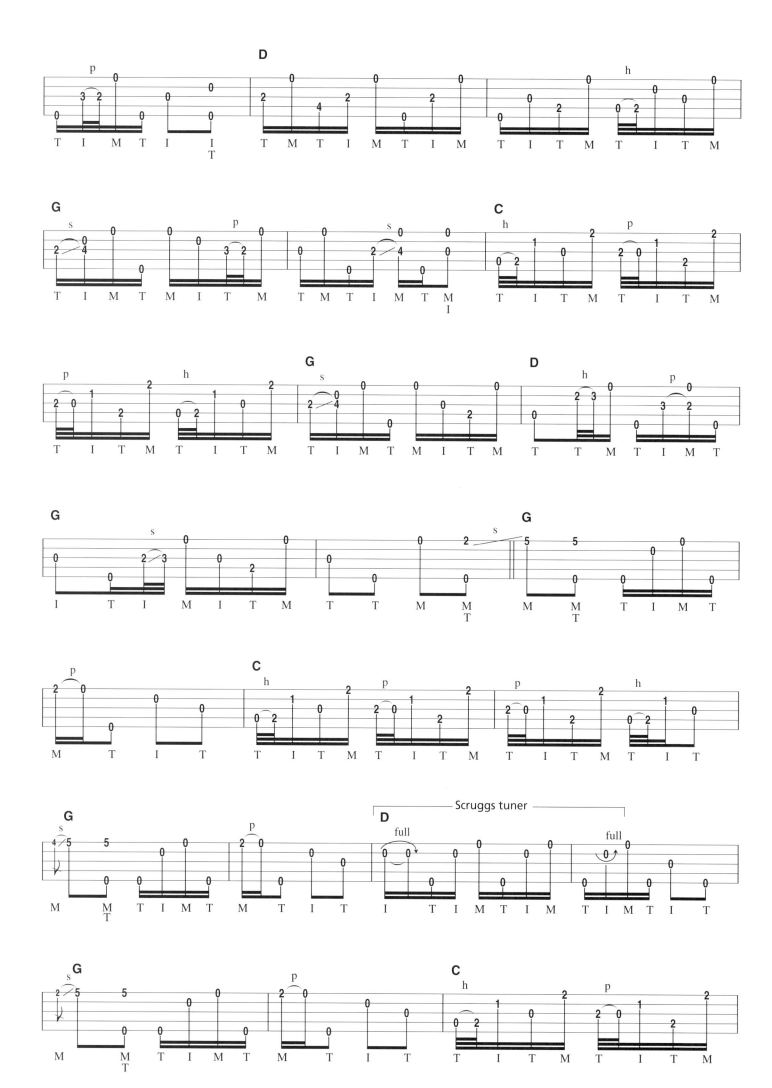

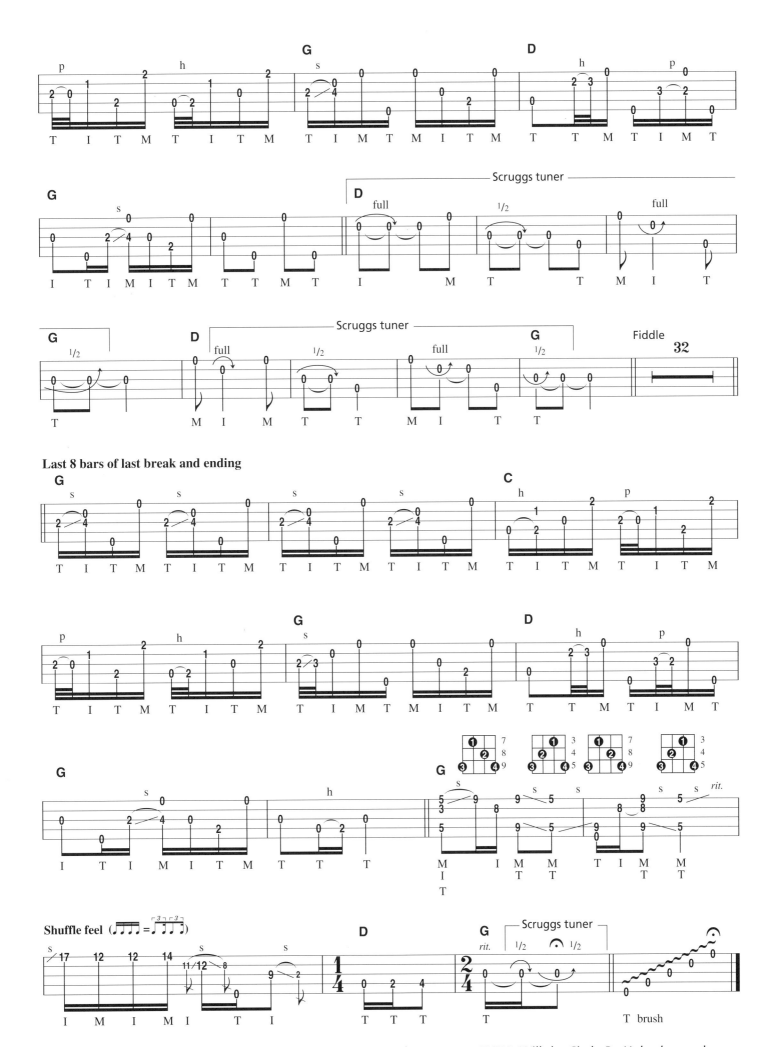

Last 8 bars of last break and ending

NOTE: Another version by Earl with the Nitty Gritty Dirt Band appears on NGDB *Will the Circle Be Unbroken* and *Flatt & Scruggs at Carnegie Hall!*

FOGGY MOUNTAIN BREAKDOWN

(Featured in the film, BONNIE AND CLYDE)

Sound sources—Flatt & Scruggs *Country Music* and *The Essential Earl Scruggs:*
First and second breaks

(G tuning)
Key of G (Recorded in G♯)

By EARL SCRUGGS

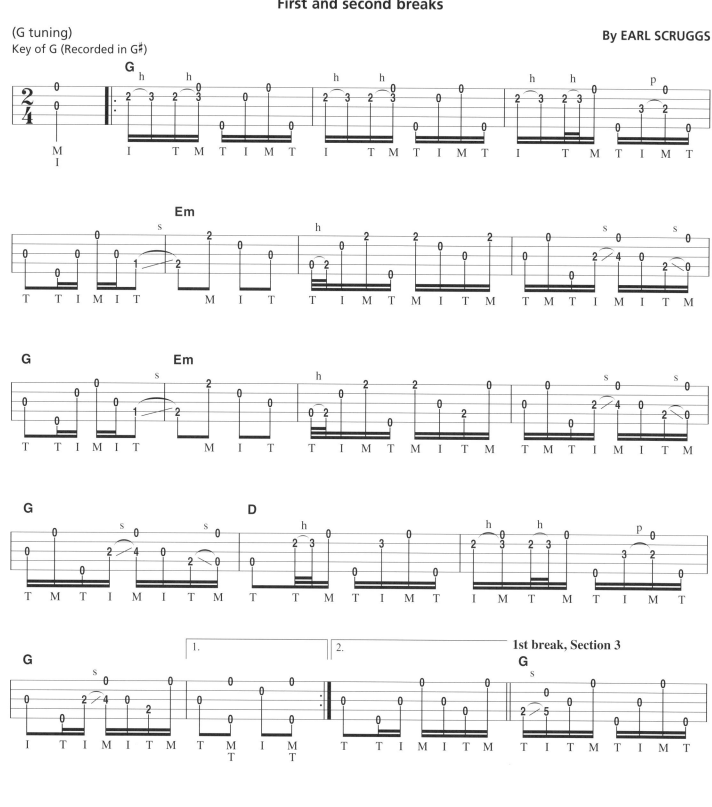

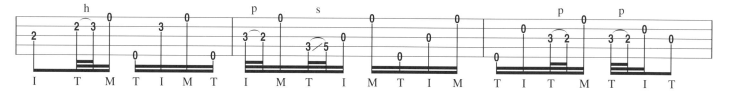

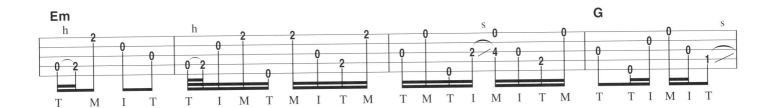

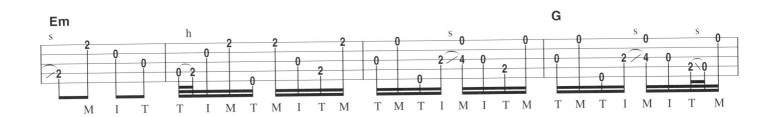

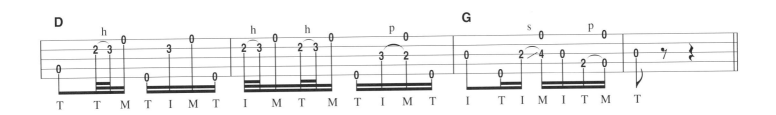

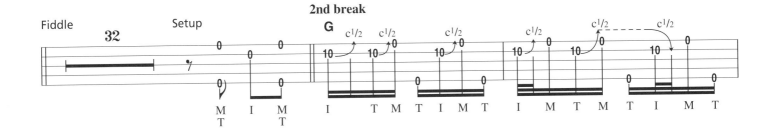

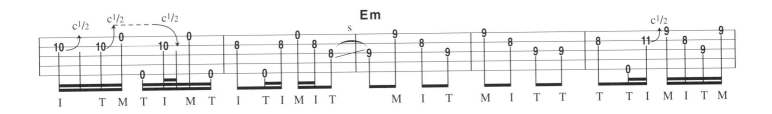

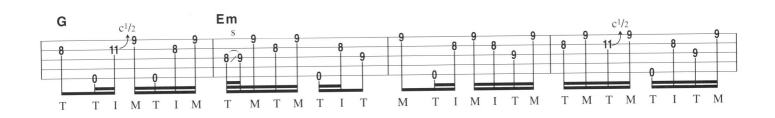

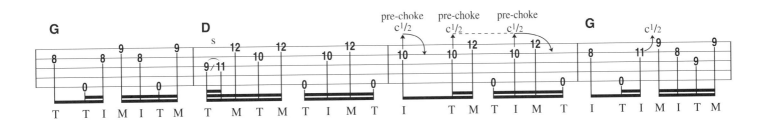

2nd break, Section 2

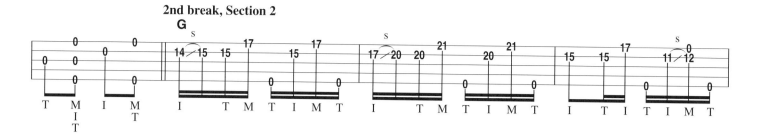

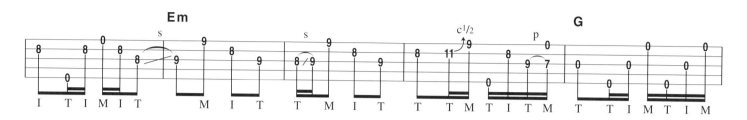

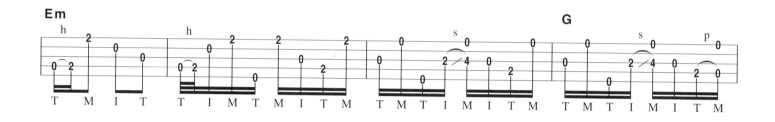

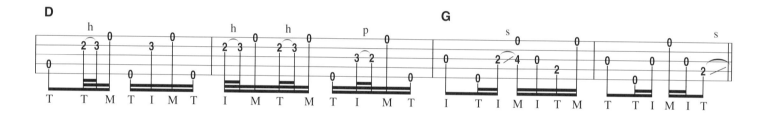

2nd break, Section 3

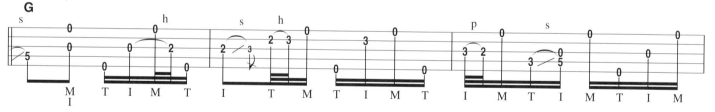

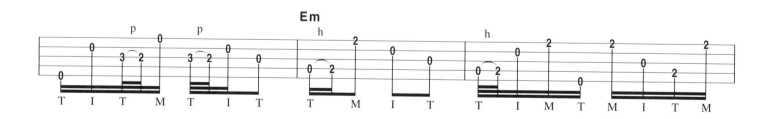

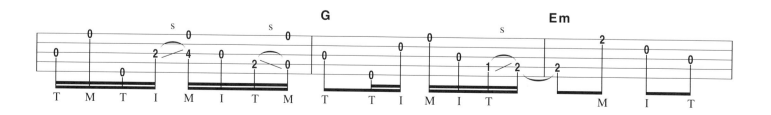

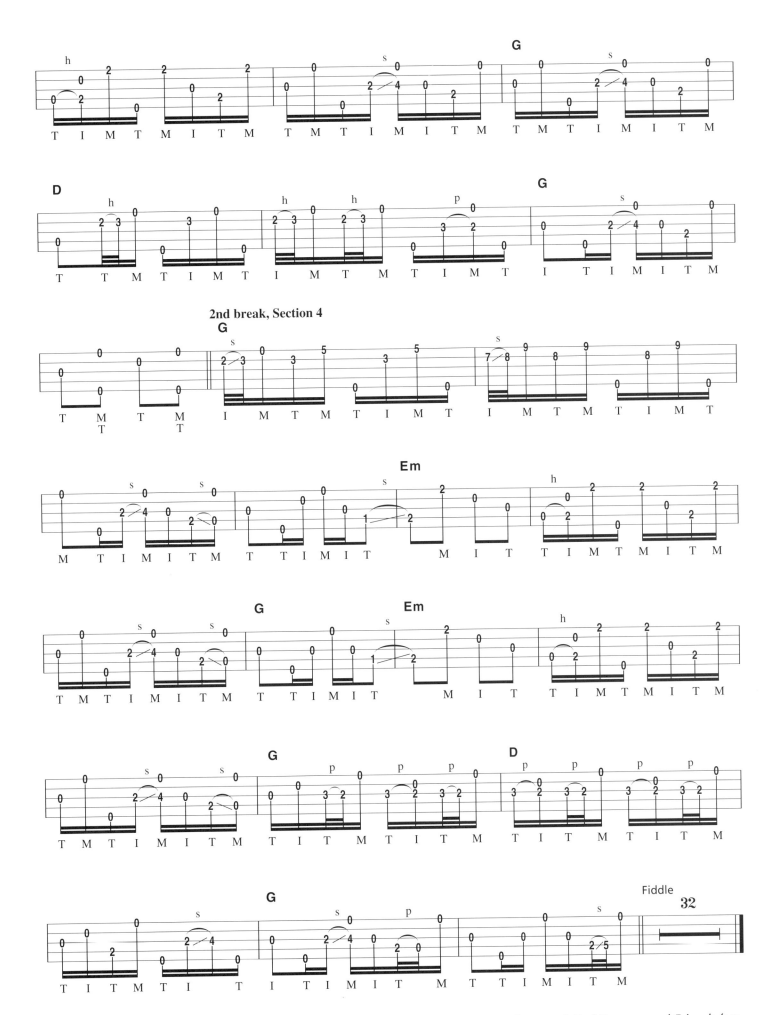

NOTE: Other versions by Earl appear on the Earl Scruggs Revue *Live at Kansas State* and *Earl Scruggs and Friends* (see page 172 for information regarding featured guest artists). The chords for this tablature reflect the way the tune is performed on *Live at Kansas State* and *Earl Scruggs and Friends*.

FOGGY MOUNTAIN CHIMES

Sound sources—Flatt & Scruggs *Foggy Mountain Jamboree* and
The Essential Earl Scruggs: Opening break

(G tuning)
Keys: G and D (Recorded in G# and D#)

By EARL SCRUGGS

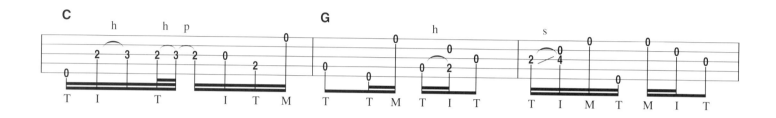

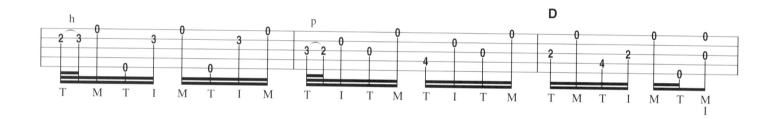

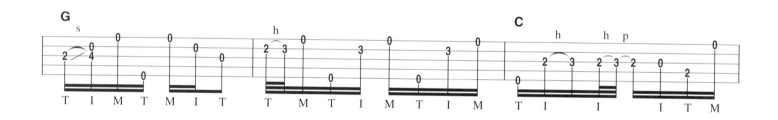

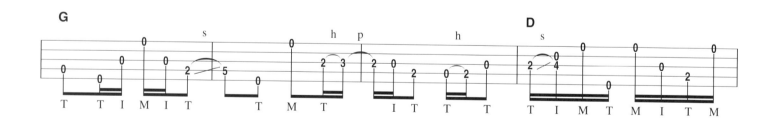

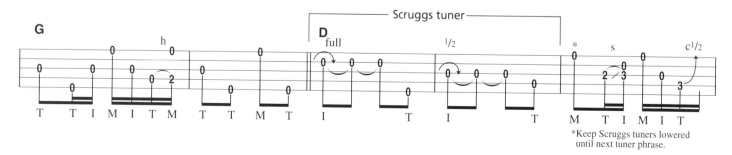

*Keep Scruggs tuners lowered
until next tuner phrase.

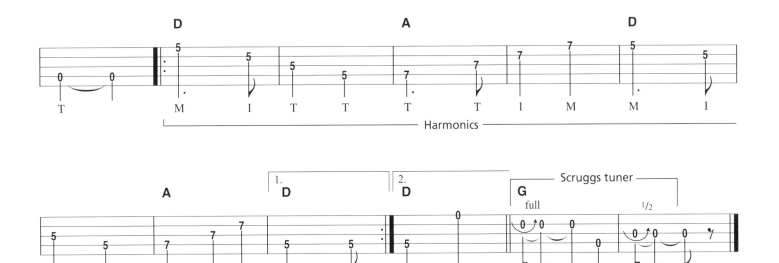

Earl Scruggs Signature Model "Golden Deluxe"

Gibson introduced the Golden Deluxe model in 1992. It features engraved 24-carat satin gold hardware.

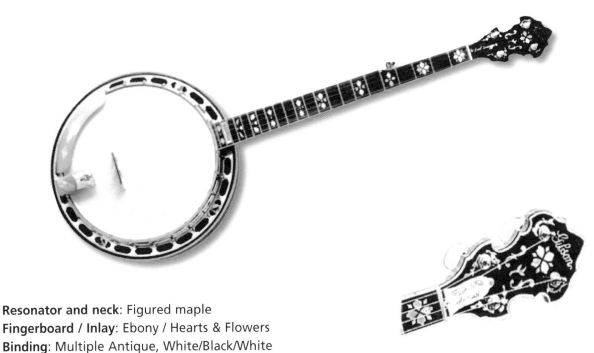

Resonator and neck: Figured maple
Fingerboard / Inlay: Ebony / Hearts & Flowers
Binding: Multiple Antique, White/Black/White
Hardware: 24k Satin Gold Engraved
Tuners: Vintage 2-band
Finish: Exact Replica, Antique Amber Brown
Case: Shaped Hardshell*

*Specifications provided by Gibson

"Golden Deluxe" peghead

GROUND SPEED

Sound source—Flatt & Scruggs *Foggy Mountain Banjo:* First and second breaks

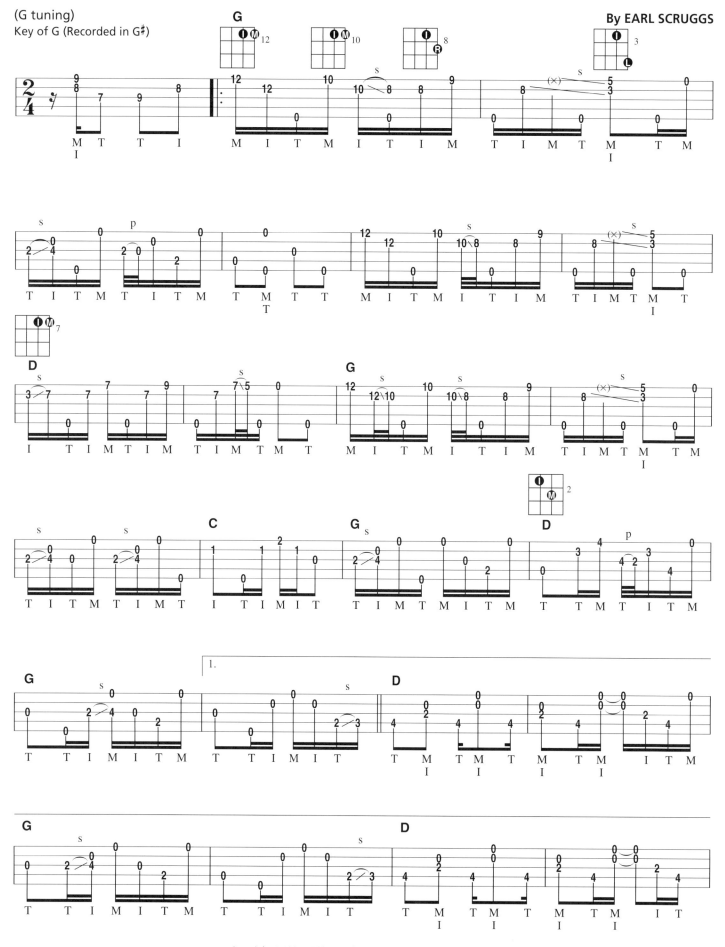

By EARL SCRUGGS

(G tuning)
Key of G (Recorded in G♯)

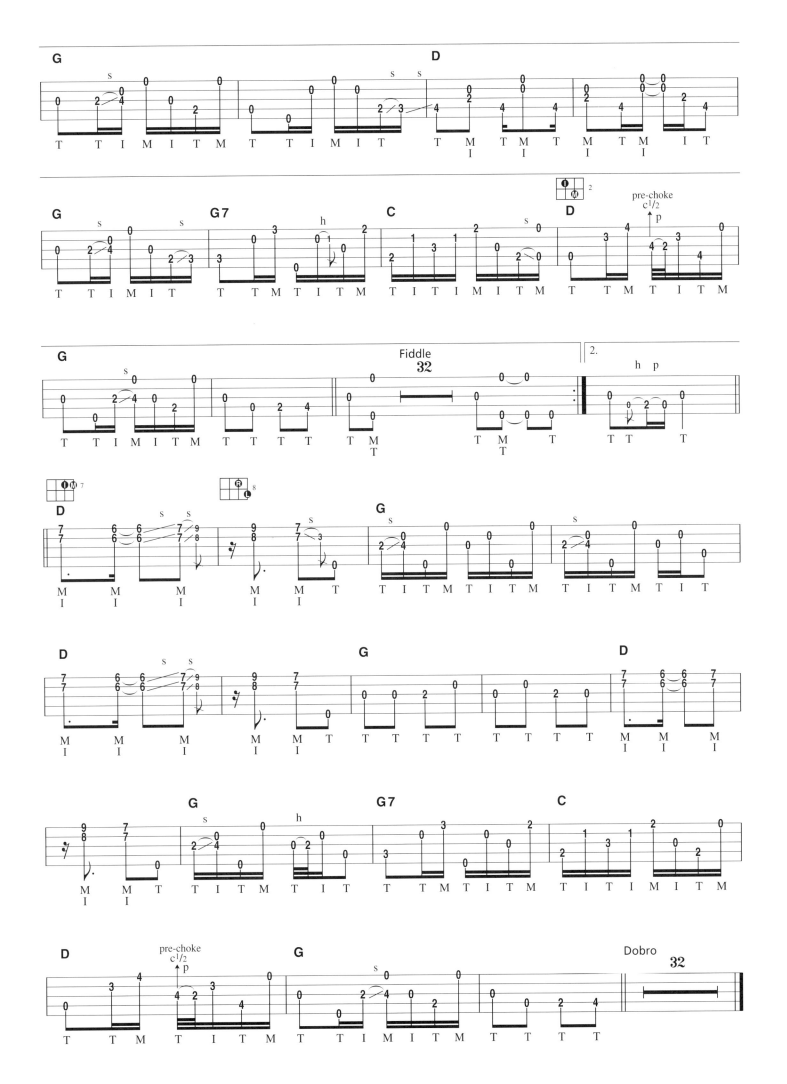

RANDY LYNN RAG

Sound sources—Flatt & Scruggs *Foggy Mountain Jamboree* and
The Essential Earl Scruggs: Opening break

(G tuning)
Key of G (Recorded in G#) Note: B tuner locks *upward* on the note C.

By EARL SCRUGGS

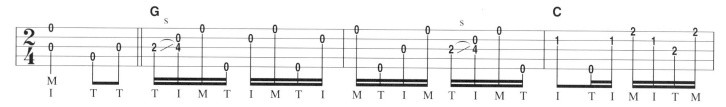

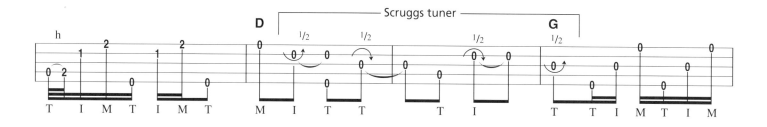

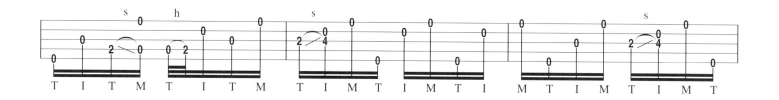

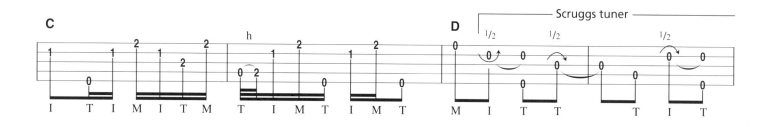

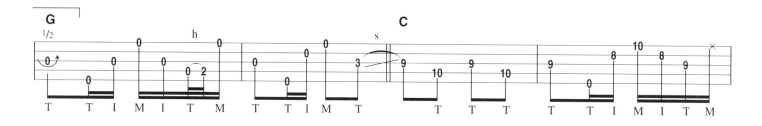

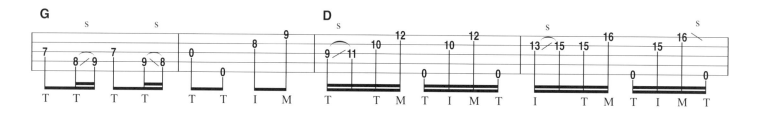

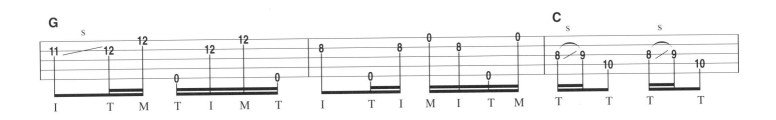

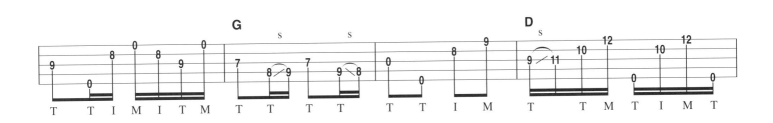

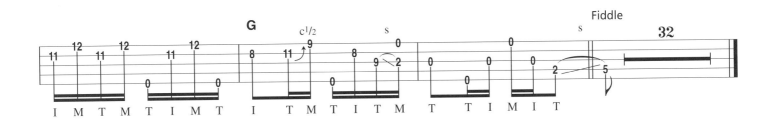

Earl Scruggs Signature Model "49 Classic"

For a period of time beginning in 1949, the fingerboard on my Granada had the then current "bow tie" inlay design. Gibson began producing the 49 Classic, which replicates that inlay styling, in 1992.

Resonator and neck: Figured maple
Fingerboard / Inlay: Rosewood / Bow Tie
Binding: Multiple Antique, White/Black/White
Hardware: Nickel Plate
Tuners: Vintage 2-band
Finish: Exact Replica, Amber Brown
Case: Shaped Hardshell*

"49 Classic" peghead

*Specifications provided by Gibson

CAROLINA TRAVELER

Sound source—John McEuen (Vanguard Records) *String Wizards* and
(The best of) John McEuen *String Wizard's Picks:* Earl's break following John's opening
frailing break + the 4-bar lead-in to the duet break by John and Earl

By EARL SCRUGGS

(C tuning)
Key of C

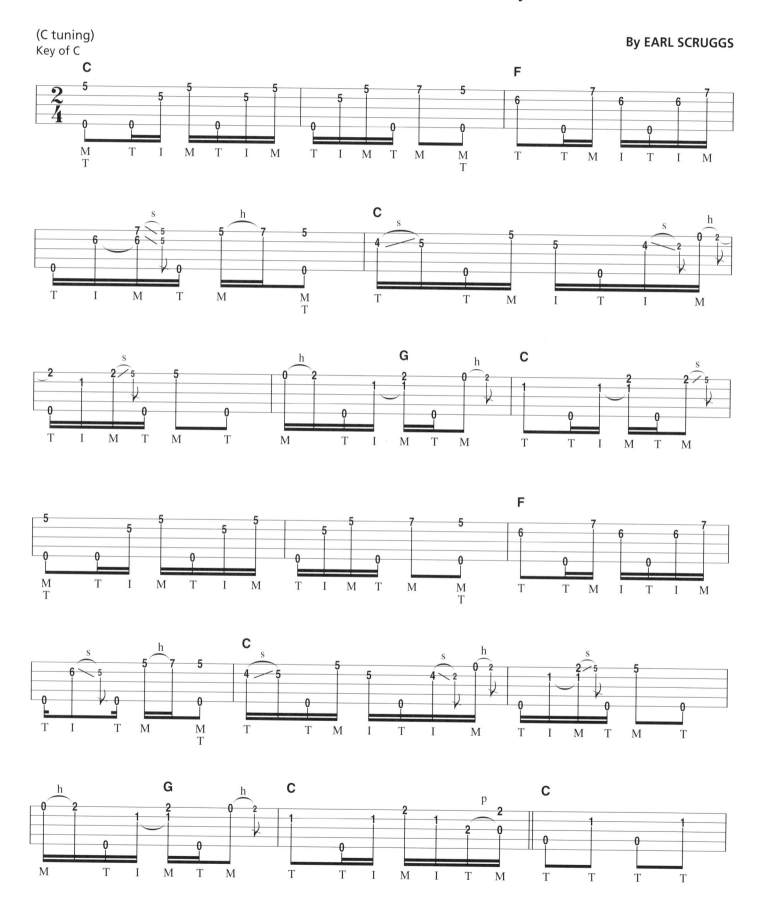

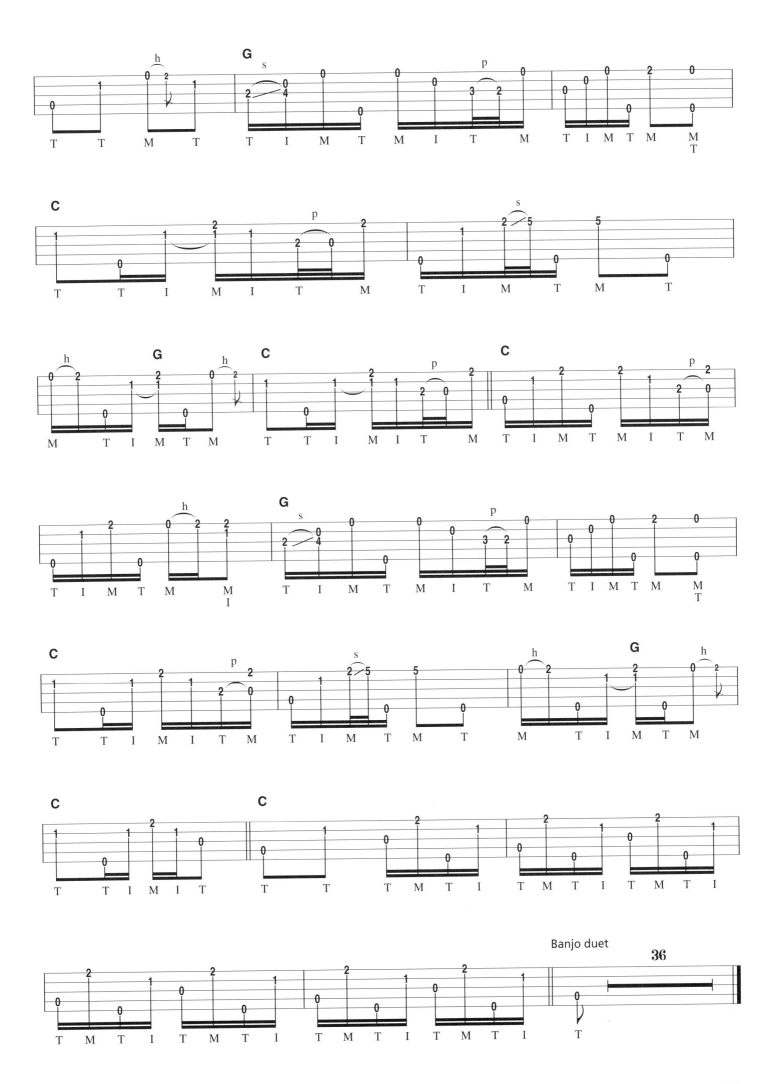

Banjo duet

36

OLD FOLKS

Sound source—Flatt & Scruggs *Live at Vanderbilt University:*
First two sections of the opening break + the last two bars of the tune

By EARL SCRUGGS

(C tuning)
Key of C

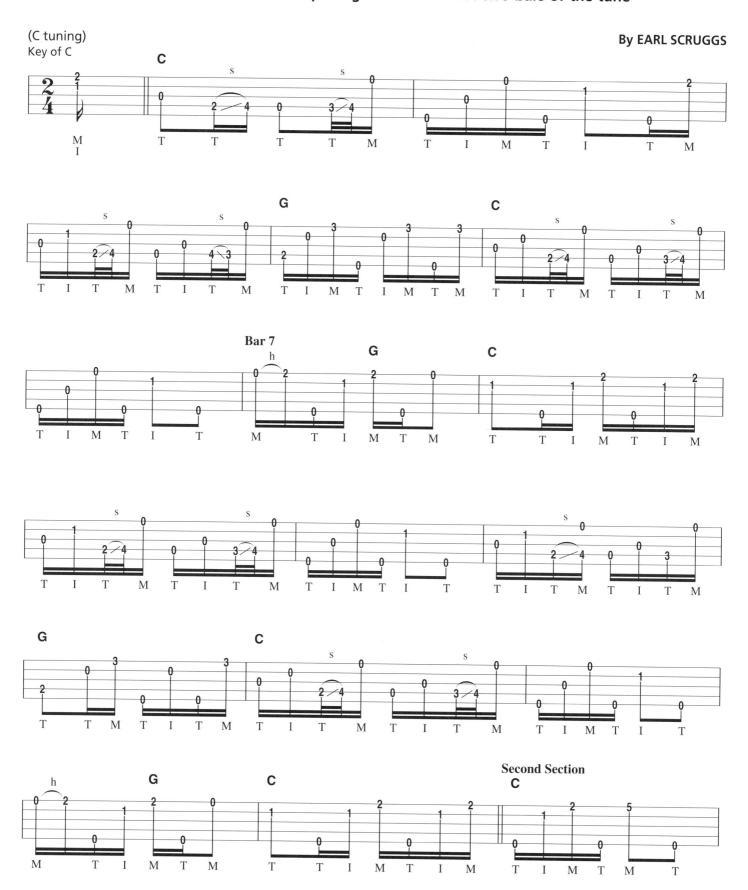

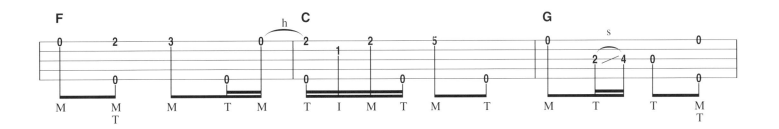

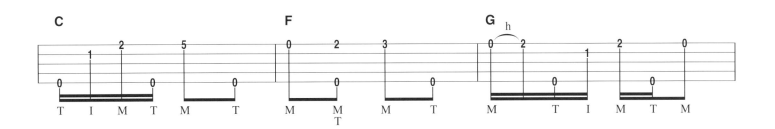

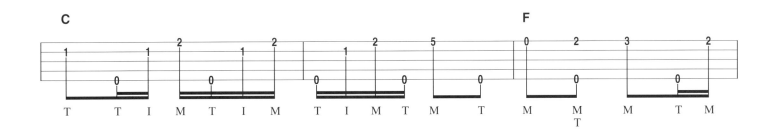

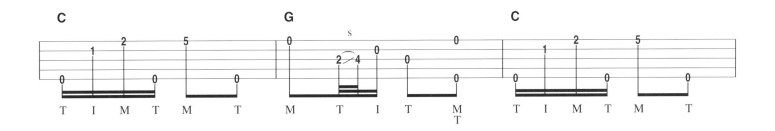

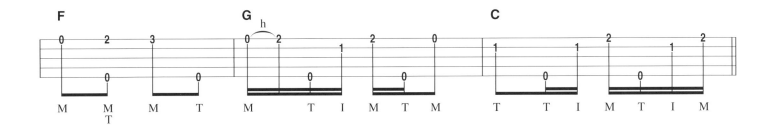

Banjo 2nd half

Last 2 Bars

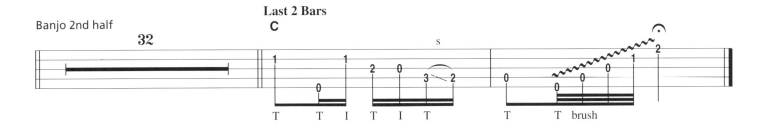

NOTE: To practice how to end the tune, play the first seven measures of the first section and then go directly to the last two bars of the tune.

ROLLER COASTER

Sound source—Earl Scruggs *Top of the World:* Opening break

(C tuning)
Key of C

By EARL SCRUGGS

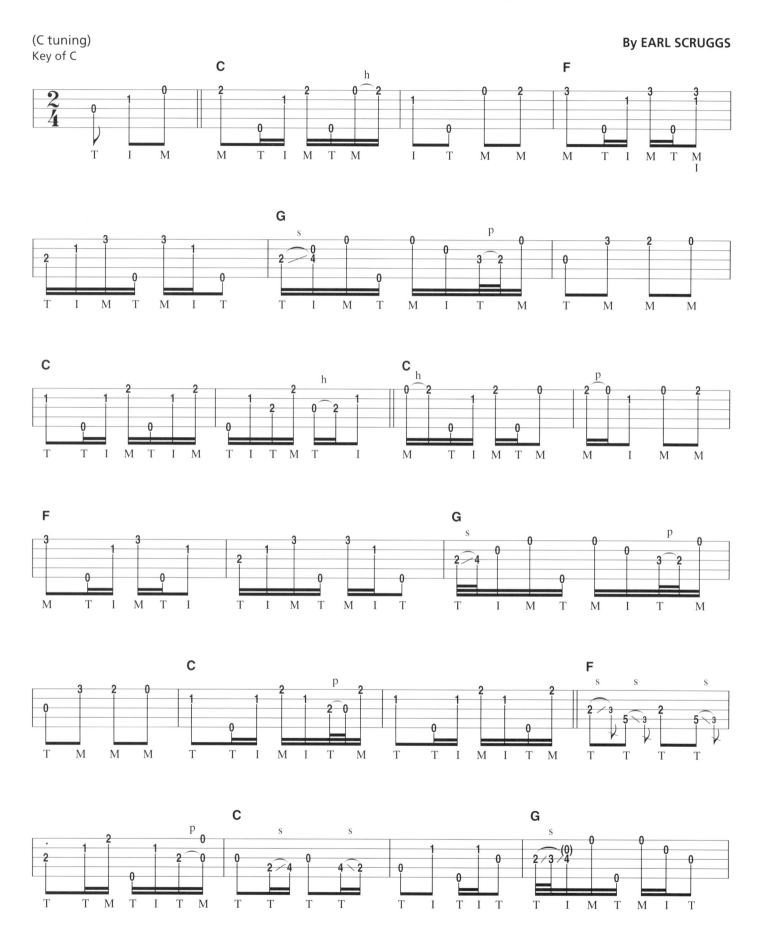

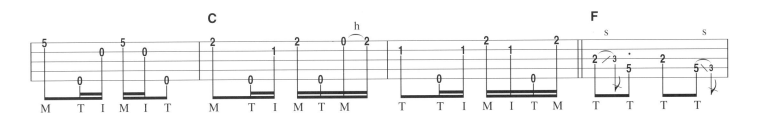

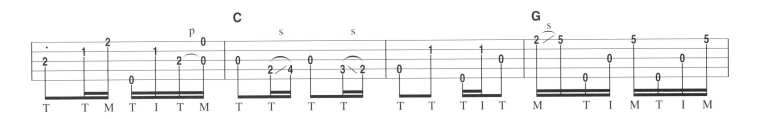

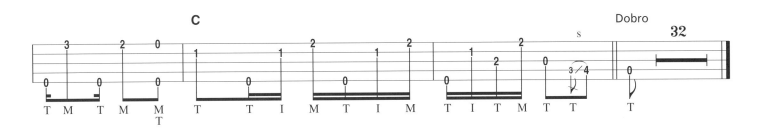

Earl Scruggs Signature Model "Special"

The Special made its debut in 1995. It is a highly ornamental instrument featuring 24-carat gold engraved hardware and binding made of abalone.

Resonator and neck: Figured maple
Fingerboard / Inlay: Ebony / Hearts & Flowers, Abalone Trim
Binding: Multiple, Abalone/White/Black/White/Abalone, Abalone bound peghead
Hardware: 24k Gold Engraved
Tuners: Vintage 2-band with pearl buttons
Finish: Exact Replica, Antique Amber Brown
Features: Earl's signature inlaid in abalone on the resonator
Case: Shaped Hardshell*

*Specifications provided by Gibson

"Special" peghead

HOME SWEET HOME

Sound source—Flatt & Scruggs *Foggy Mountain Banjo:* First and second breaks

By EARL SCRUGGS

(C tuning)
Key of C

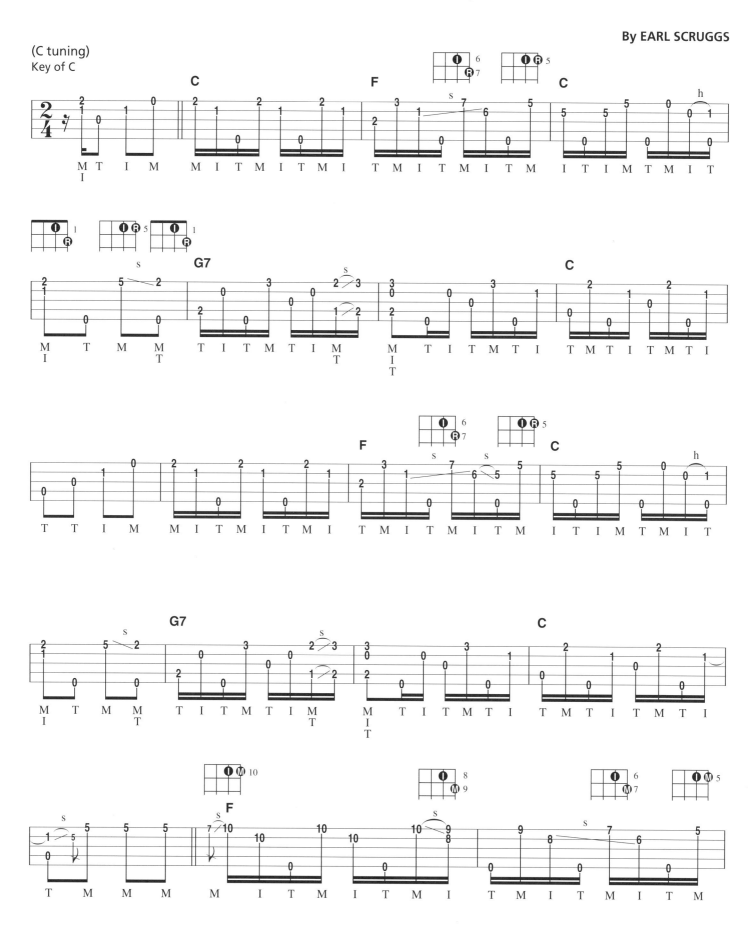

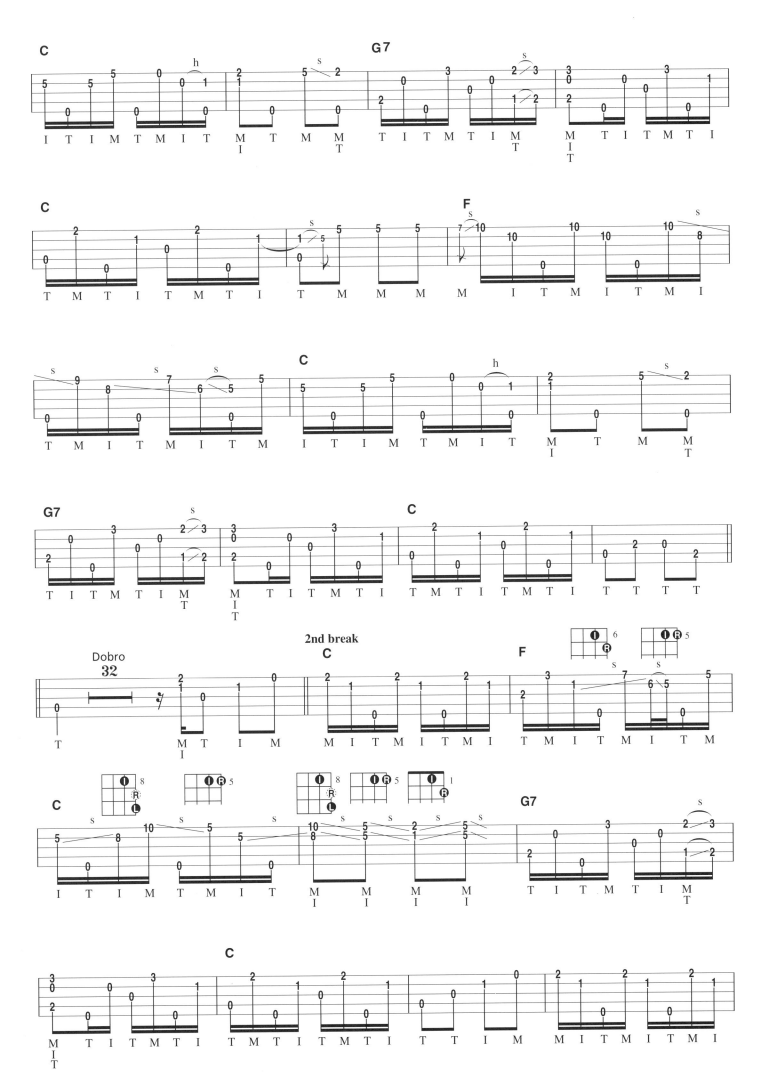

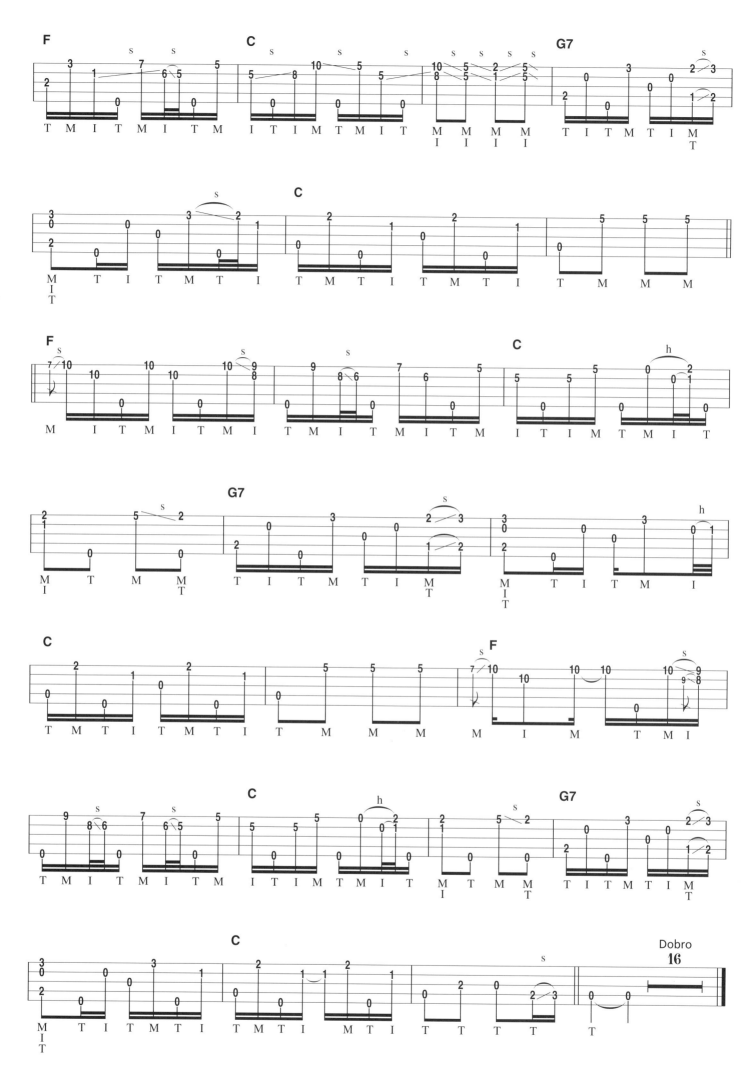

BROAD RIVER

Sound source—*Earl Scruggs Revue Volume II:* Opening break

By EARL SCRUGGS

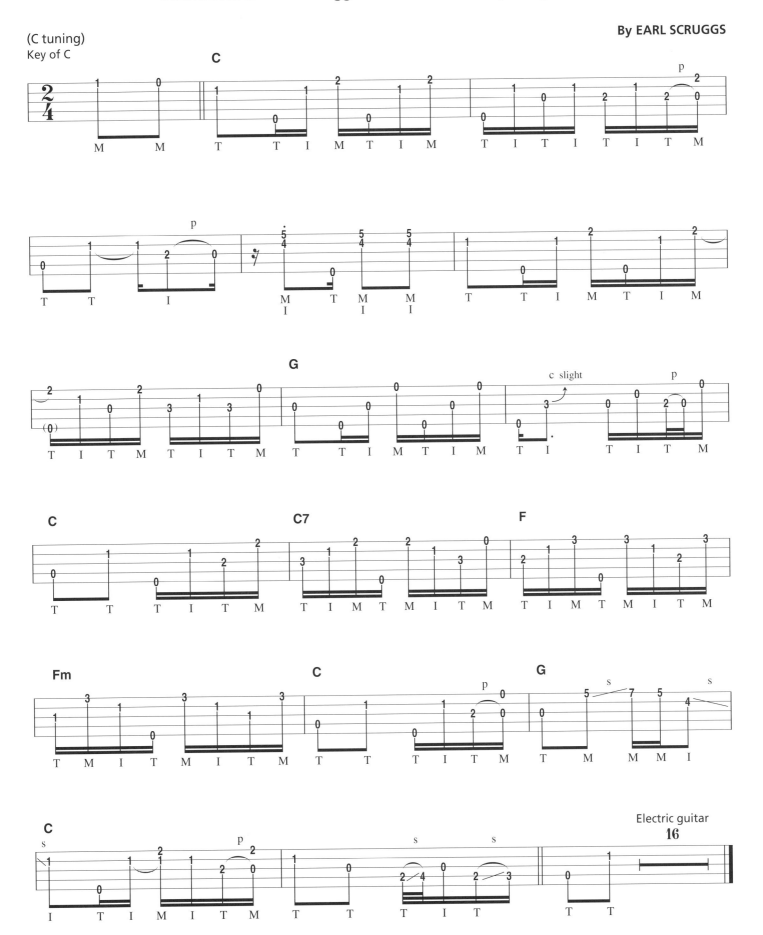

PEDAL TO THE METAL

Sound source—Earl Scruggs *American Made – World Played:* Opening break

By EARL SCRUGGS
and STEVE SCRUGGS

(G tuning)
Key of G

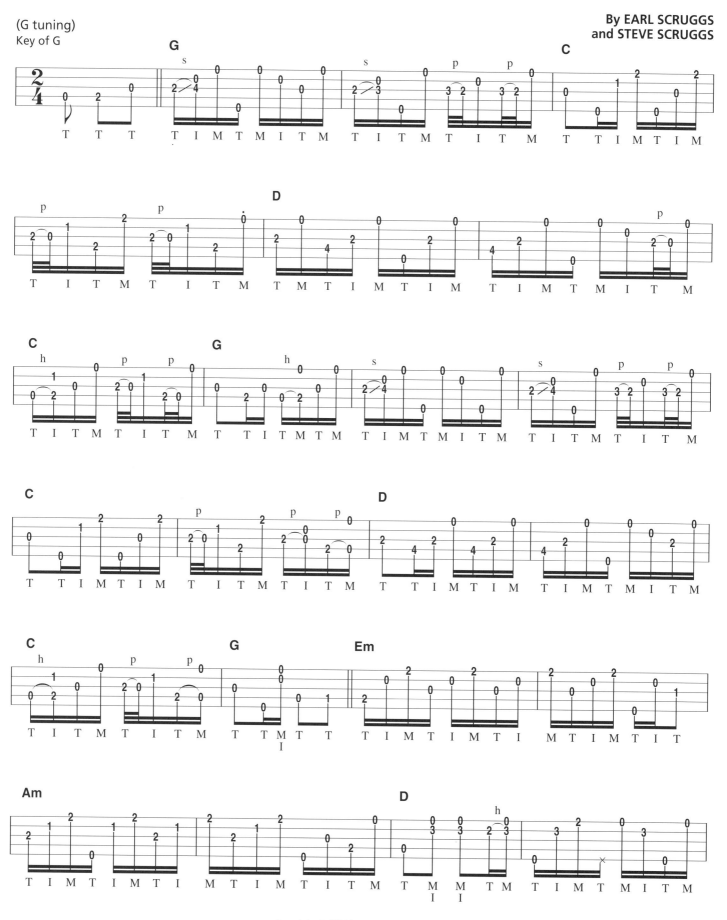

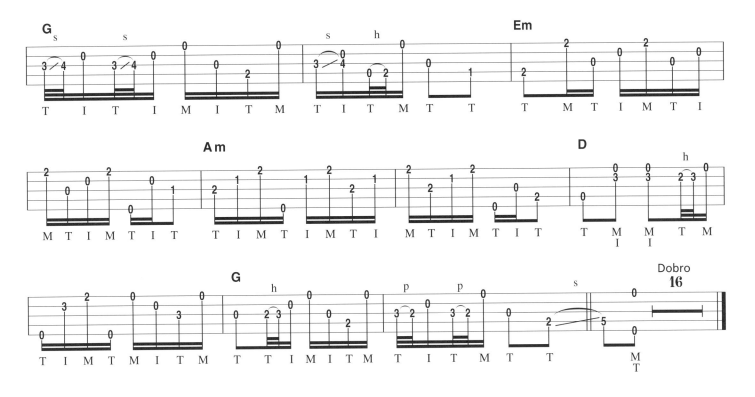

CAROLINA BOOGIE

Sound source—Earl Scruggs Revue *Live at Kansas State:* First banjo break

(G tuning)
Key of G

By EARL SCRUGGS

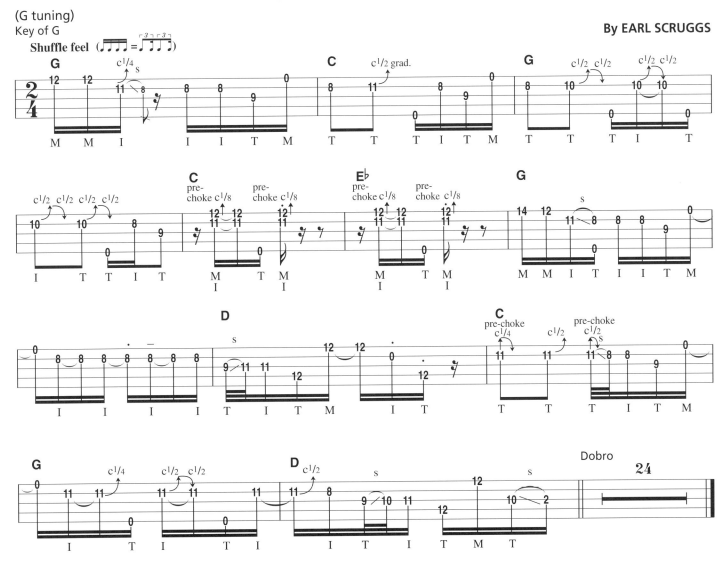

SALLY ANN

Sound source—Flatt & Scruggs *Foggy Mountain Banjo:*
Opening break and last 2 measures of the last break + ending

By EARL SCRUGGS

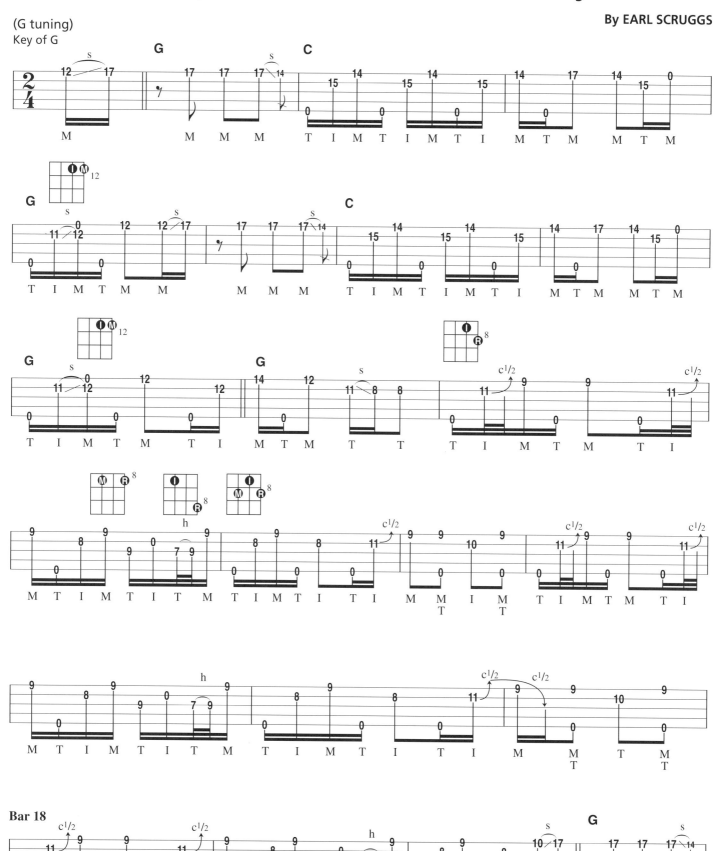

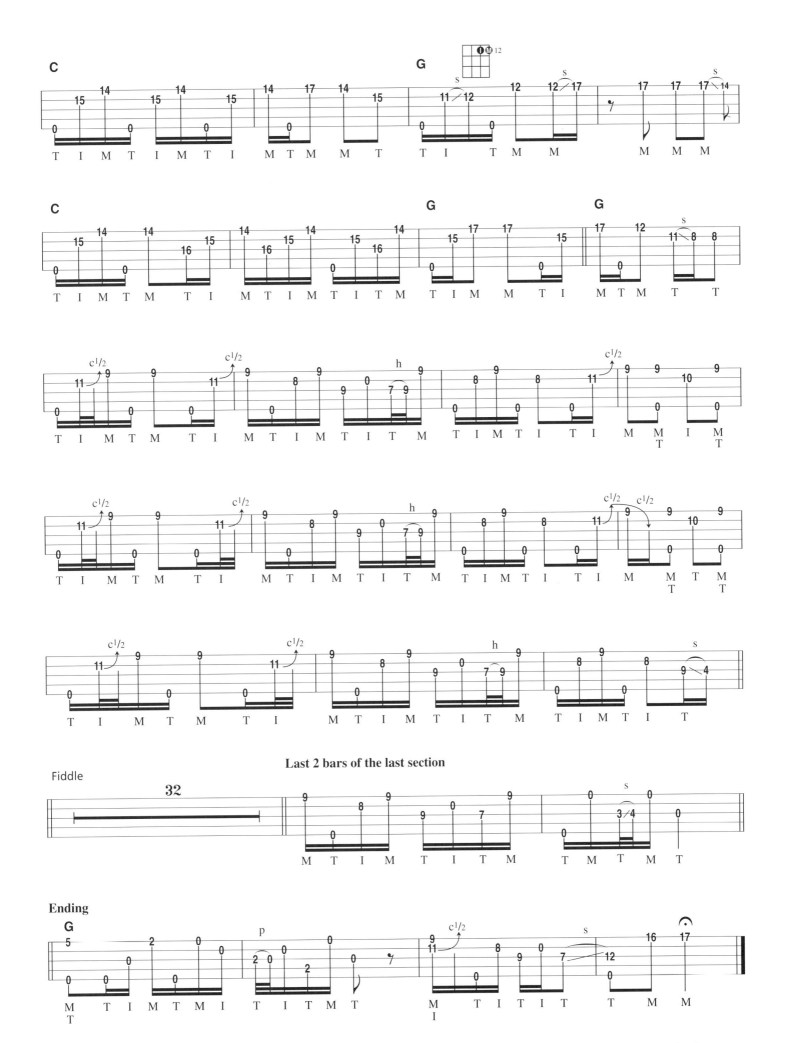

NOTE: To practice how to end the tune, play the first eighteen bars of the tune and then go directly to the last two bars of the last section.

SHUCKIN' THE CORN

Sound sources—Flatt & Scruggs *Foggy Mountain Jamboree* **and**
The Essential Earl Scruggs: **Opening break**

By GRAVES,
CIRTAIN and STACEY

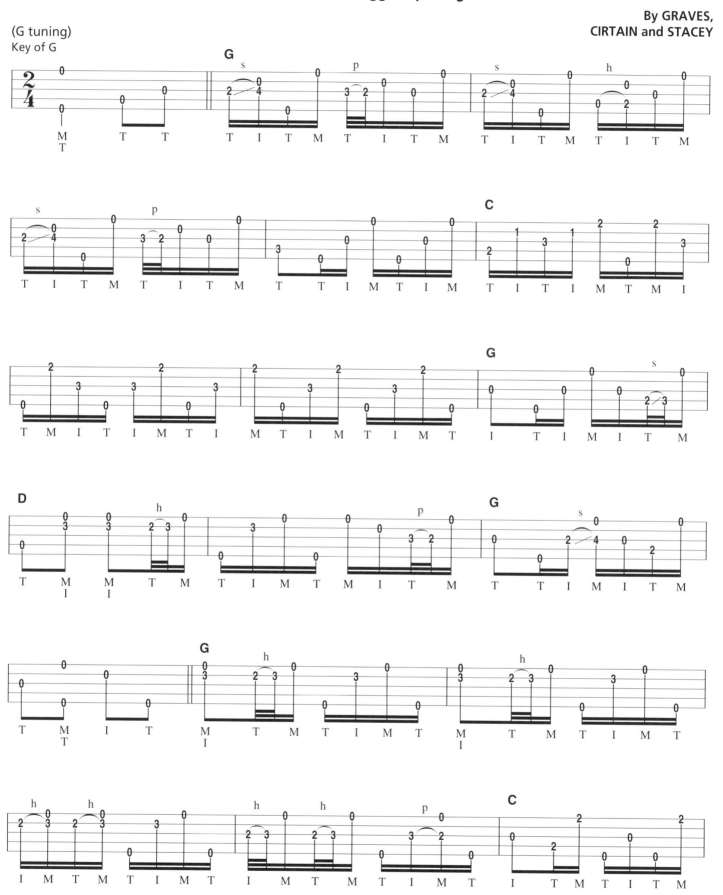

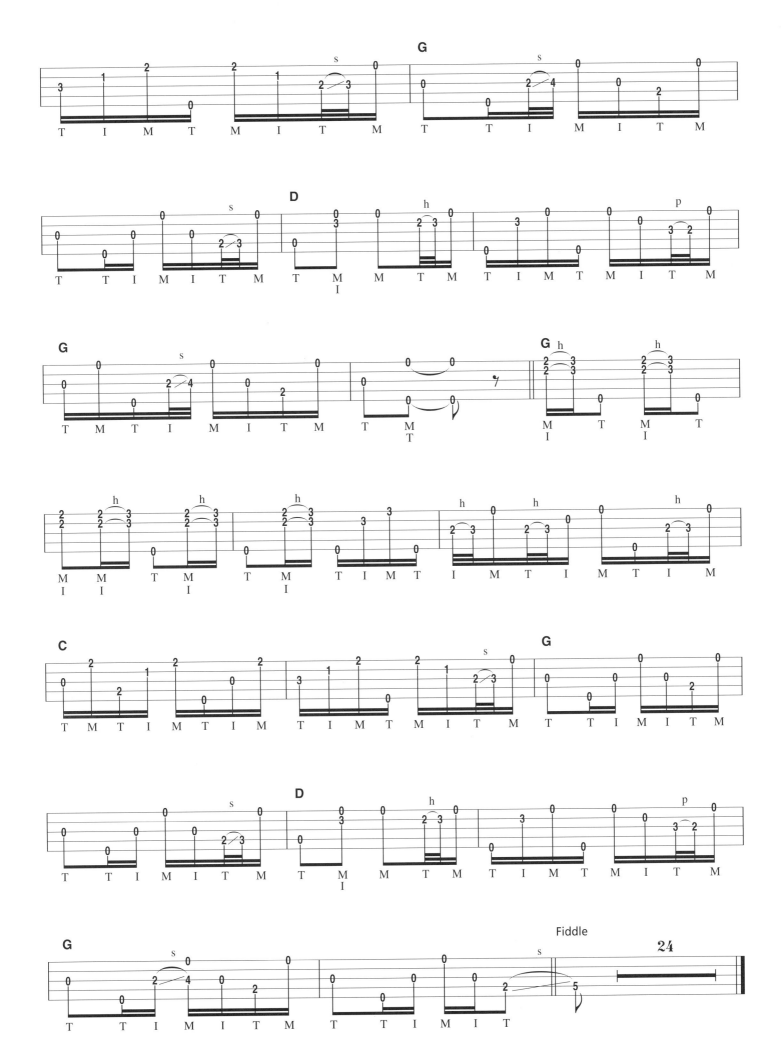

TRAIN NUMBER FORTY-FIVE

Sound source—Earl Scruggs *Nashville's Rock:* Intro and opening break

(G tuning)
Key of G

By EARL SCRUGGS

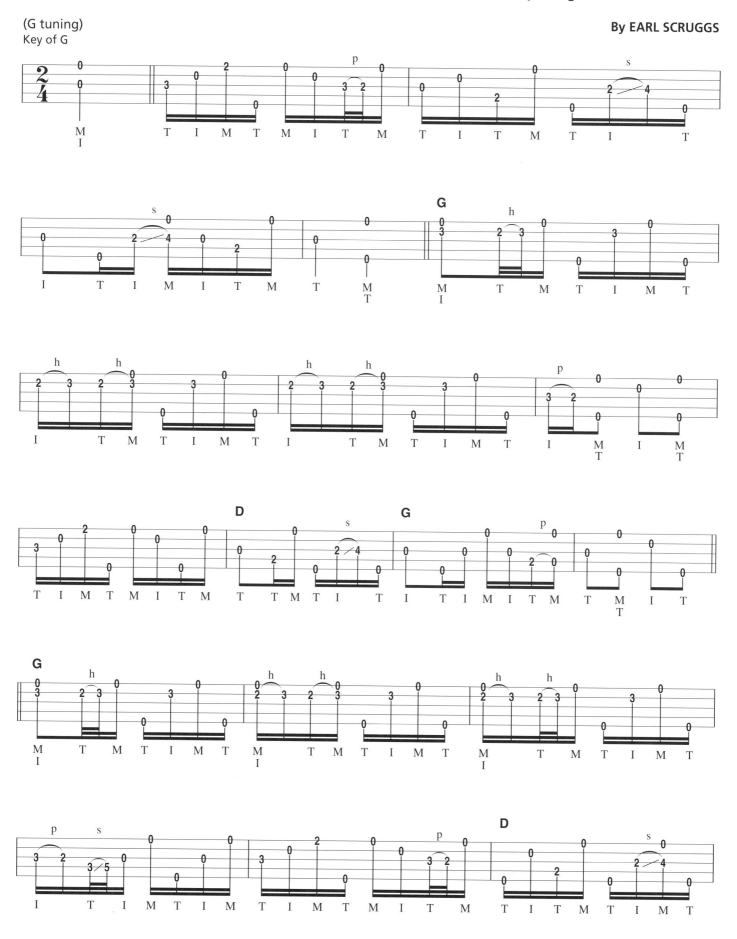

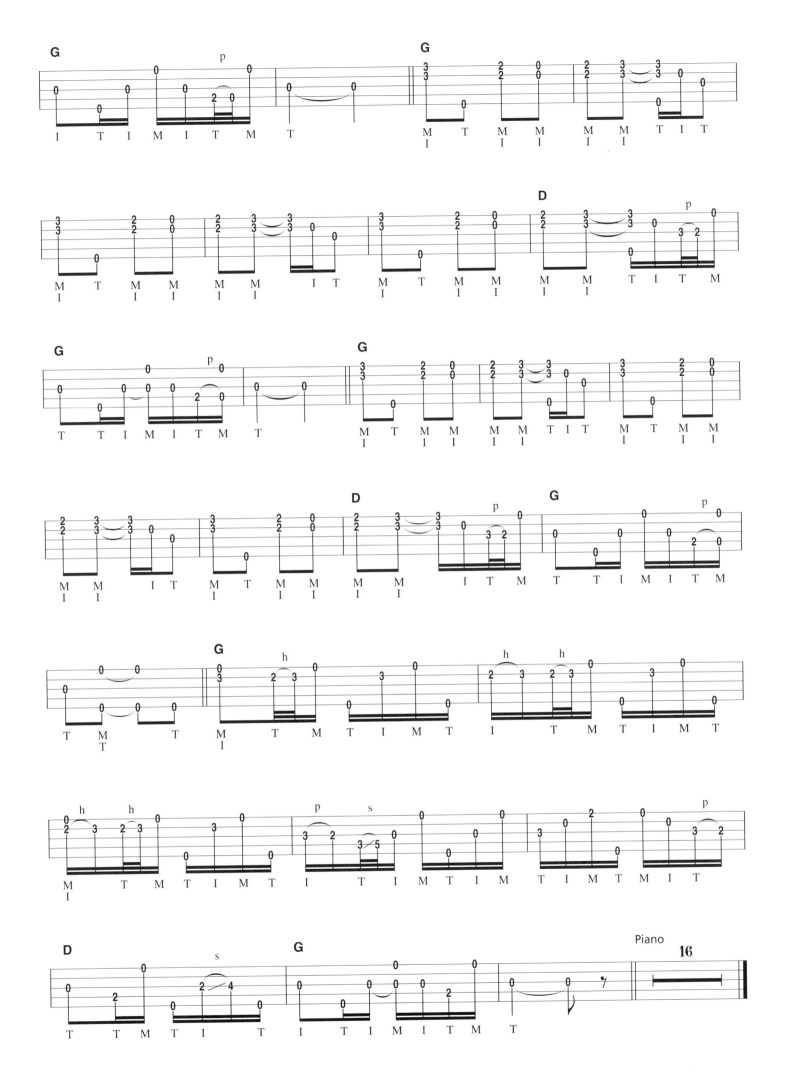

AMERICAN MADE – WORLD PLAYED

Sound sources—Earl Scruggs *American Made – World Played* and *The Essential Earl Scruggs:* 8 bar intro and opening break

By EARL SCRUGGS

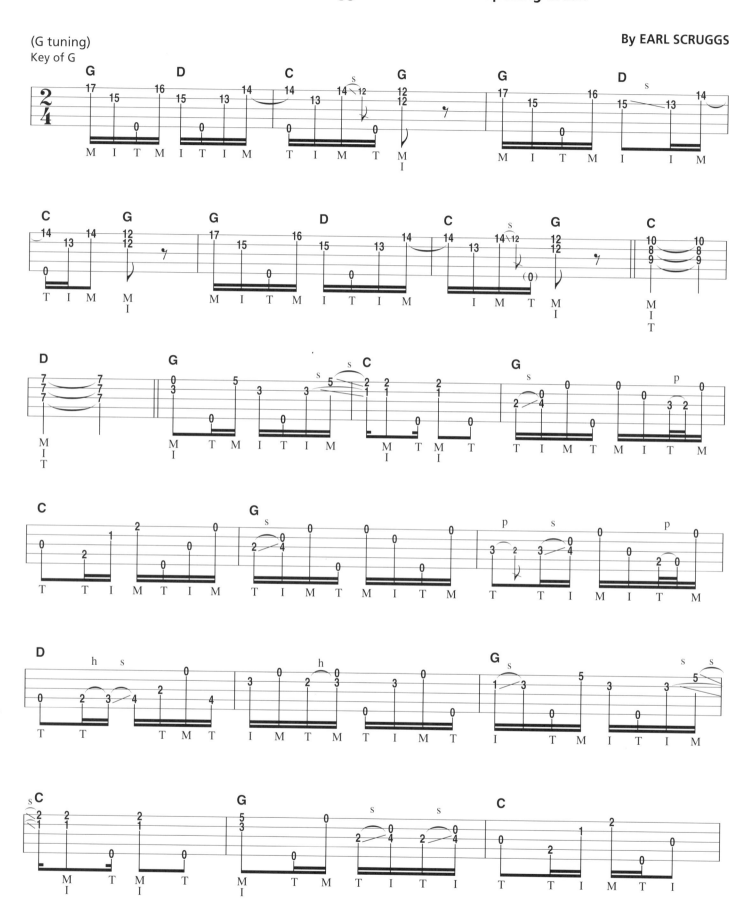

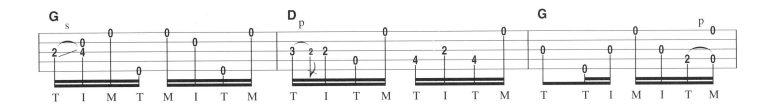

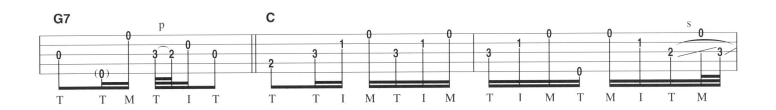

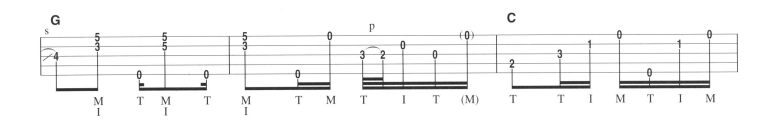

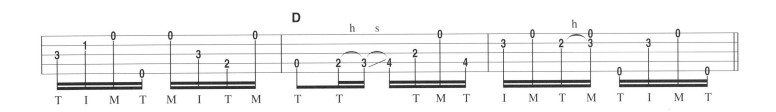

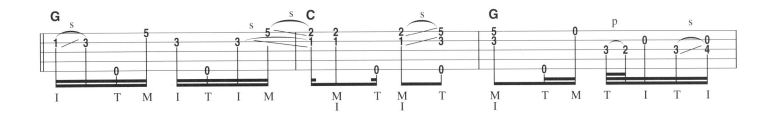

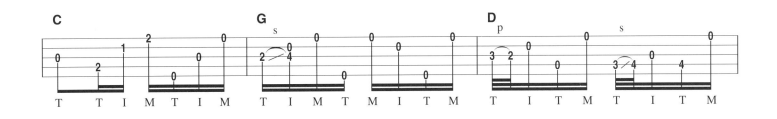

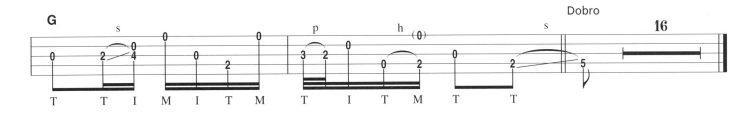

BLEEKER STREET RAG

Sound sources—Earl Scruggs *Anniversary Special* and Earl Scruggs Revue
Artist's Choice: The Best Tracks, 1970–1980: Last banjo break and ending banjo tags

By RANDY SCRUGGS

(G tuning)
Key of C

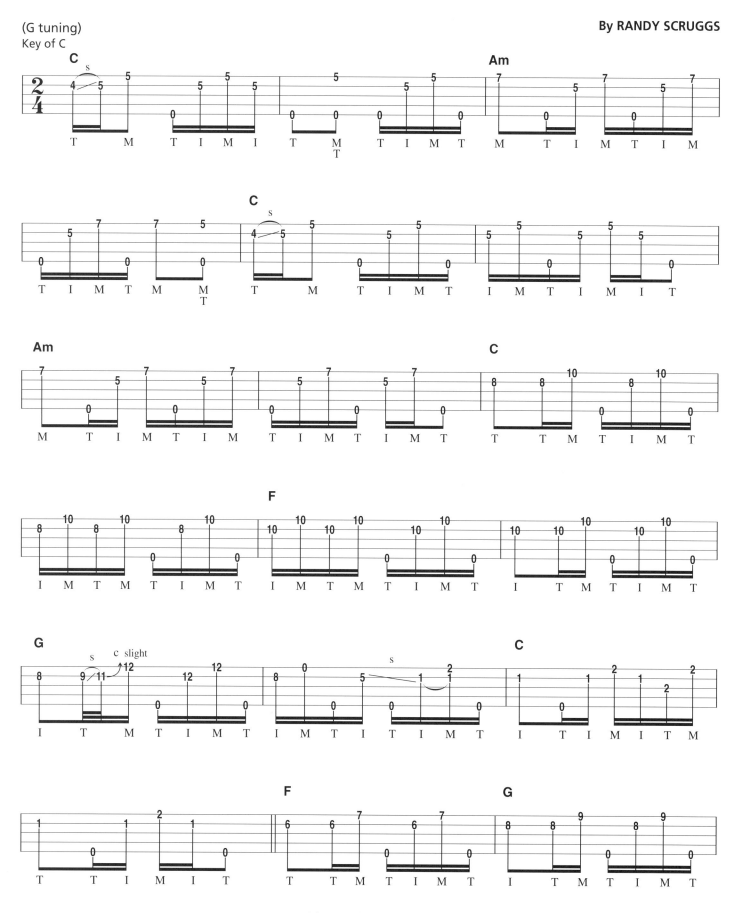

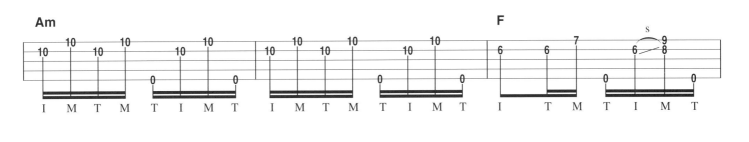

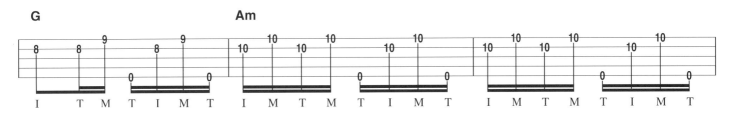

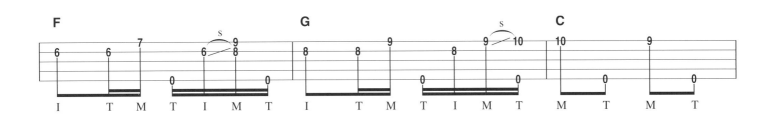

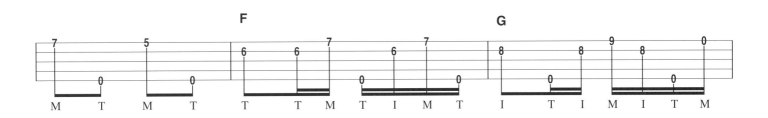

First tag

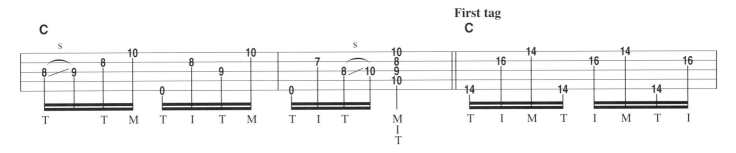

Second tag

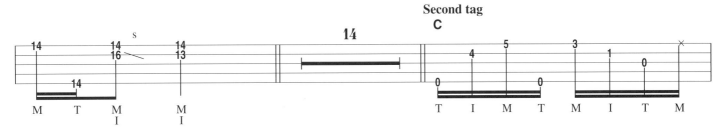

Last tag

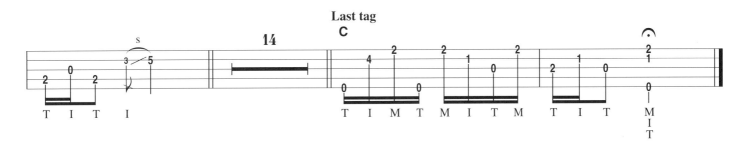

LONESOME ROAD BLUES

Sound source—Flatt & Scruggs *Foggy Mountain Banjo:* Opening break

By EARL SCRUGGS

(G tuning)
Key of G

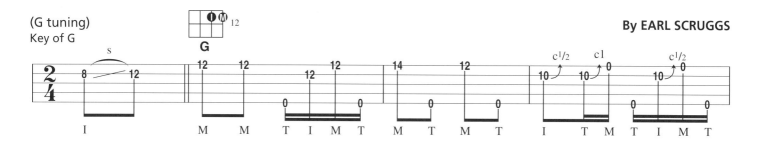

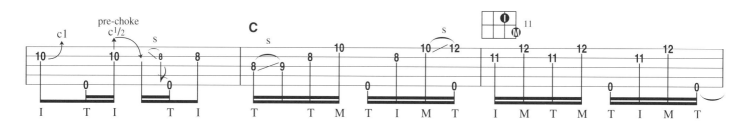

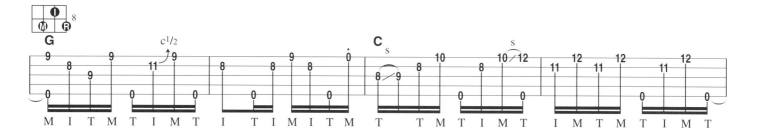

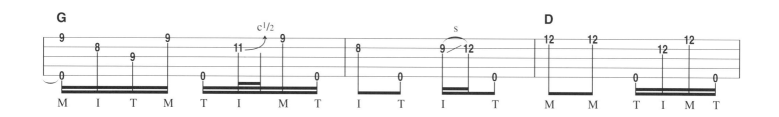

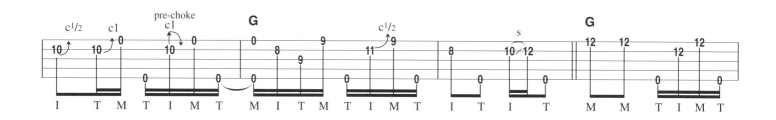

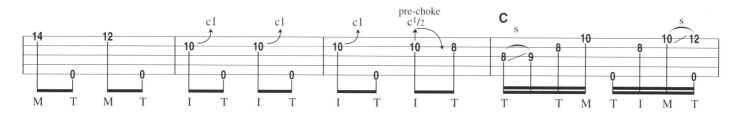

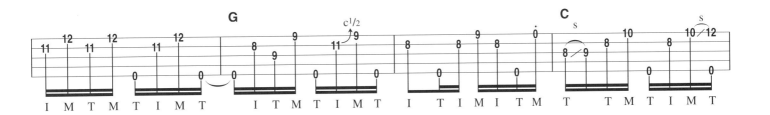

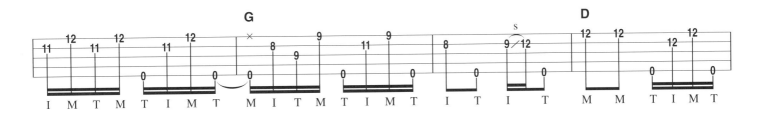

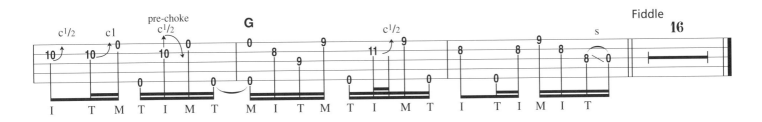

GROUND HOG

By EARL SCRUGGS

(G tuning)
Key of G

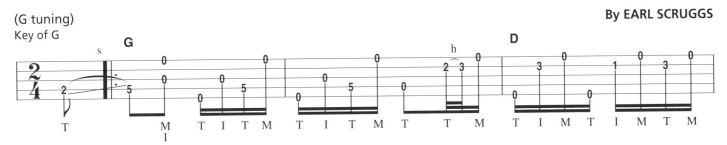

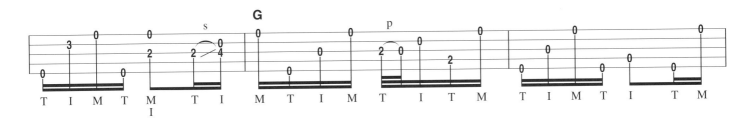

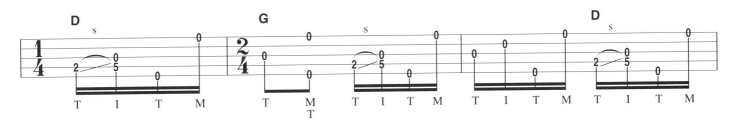

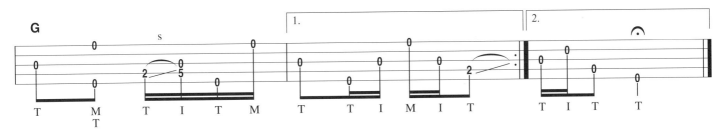

LORADEROJOST III BREAKDOWN

Sound source—Earl Scruggs *Nashville's Rock*: Opening break

By RANDY SCRUGGS

(G tuning)
Key of G

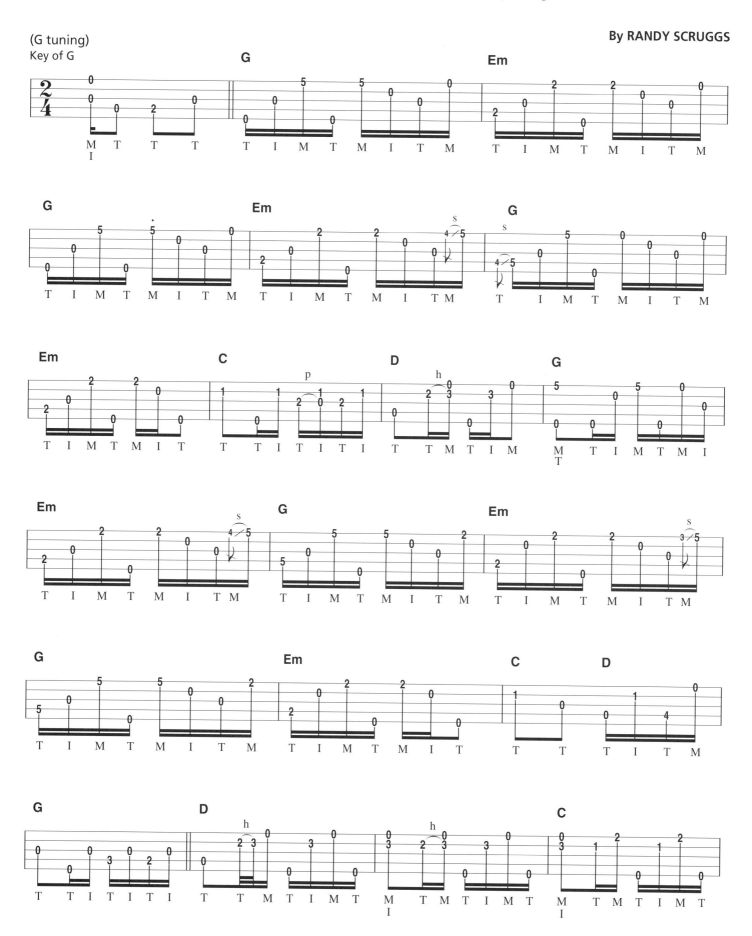

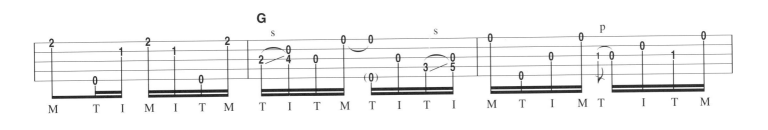

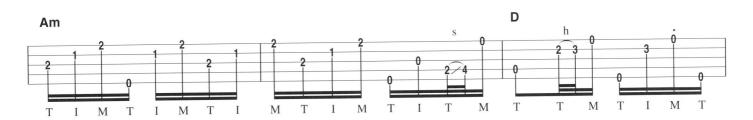

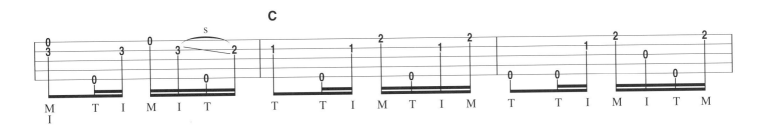

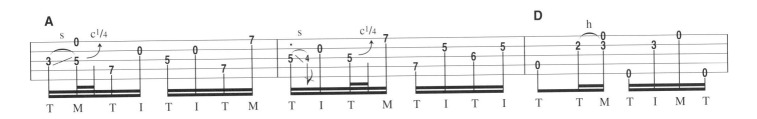

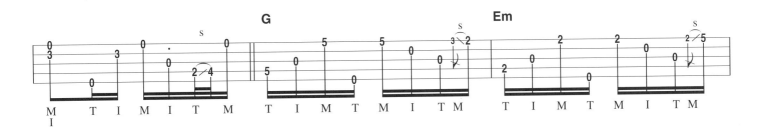

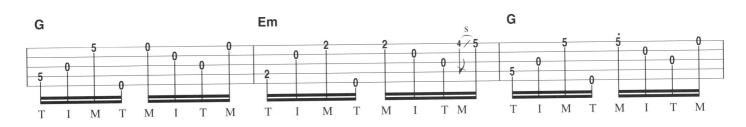

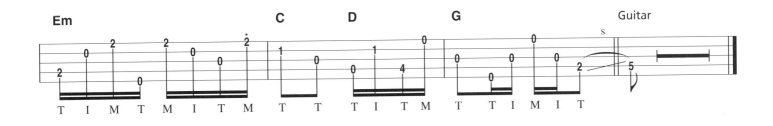

STRING BENDER

Sound source—Earl Scruggs (with the Earl Scruggs Revue) *Dueling Banjos:*
First banjo break

By RANDY SCRUGGS

(Tuning: aDGBD)
Key of D: Hook the 5th string at the 7th fret

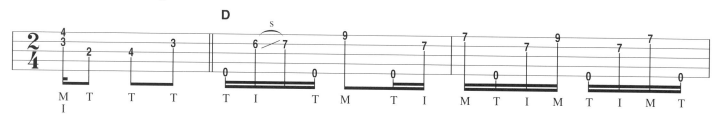

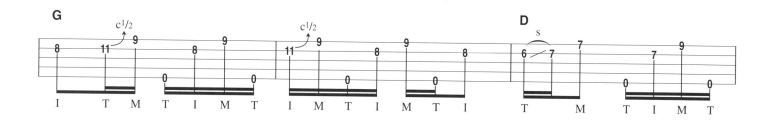

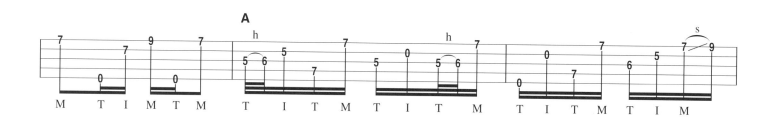

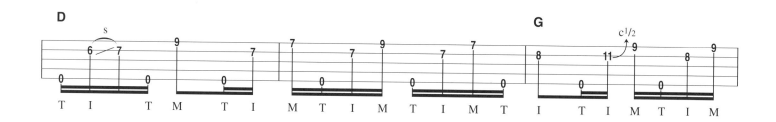

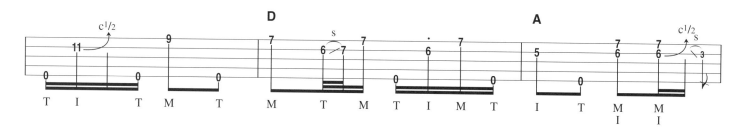

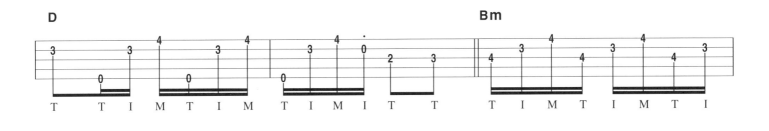

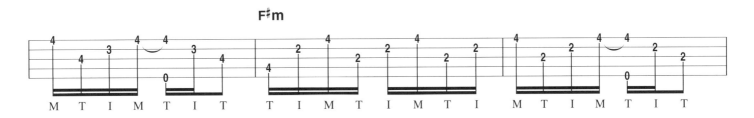

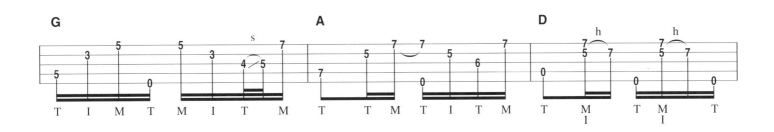

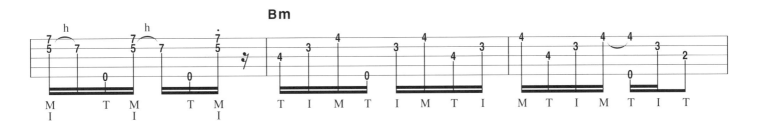

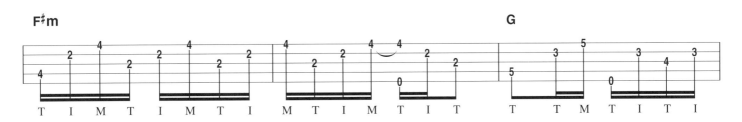

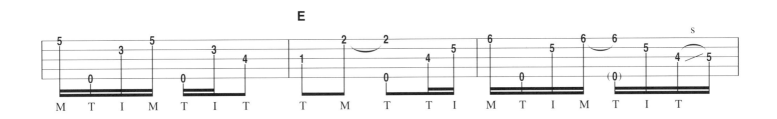

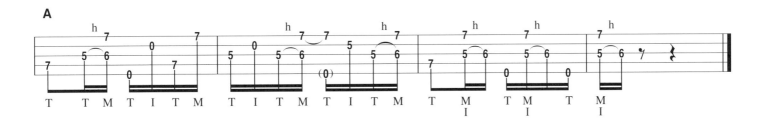

STATION BREAK

Sound source—Earl Scruggs Revue *Earl Scruggs Revue:* Intro and opening break

(Tuning: aDGBD)
Key of D: Hook the 5th string at the 7th fret

By EARL SCRUGGS

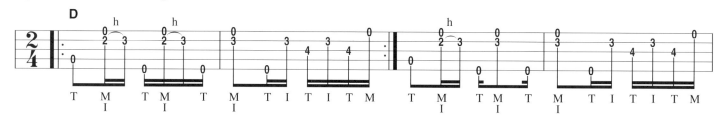

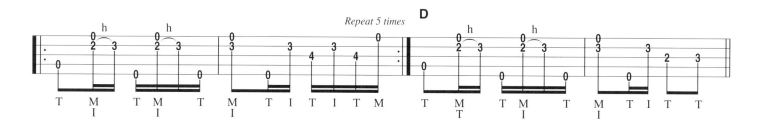

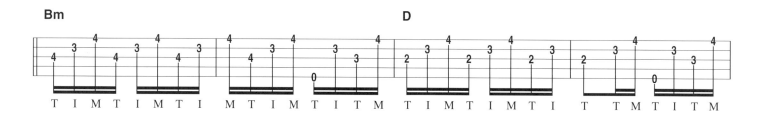

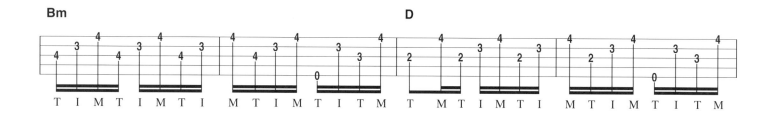

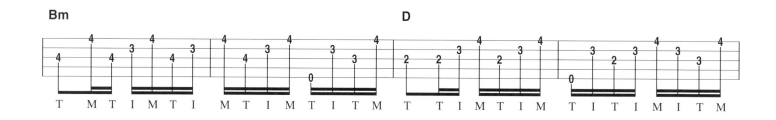

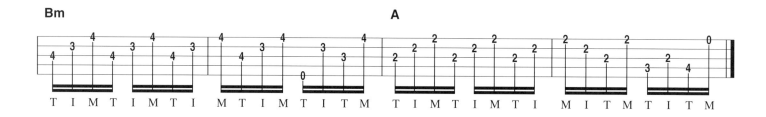

PRETTY POLLY

By EARL SCRUGGS

(G modal tuning)

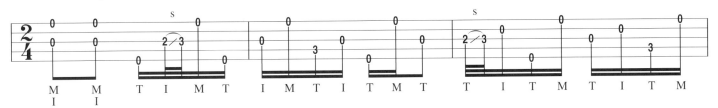

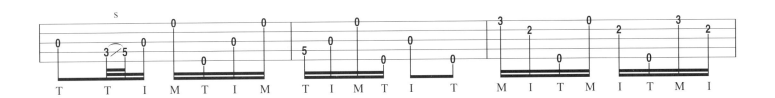

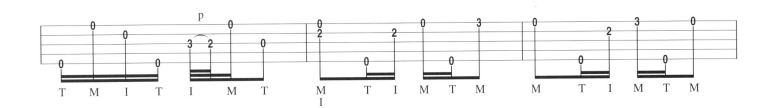

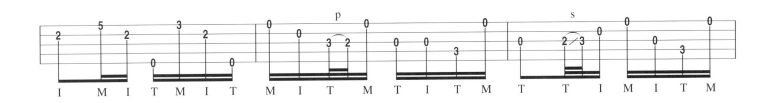

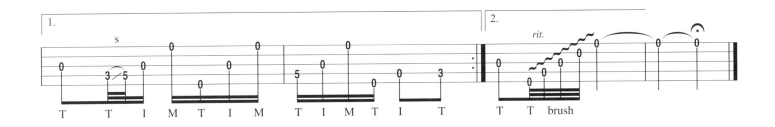

JOHN HENRY

Sound source—Flatt & Scruggs *Foggy Mountain Banjo:* First and last breaks

By EARL SCRUGGS

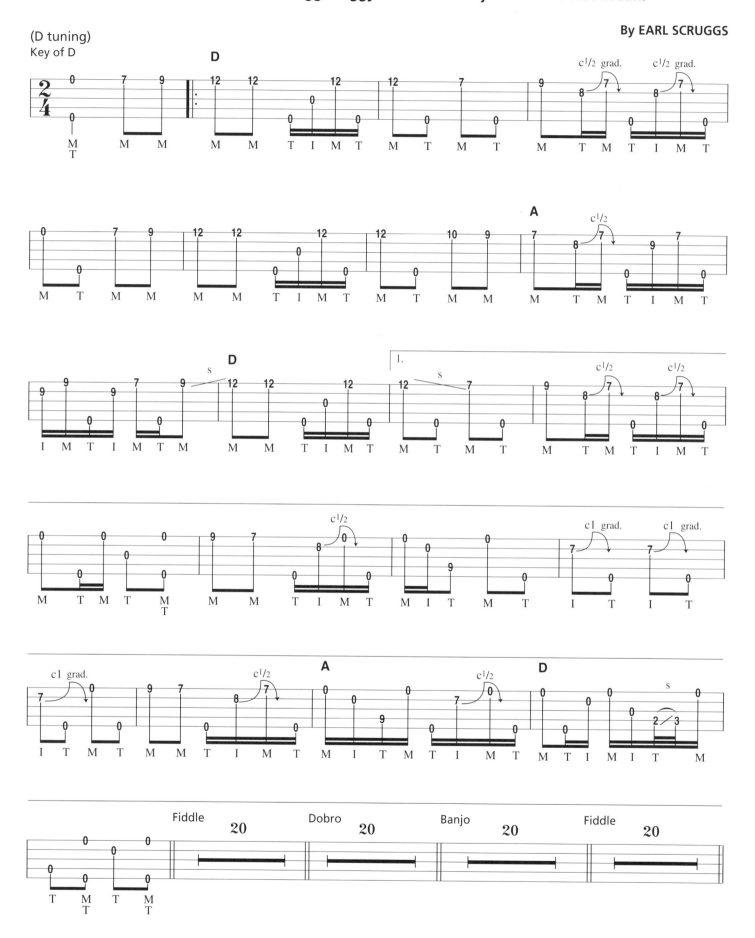

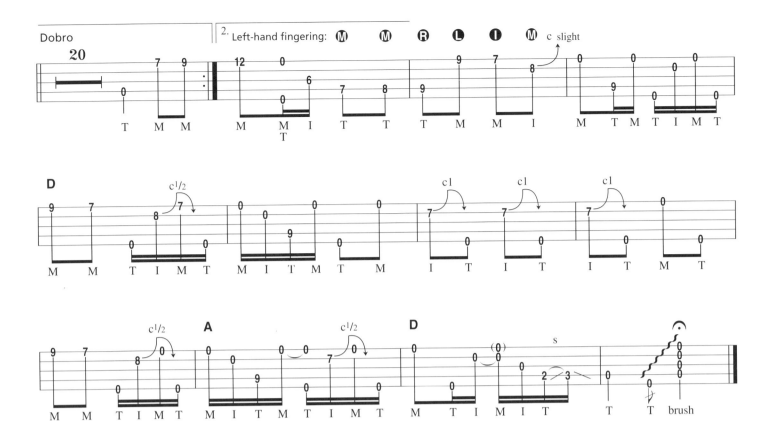

Earl Scruggs Signature Model "Flint Hill Special"

Gibson introduced the Flint Hill Special model in 1997. Its hardware is gold-plated, the armrest is engraved, and the headstock is bound with mother-of-pearl.

"Flint Hill Special" peghead

Resonator and neck: Figured maple
Fingerboard / Inlay: Ebony / Hearts & Flowers
Binding: Multiple, White/Black/White, Mother-of-pearl Bound Peghead
Hardware: Gold Plated
Tuners: Vintage 2-band
Finish: Exact Replica, Amber Brown
Case: Shaped Hardshell*

*Specifications provided by Gibson

REUBEN

Sound sources—Flatt & Scruggs *Foggy Mountain Banjo* and
The Essential Earl Scruggs: Opening break, first 16 bars of the third break, and last break

(D tuning)
Key of D

By EARL SCRUGGS

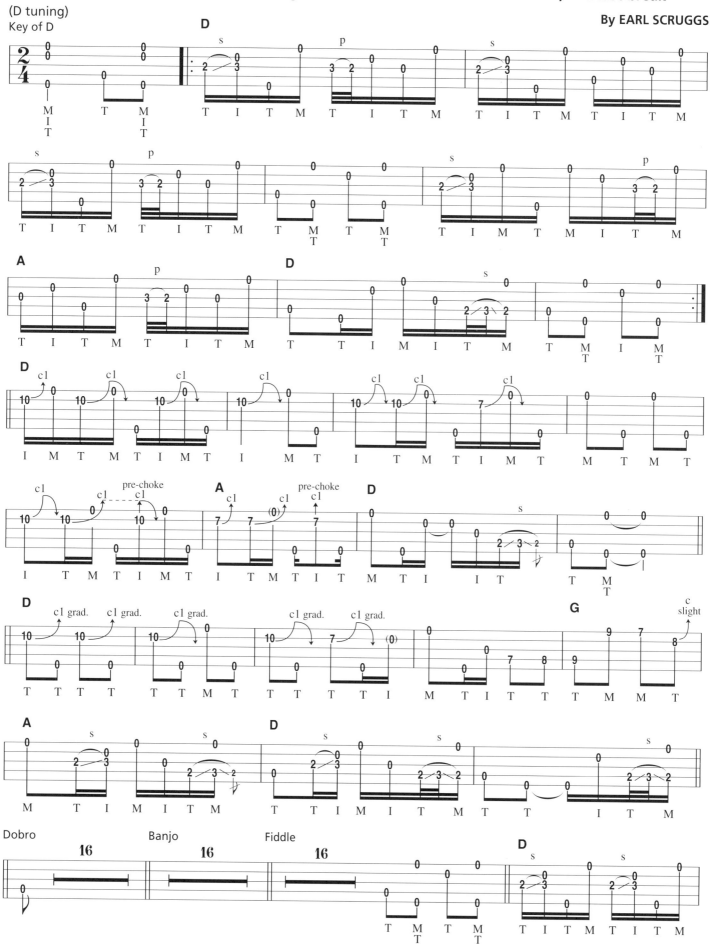

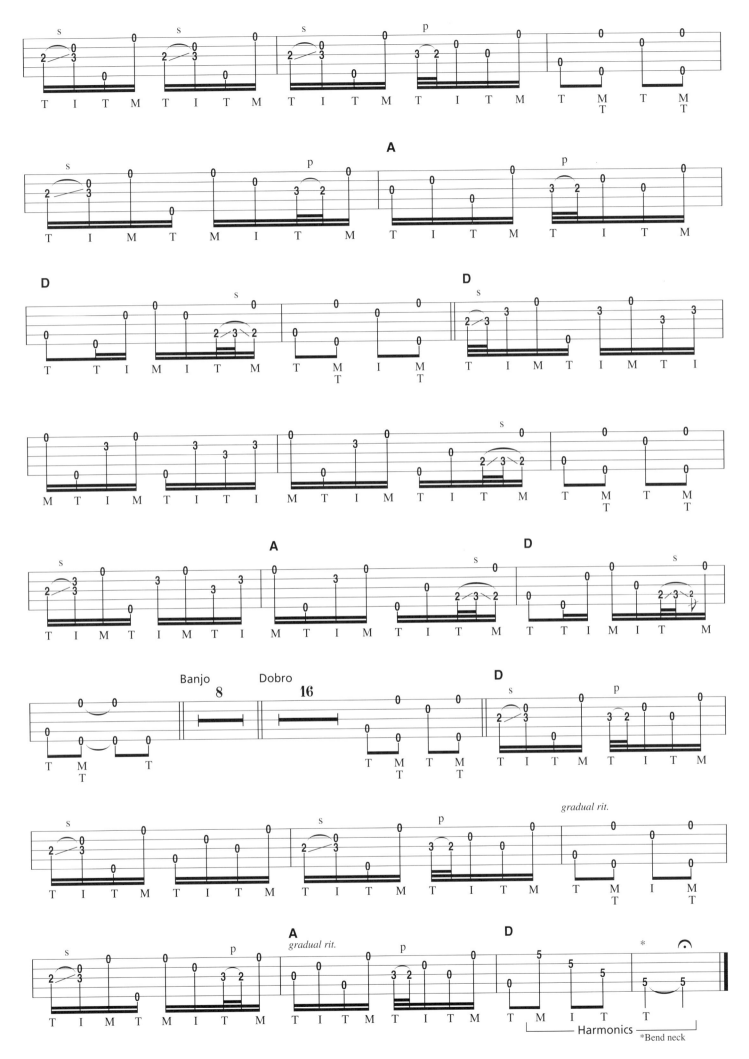

CARELESS LOVE

Sound source—Flatt & Scruggs with Doc Watson *Strictly Instrumental:* **Opening break**

(D tuning)
Key of D

By EARL SCRUGGS

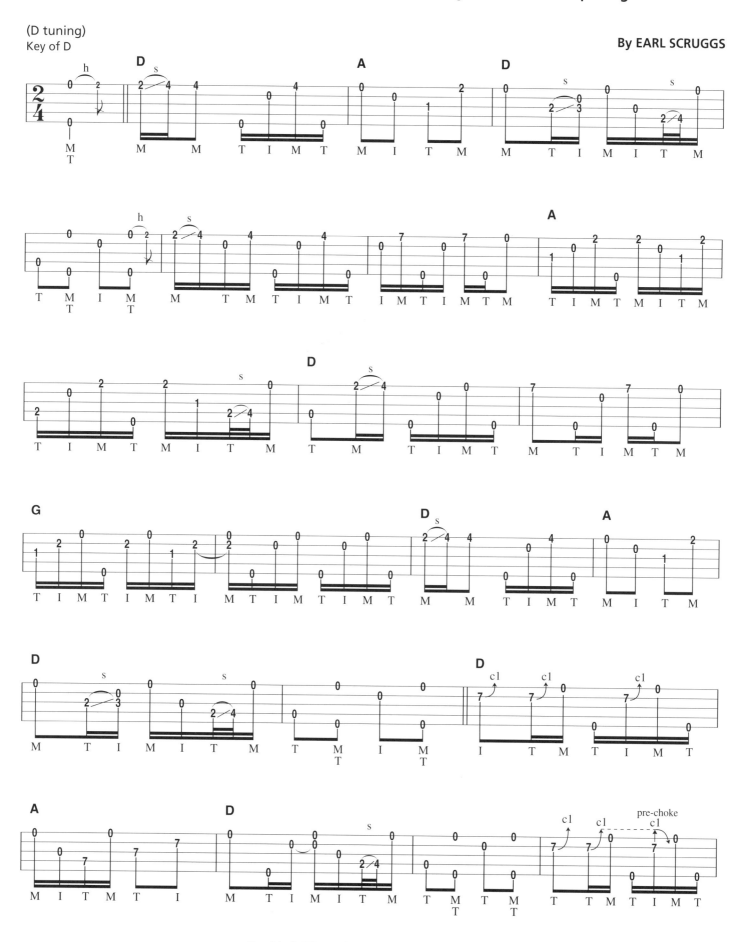

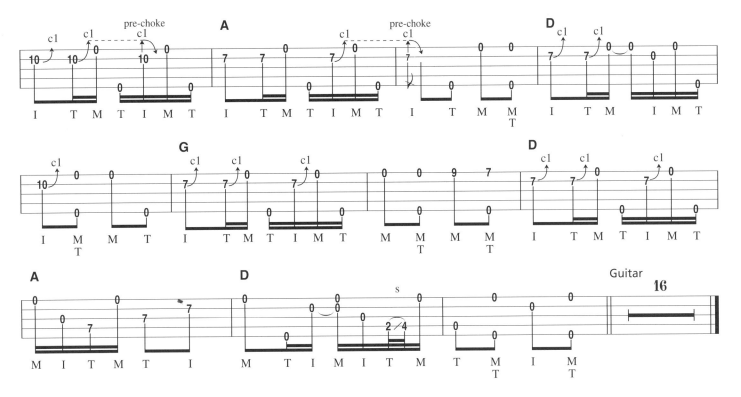

Earl Scruggs Signature Model "The Earl"

I felt very honored when Gibson designed a banjo they described as "a new, limited edition, collectible/tribute banjo model," named "The Earl."

Gibson Chairman and CEO Henry Juszkiewicz presented the very first "The Earl" banjo to me in Nashville during a special ceremony held at the Gibson Bluegrass Showcase, home of Gibson's Original Acoustic Instruments division, in July of 2002.

Resonator and neck: Indian rosewood

Fingerboard / Inlay: Green abalone inlay with 14K gold outlines on neck and headstock veneer / 14K gold "Mastertone" inlay block

Binding: Maple binding with marquetry

Hardware: Pure silver and silver-plated hardware

Tuners: Vintage 2-band with pearl buttons

Finish: Hand-drawn portrait of Earl Scruggs by world-renowned artist Randall Martin

Features: Custom engraving pattern – never to be reused on any other model Gibson banjo / Autographed by Earl Scruggs

Case: Leather case with humidity gauge*

*Specifications provided by Gibson

"The Earl" peghead   *Portrait of Earl on the resonator*

NASHVILLE BLUES

Sound sources—Nitty Gritty Dirt Band *Will the Circle Be Unbroken* and
The Essential Earl Scruggs: First break and last 4 measures of last break

(D minor tuning)
Key of Dm: Hook the 5th string

By EARL SCRUGGS

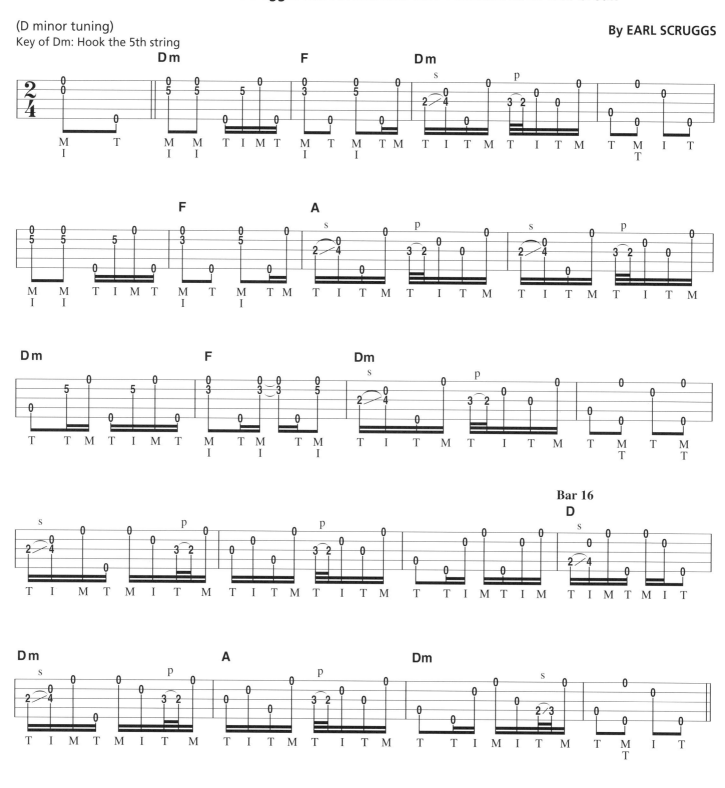

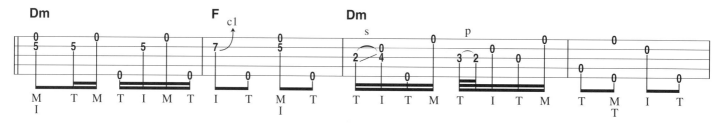

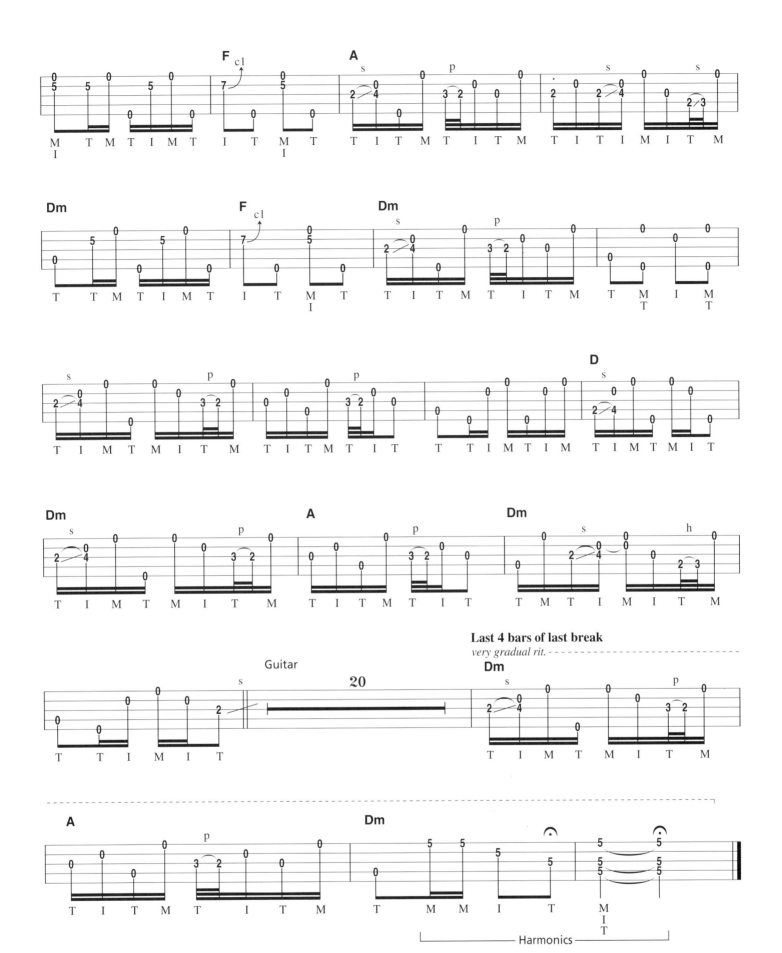

NOTE: To practice how to end the tune, play the first sixteen bars of the tune and then go directly to the last four bars of the last break.

NOTE: Another version appears on Flatt & Scruggs *Town and Country.*

INSTRUMENTAL IN D MINOR

Sound sources—*Earl Scruggs Revue Volume II* and *Earl Scruggs Revue*
Artist's Choice: The Best Tracks, 1970–1980: First break and ending

By EARL SCRUGGS

(D minor tuning)
Key of Dm: Hook the 5th string

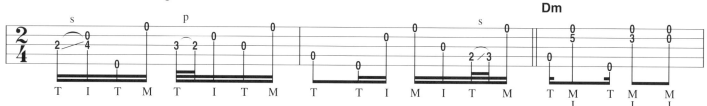

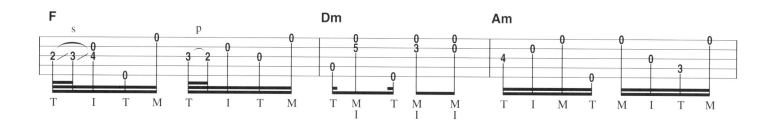

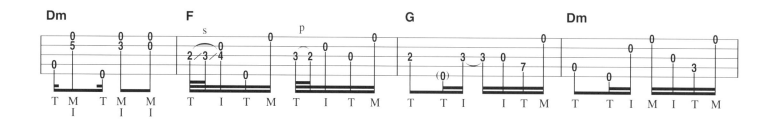

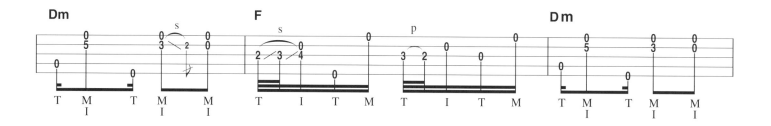

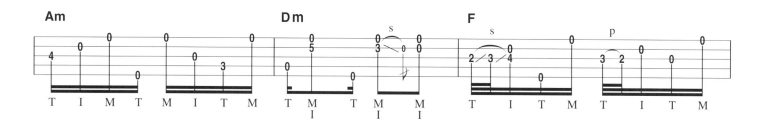

B Section (see note on next page)

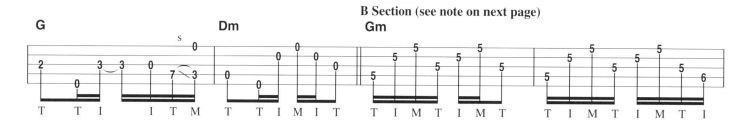

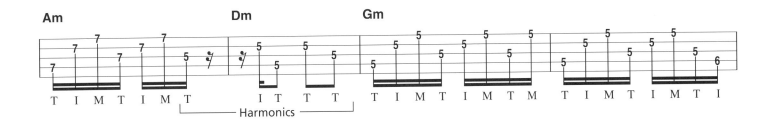

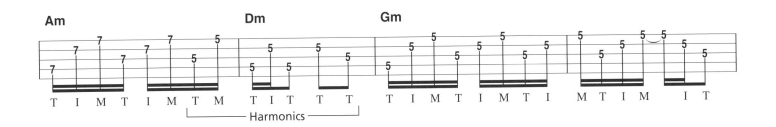

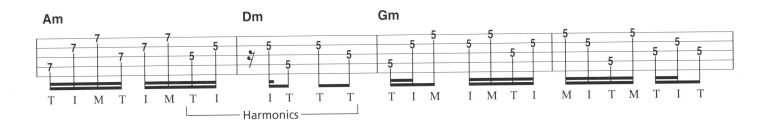

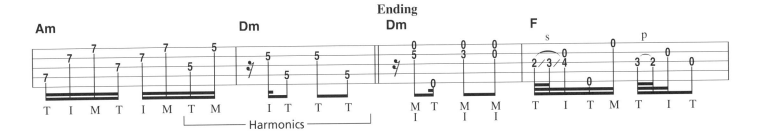

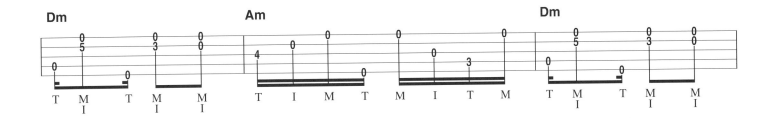

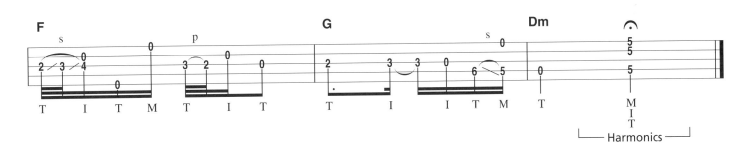

NOTE: Four passages in the 16-bar B section incorporate harmonic chimes. In the other measures of section B, position your barred finger directly over the frets—but instead of lightly touching the strings as you do when chiming, use the fully muted vamping technique taught on page 69. Listen to the recording if you have it in order to hear how vamping directly over the fifth and seventh frets produces not only a muted effect, but harmonic overtones as well.

MY LIFE AND TIMES

THEY SAY THAT TIME FLIES BY. "They" are right. Sometimes it's hard for me to believe that I've been playing banjo for over seventy-five years.

I grew up in the southwestern Piedmont section of North Carolina, and for some reason that region was a hotbed for 5-string banjo pickers. I've never heard of any other place in the world at that time where so many banjo players were picking two- and sometimes three-finger styles like they were in that one remote area of the United States.

The old home place

I began learning to play banjo at the age of four. I learned to pick with two fingers, using my thumb and index finger. As I grew older I dreamed of playing three-finger style, which I had heard from time to time. The year was 1934, and I was ten years old on the day my dream finally came true.

My brother, Horace, and I had been arguing as kids will sometimes do. I grabbed a banjo and took it into another room. I was angry and wanted to be left alone. I sat down and began to pick, hoping to get the argument out of my mind.

Anyway, I was sitting there in the room picking the tune "Reuben" in D tuning and daydreaming at the same time. I remember looking down at my right hand and waking up from the daydreams. My eyes must have gotten bigger than baseballs—I was picking with three fingers!

I had never felt as excited in all of my ten years of life as I did at that moment. I just kept staring at my right hand as I picked because I wanted to remember exactly what it was that my fingers were doing. It was then that I started shouting, "I got it! I got it!" I always took the banjo very seriously.

I was born into a musical family on January 6, 1924. We all lived and worked on a forty-acre farm in a little community called Flint Hill, North Carolina. There are more areas than one called "Flint Hill" in North Carolina, and the one I'm referring to isn't found on any map that I've ever seen. It's located a few miles southwest of Shelby, North Carolina in Cleveland County.

The community had a two-room school, a church, and a grocery store, so there really wasn't much to do there as far as entertainment was concerned. My family didn't even have a radio for years, but we did have a lot of fun by entertaining ourselves with all the music we made. It's hard to imagine a family enjoying playing music and singing together any more than we did.

Brothers Horace on guitar and Earl on banjo

We all played music except for my younger sister. My father, George Elam Scruggs, played fiddle and banjo. He died when I was four years old. He had been sick for the eight months leading up to his death, so I don't remember him playing any music; but I do have a few good memories of him. My mother, Lula Ruppe Scruggs, played pump organ. My older brothers, Junie and Horace, both played guitar and banjo as did my two older sisters, Eula Mae and Ruby. I learned to play banjo and guitar and every now and then I would play my father's fiddle. An old Autoharp was there for anyone who wanted to take the time to tune it.

George Elam Scruggs   *Lula Ruppe Scruggs*

My brothers and sisters could pick for awhile and then seem to forget about it more easily than I could. Picking the banjo stayed on my mind a lot of the time, even when I was playing with friends or working on the farm or going to school.

There were a few good three-finger banjo pickers I admired who lived near Flint Hill. Mack Woolbright, a blind banjo picker who recorded with Charlie Parker for Columbia Records in the late 1920s, stands out in my mind. I remember him from a visit he made to my Uncle Sidney Ruppe's home. Mack rocked in a rocking chair while picking "Home Sweet Home" in the key of C while in C tuning. The G7 chord he played in that tune sent chills down my spine. I was six years old then and couldn't help but wonder how a blind person could pick a banjo so beautifully.

Some other good banjo players in that region were Leaborn Rogers, Rex Brooks, DeWitt "Snuffy" Jenkins, Mack Crow, and Smith Hammett.

Earl

The player who inspired the most people at that time was probably Smith Hammett. He was born in 1887 in Gaffney, South Carolina and died in 1930 when I was six years old. Smith played several instruments including banjo, fiddle, and organ. As far as I can trace it back, he was the first banjo player I know of to pick with three fingers.

Smith's wife, Ola Hammett, and my mother were cousins. Our families visited each other fairly often, and we always ended up playing some music before the visits were over.

Smith inspired my oldest brother, Junie, to pick. Junie began playing in 1927 and bought a pretty good banjo for that day and time for around seventeen dollars from a mail order company.

Smith's banjo picking inspired me, too, but what I remember most about him was a little banjo that he owned.

When I was a little boy, the only way I could pick Junie's banjo or the old banjo my father had played was to sit down with the body of the banjo resting to my right. I would slide it around quite a bit depending on which position on the neck I was trying to reach. That was pretty rough on a banjo if I happened to be sitting on the hardwood floor or outside on the porch or in the yard. Needless to say, Junie wasn't too pleased with me whenever he caught me playing his banjo.

The banjo head on Smith's little banjo was about nine inches in diameter, and the neck was quite a bit shorter than the length of a standard banjo neck. It always thrilled me to pick that little banjo because I could hold it in my lap and pick just like the grownups did with their regular-sized banjos.

John Ross on fiddle, Smith Hammett on banjo, and Brooker Self, jug

The first time I ever picked before an audience was in 1930. I was six years old, and a fiddler's convention was held in Boiling Springs, North Carolina, which is a couple of miles or so from Flint Hill. Fiddling, picking, and singing contests were held during the convention, and I had made up my mind to enter into the banjo category.

I walked that trip with a banjo strapped around me and picked a little as I made my way along the old dirt road. First, second, and third prizes were given in each category. Three people judged the contest. I played "Cripple Creek" and won either first or second prize, which was probably due to my young age. I also later learned "Cripple Creek" was a favorite of a couple of the judges.

Around that same time, Junie was playing one or two nights a week for square dances near home. I played rhythm guitar for him on one of those nights, and soon after that Junie and I played on radio station WSPA in Spartanburg, South Carolina along with my other brother, Horace.

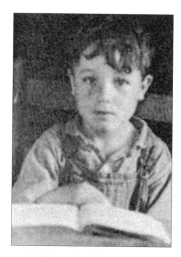

Earl at school in Flint Hill

I played again on WSPA with Horace and a friend named T.W. Bryant when I was eleven. T.W.'s father drove us to Spartanburg in his rumble seat Model T Ford for a talent show that aired at 7:00 in the morning. The trip was an exciting experience, as I was pretty much living and breathing banjo. By that time, I was playing three-finger style.

When I first began picking with three fingers, I wasn't completely happy with my sound because it didn't sound exactly like the other three-finger pickers I had heard. However, the more I played, the more I realized I could play some things I had never heard before. It also worked well with slow songs as well as fast ones.

Brothers Earl on fiddle, Junie on banjo, Horace on guitar

I didn't have a banjo of my own until 1937 when I was thirteen years old. I bought one for ten dollars and ninety-five cents from a mail order company. I'll never forget the aroma that came out of that new banjo when it finally arrived at the house.

I played that banjo until 1941 and then bought a much better one: a Gibson RB-11 model that I found in a pawnshop. At that time, a lot of very good banjos could be found in pawnshops in both North and South Carolina. They could be bought at prices ranging from twenty-five to ninety dollars depending on how long they had been hanging on the pawnshop walls.

Earl on banjo and brother Horace on guitar

I jumped at any chance that came along to play before an audience. An employee of Lily Mills, a thread mill in Shelby, built a small recreational building on the banks of Broad River near where we lived. He rented out the building for fish fry's, private parties, and other social events. There was space for thirty or forty couples to dance. It was there that I started making money for picking banjo. He would pay me three dollars to pick for a couple of hours, which usually ran into three or four hours. But I didn't mind; it was a good experience, and I enjoyed it, even though it was sometimes very tiring to pick alone. At that time there were no amplifiers or microphones around; in fact, there was no electricity within three miles of the place, so I soon learned to pick hard and aggressively in order to be heard.

I was fifteen or sixteen years old when our family got its first radio, and it opened up a whole new world to me. I enjoyed listening to Fisher Hendley on WIS in Columbia, South Carolina. He was in a group called the "Aristocratic Pigs." The name was derived from their sponsor, which was a meat-packing company whose advertising slogan was "Our meats come from aristocratic pigs."

Fisher played banjo and did the emcee work for the group. They usually played music with a touch of Western atmosphere to it. What I really looked forward to was the two or three times during the week when Fisher would play a tune on his banjo along with the fiddle player. To me, that always made the listening really worthwhile. I loved the interplay between the two instruments and I've always enjoyed including a fiddle-and-banjo tune in my shows. It really takes me back home.

Another sound that I heard later in the 1930s and 1940s on WIS was the three-finger banjo style of the late Snuffy Jenkins. Hearing him play was always a treat for me, and I enjoyed his comedy routines as well.

Snuffy was born in 1908 in Harris, North Carolina. He was the youngest in a family of ten, and all the children played music. Snuffy started playing fiddle when he was very young and too small to use the bow. He once told me in a letter, "I picked it like a mandolin. Soon after that I took up playing the guitar with my brother. In 1927, we started playing with two fellows who both played a three-finger style of banjo. Their names were Smith Hammett and Rex Brooks. This is when I started playing my style of banjo."

Snuffy Jenkins

When I was fifteen, I played with a group called the "Carolina Wildcats" for eleven months, and we played on a radio station in Gastonia, North Carolina on Saturday mornings. It was fun to arrive at the station and read the fan mail (which usually consisted of letters from our relatives).

On Saturday nights I would often pick with a friend named Dennis Butler who played an excellent old-time fiddle style. We sometimes played for parties at the homes of friends until after midnight just for the experience. A guitar player named Marvin White would often accompany us, and those times were a great help to me in learning to play backup and lead breaks on the banjo.

I also worked for a while with the Morris Brothers, Wiley, George, and Zeke, on WSPA in 1939. The program aired from 6:00 to 7:00 in the morning. I was fifteen years old and sitting on top of the world because I was playing with real professionals.

When America entered into World War II, I left the farm to help support my mother and younger sister. I got a job at the thread mill in Shelby, working seventy-two hour weeks. During that time I didn't do much playing away from home.

I stayed on at the mill until the war ended in 1945. By that time I knew that I wanted to make music my career. I went to Knoxville, Tennessee and was hired by "Lost John" Miller to play in his band, the Allied Kentuckians. A couple of weeks later, he also started doing a Saturday morning radio program in Nashville, Tennessee.

I enjoyed those weekly trips to Nashville with Lost John and the band even though the trips were usually quick turn-around drives back to Knoxville. When in Nashville I would sometimes see a friend named Jim Shumate, who was also from North Carolina. Jim played fiddle for Bill Monroe and the Blue Grass Boys.

Jim asked me several times to audition for Bill's band. I had heard Bill and the Blue Grass Boys a few times on the radio and thought they were one of the better string bands playing "hillbilly" music as it was called back then. Another old-time string band that I liked listening to was J.E. Mainer and the Mountaineers, a group based in North Carolina. Whenever Jim asked me to audition for Bill, I always told him I was happy working with Lost John and I didn't want to leave his band.

On December 1, 1945, John told the band he was going to quit working the road full time. I needed and wanted full-time work so I called Jim and told him I would like to try out for Bill's group. Jim arranged for an audition, and Bill hired me at a salary of sixty dollars a week.

My first appearance with Bill and the Blue Grass Boys was to be on WSM's Grand Ole Opry at the Ryman Auditorium, on December 8, 1945. I was confident my three-finger picking would fit in with Bill's band but I didn't know how Bill's fans would take to it. Up until that time, Bill had only used two banjo players in his band, and their playing styles were very different than mine.

"Stringbean" Akeman was Bill's banjo player from 1942 to 1945, playing old-time frailing and two-finger picking styles. When String quit, Bill hired a tenor banjo player, Jim Andrews, to replace him.

We played the Opry show, and the response was great. Playing at the Ryman was a big thrill for me. I'd never been on a stage so big, and the applause was the loudest I had ever heard in my life.

George D. Hay, who was known as "The Solemn Old Judge," was the announcer for the Grand Ole Opry back in those days. There were many times that he introduced the group as "Bill Monroe and Earl Scruggs with his fancy banjo," and that always made me feel real good.

Working in Bill's band was a lot of fun at first. Lester Flatt, from Sparta, Tennessee, sang most of the lead vocals and played rhythm guitar. He had previously sung and played mandolin in Bill's brother's string band, Charlie Monroe and the Kentucky "Pardners."

I've heard that when Bill told Lester he was going to try me out on banjo, Lester had said, "Well, as far as I'm concerned, he can leave the damn thing in the case." Lester felt the Blue Grass Boys would be better off without another banjo player. After Lester heard me play a couple of tunes, he encouraged Bill to hire me.

Robert "Chubby" Wise, a great fiddle player from Florida, joined the group three or four months after I did. Chubby, who had already been a Blue Grass Boy, replaced Howard "Howdy" Forrester who left the group, along with his wife, Wilene "Sally Ann" Forrester. Sally Ann had been Bill's accordion player since 1943.

Howdy had rejoined Bill and the Blue Grass Boys (replacing Jim Shumate on fiddle) on the night I made my debut on the Opry. He had been overseas serving in the military for the previous three years and Sally Ann had stayed with Bill during Howdy's absence.

It was always fun when Howard Watts, who went by the stage name "Cedric Rainwater," was the bass player in the band. Cedric rejoined the Blue Grass Boys around the same time that Chubby came back to the band.

The first recording session I did as a Blue Grass Boy was with Bill, Lester, Chubby, and Cedric in September 1946. The first song we recorded was "Heavy Traffic Ahead." There's a line in the song that says the Blue Grass Boys are never late. The truth is, the Blue Grass Boys were almost *always* late for a show during my time with the band.

We traveled in a 1941 custom-made stretch Chevrolet automobile, and that was long before interstate highways were built. Traveling was slow, and Bill was bad about disappearing after a show and then showing up late for departure times when we left one town for the next.

Sometimes Bill would be hours late, and we would have to drive pedal-to-the-metal on the two-lane roads that led to the next show date. Looking back on all of that, I'm surprised we weren't all killed. We did have a couple of wrecks, but luckily no one was seriously injured.

We rarely stayed in hotels while we were on the road, so that meant many nights of sleeping in the car while we traveled. There were times we didn't see a bed for a week. When we did check in to hotels, the band members had to pay for their own rooms. My salary stayed at sixty dollars a week, and I was still helping my mother and younger sister with their weekly expenses. I was barely making ends meet.

By the time February of 1948 rolled around, I felt way overworked and way underpaid. I was totally burned out and ready to quit the band and move back to North Carolina to go back to work in the thread mill. I gave Bill my two-weeks notice to leave the group.

Bill wasn't very happy with that news and tried to talk me in to staying in the band, but my mind was made up. Bill told me that if I left his band, the name "Earl Scruggs" would never be heard of again. "Whoever picks banjo with Bill Monroe will be the only banjo player anyone will ever know," were his words to me. I didn't care. I'd had it.

Bill didn't speak to me or even look at me until the two-weeks notice was almost up. He then asked me to stay on for two more weeks, which I agreed to do. That meant two more weeks of Bill not speaking to me.

When those final two weeks had passed and as I was leaving to head back to North Carolina, Lester told me that he, too, was going to quit the band. I didn't know if he was serious or not about leaving, but a few days after I returned home to North Carolina, Lester called and asked me if I would be interested in us starting a band together. I knew in my heart I still wanted to make my living by playing music so I told him I was willing to give it a try.

~

Lester and I had become close friends while working together with Bill. Lester had a very easygoing stage presence, and I had a lot of confidence in him to do our emcee work.

I had observed Bill's business practices during my time with his band and felt I had learned what to do and just as importantly what *not* to do when it came to doing business. It would be my job to deal with concert promoters and oversee the bookings for our new act.

The early Flatt & Scruggs years were a big challenge and at times somewhat of a struggle, but we managed to survive. It was important for many bands in those days to be connected with a radio station. If a band had its own radio show, the chances for booking live performances greatly increased in the areas that the station's signal reached. The downside to that, especially with smaller stations, was that a band couldn't expect to keep getting booked time and time again in the same region. It would eventually have to move on to another radio station in another area.

Moving meant uprooting families, and that made holding a band together more difficult at times. In the years from 1948 to 1955 we moved a dozen times, living in Virginia, North Carolina, Kentucky, Florida, and Tennessee.

Lester and I formed our first band and started out working in Danville, Virginia on radio station WDVA. One of my favorite groups at that time was the original Carter Family. We chose their song "Foggy Mountain Top" as the theme song for our radio show and called the band "The Foggy Mountain Boys."

The original "Foggies" were Jim Shumate on fiddle and Howard (Cedric Rainwater) Watts on upright bass. Jim was the one who had encouraged me to audition for the Blue Grass Boys in 1945. Cedric, another ex-Blue Grass Boy who I also mentioned earlier, did comedy routines as well. Jim Eanes, a guitar player, was also with us, but only very briefly. We soon moved to Hickory, North Carolina and worked on WHKY. Mac Wiseman joined the group and played guitar and sang tenor.

L–R: Earl, Howard Watts, Jim Shumate, and Lester Flatt

It was while working in Hickory that I married Louise Certain. I had met Louise in Nashville at the Grand Ole Opry in 1946. She was living in Nashville and employed as an accountant at that time. We were married on April 18, 1948 in Gaffney, South Carolina.

Louise was the only child of Ewing and Mamie Certain and she grew up on a farm in Grant, Tennessee, a small community located forty-five miles east of Nashville. Louise, like me, grew up admiring old-time music. Her grandfather had one of the first radios in their community, and all the neighbors would gather in on Saturday nights to listen to the Grand Ole Opry or the WLS Barn Dance out of Chicago, Illinois.

Newly-wed

The group stayed in Hickory for about a month, and due to financial reasons we decided that Hickory wasn't the place for us to be. For example, one date we worked was in a small theater, which was booked on a percentage. After advertising expenses were taken out of the gate receipts, our grand total profit for the night was seventeen cents each. We moved to Bristol, Virginia and began working on radio station WCYB.

Shortly after we started our radio programs in Bristol, Lester and I signed a recording contract with Mercury Records. We recorded four songs on our first session in the fall of 1948 in Knoxville. I played guitar on the very first two Flatt & Scruggs recordings, which were "God Loves His Children" and "I'm Going to Make Heaven My Home." We eventually recorded twenty-eight sides for Mercury over the next two years.

While we were at WCYB, I got the banjo that I still play to this day. Bill Monroe and his band came through the area in early 1949. Lester and I invited Bill to be a guest on our radio show, and he accepted the invitation. Don Reno, who had his own unique picking style, was playing banjo in Bill's band at that time, and I traded a Gibson RB-3 that I had bought a couple of years earlier for Don's Gibson Granada and a Martin guitar.

We stayed on at WCYB until March 1949 and then moved to Knoxville, where we worked on WROL. My first son, Gary, was born on May 18, 1949.

Earl & son Gary and two-tone shoes–1951

Lester and I recorded three more sessions for Mercury that year—one in the spring and two in December. It was during the December sessions that we recorded "Foggy Mountain Breakdown," which I had just recently written.

Columbia Records, a much larger recording company than Mercury in those days, offered us a recording contract in the summer of 1950. Lester and I wanted to accept the offer. Mercury agreed to release us provided that we would record twelve more songs for them. We did so in Tampa, Florida in October of 1950 in what some have called the "hurricane sessions." (We were just as anxious to get *out* of town, as an approaching hurricane was to get *in* to town). We recorded our first session for Columbia in November of 1950.

During the next few years we made several moves, working on radio stations in Lexington, Kentucky; Roanoke, Virginia; Tampa, Florida; and Raleigh, North Carolina. We moved back to Knoxville in the fall of 1952 and began working a noontime radio program along with doing our road shows most every night.

In 1953, Martha White Mills, a flour company based in Nashville, Tennessee, asked us to host their WSM radio programs in Nashville, and we moved there in June. My second son, Randy, was born on August 3 of that year.

We did the radio programs live, seven days a week. The five weekday shows aired at 5:45–6:00 in the morning. We also had a Saturday evening

show and an all-hymn program on Sunday mornings. We were doing personal appearances most every night as well, and the grinding schedule was getting the best of us. In September 1954, Martha White agreed to let us tape the shows.

We then moved to Virginia and taped a daily program on WRVA in Richmond and did two daily shows at WSVS in nearby Crewe, Virginia. We taped the Martha White shows in Crewe and sent them to Nashville, producing a total of four fifteen minute shows a day.

We joined the cast on the WRVA Saturday Night Barn Dance and of course continued to make personal appearances.

The WRVA Barn Dance cast was booked into New York City for two weeks. That was the first time we ever performed there, and the audiences were very enthusiastic. What was really satisfying about that trip to me was finding out that our records were being heard in that part of the country and that we had quite a few fans there that were learning my banjo style.

Teenager Randy Scruggs playing a 12-string guitar

We moved back to Nashville in January of 1955. Martha White had expanded into several areas, and we began doing live television shows for them six days a week. Our weekly circuit took us to six southeastern cities, including Nashville, and involved twenty-five hundred miles of travel each week. We also played show dates during those trips. We later taped all the shows in Nashville, which allowed us to book more concert dates in other parts of the country as well. We also became members of the Grand Ole Opry and hosted the Martha White segment of the show.

The year 1955 stands out in my mind for a number of reasons. Becoming members of the Opry gave Lester and me the confidence to finally settle down after all those early "gypsy" years of moving from town to town.

There were, of course, no cell phones or emails back in those days, so when we were on the road it was very difficult for me to tend to our bookings and other business matters. It sometimes seemed that if I wasn't working on the road, I was at home working on the phone. I remember one day we were about to leave for a show and as I was walking out the door I handed Louise the name and number of a promoter. I asked her to call him and see if she could book the band for a show.

When I got home from the trip late that night, Louise said, "I booked that date for you. Are there any other people you want me to call?"

I gladly gave her a list of some other contacts, and again she was successful in getting the dates booked. It wasn't long until Louise was doing all of the bookings for Lester and me as well as managing our other business affairs.

We hired Burkett "Uncle Josh" Graves in that year to play upright bass. Josh always brought his Dobro guitar along on our road trips and he enjoyed jamming with it. The more I heard him play, the more I liked the way he had adapted some of my three-finger banjo rolls to his Dobro style. After about a month's time, I told Lester I thought Josh would be a greater asset to the band playing his Dobro instead of bass. Lester agreed, and Josh was very happy to make the switch. The change helped identify our sound even more, and it wasn't long before other string bands were adding resophonic guitars to their instrumentation.

Paul Warren was already playing fiddle in the group when Josh joined the band. English P. "Cousin Jake" Tullock started playing upright bass for us not long after Josh switched over to Dobro. Josh, Jake, and Paul were the core members of the Foggy Mountain Boys for the most part of the remaining Flatt & Scruggs years.

Others who had been or would become band members included Jody Rainwater, Benny Martin, John "Curly" Seckler, Benny Sims, Everett Lilly, Chubby Wise, Howdy Forrester, and Billy Powers.

My mother suffered a serious stroke in October of 1955. Louise and I packed our car and we, along with Gary and Randy, headed to North Carolina to be with her. We were just outside of Knoxville when a car ran a stop sign and pulled out into the highway just in front of us. We crashed into the other car.

Gary and Randy were riding in the back seat and were not seriously injured, but Louise and I were both hospitalized for almost a month. Both of my hips were dislocated, and my pelvis bone was broken. My mother died while we were in the hospital, and I was off the road for eight months.

I returned to the road in late spring of 1956. I couldn't continue to travel our schedule by car, so Lester and I bought a bus and had the seats in the rear section stripped out and replaced with bunk beds. It wasn't a fancy bus by today's tour bus standards, but at least a person could stretch out and rest when feeling tired or sleepy.

L–R: Jake Tullock, Billy Powers, Paul Warren, Josh Graves, Earl Scruggs, and Lester Flatt—circa 1963

Columbia Records released our first album, *Foggy Mountain Jamboree*, at the end of 1957. Up until then, all of our records had been single releases. The band was becoming more and more popular, and in the next couple of years Mercury, too, was releasing our old catalogue as LPs.

My youngest son, Steve, was born on February 8, 1958. I decided I would learn to fly that year. The bus was a lot more comfortable than a car, but the travel was still taking its toll on me. I started taking flying lessons and bought an airplane. I obtained single and multi-engine instrument licenses and whenever possible I used my plane or flew commercially to get to our concerts.

Earl giving youngest son Steve a banjo lesson—1965
– Cover photo by Burt Brent

The only concert I ever performed without Lester and the Foggy Mountain Boys during the Flatt & Scruggs years was at the first annual Newport Folk Festival in July of 1959. The "folk boom" was underway, and with it came a renewed national interest in the banjo. I was amazed at the number of young fans there that were learning my style of banjo. The following year I was invited back to the festival along with Lester and the band.

The first national television exposure that Lester and I had was on CBS in 1960 on the Revlon Revue's *Folk Sound, U.S.A.* show. King Curtis, a great rhythm & blues saxophone player, was also on the show. King and I hit it off immediately. We jammed every chance we could during the couple of days of rehearsals before the live airing of the show. The jams, which at times included his piano player, were a lot of fun and got me to thinking that the banjo was not limited to country music.

Interest in the banjo continued to grow, and the first Flatt & Scruggs all-instrumental album, *Foggy Mountain Banjo,* came out in 1961. It became one of our most popular recordings. *Songs of the Famous Carter Family* also came out that year, and it was a lot of fun for me to record with one of my musical heroes, "Mother" Maybelle Carter of the original Carter Family.

That same year Lester and I worked two weeks in Los Angeles, California. Paul Henning, who was then creating *The Beverly Hillbillies* for CBS television, came to a few of our shows. He liked the sound of our music and asked us to play the music for the show's theme song, "Ballad of Jed Clampett."

L–R: Irene Ryan, Lester Flatt, Buddy Ebsen, Earl (in foreground), Donna Douglas, and Max Baer, Jr.

We recorded the theme, and Louise suggested that Lester and I also record the song for a single. We did and it was released shortly after the show premiered on television in 1962. The series was a hit right away, and our single went to #1 on the country charts and was in the pop charts also. We eventually appeared in seven episodes during the show's run. Those were special times for me

working with cast members Buddy Ebsen, Irene Ryan, Donna Douglas, and Max Baer, Jr.

Lester and I played Carnegie Hall on December 8, 1962. Louise asked Columbia to record the concert for release as a live album, but Columbia rejected the idea at first, saying that they didn't know if that could be done. She eventually talked them into doing it and the album *Flatt and Scruggs at Carnegie Hall!,* and the single "Ballad of Jed Clampett" received Grammy award nominations.

At Carnegie Hall

The days of being limited to performing in rural schoolhouses, small theaters, and on top of drive-in movie concession stands were long over. One music critic described our music as "folk music with overdrive." Great things continued to happen during the next few years, including another live album that we recorded at Vanderbilt University in Nashville. Another favorite Flatt & Scruggs album of mine was *Strictly Instrumental,* recorded with our guest artist Doc Watson.

The movie *Bonnie and Clyde* came out in 1967. Warren Beatty, who produced it and acted the part of outlaw Clyde Barrow, had called during its production and told us he wanted to feature our 1949 recording of "Foggy Mountain Breakdown" in the film, and we agreed to his request.

1967 also proved to be the beginning of the end for the Flatt & Scruggs Show. Columbia Records wanted us to record more contemporary material in hopes of expanding our market to a younger record-buying audience. We agreed to do so, but the results were mixed. I liked the idea because I was interested, as I'd always been, in exploring new musical ideas. I remembered how much fun I'd had jamming with King Curtis back in 1960. Lester, however, didn't feel comfortable singing the songs that Columbia wanted us to do.

As much as I liked Lester, one thing that had begun to bother me was his reluctance to perform new material on our stage shows. He was happier singing songs that we had recorded long ago, and at times it felt to me that we were doing the same show night after night and year after year. The situation seemed to get worse as time went on.

Bonnie and Clyde came out and was a box-office hit, and "Foggy Mountain Breakdown" became a radio hit. The new albums were being released, and our fan base was definitely growing.

We were even being booked into rock venues and festivals. The audience response was great, and I enjoyed seeing more and more younger faces in the crowd, but Lester wasn't happy with the path we were on. He expressed his desire to get back to the more rural circuit that we had once traveled.

By the time 1969 rolled around, Lester and I were both ready to end our partnership. We did our last performance together at the Grand Ole Opry in February of that year on the stage of the Ryman Auditorium, the same stage where we had first performed together in December 1945. A few days later, "Foggy Mountain Breakdown" won Lester and me a Grammy award during the same week it was announced that we had called it quits—so I guess you can say we ended on a high note.

～

As great as most of the Flatt & Scruggs years had been, there was always a negative side to them in my mind. Because of all the touring, I often had a sense of guilt about being away from Louise and our sons Gary, Randy, and Steve for so many days out of every year. I missed out on a lot of anniversaries, birthday parties, holidays, Little League games, and so on.

Having my sons tour with me in the Earl Scruggs Revue was a real treat in more ways than one. They brought a fire and an enthusiasm to the music that I felt was lacking in the latter years of Flatt & Scruggs. Suddenly the old songs felt new again, and they were eager to work up new songs and new arrangements with me.

The Revue merged acoustic instruments with electric instruments, and the band is considered by some to have been one of the pioneer acts of what came to be known as country-rock music.

(L–R) Earl with sons Steve, Gary, and Randy—circa 1965

In the summer of 1969, a video production team called to say they wanted to do a documentary on me for the National Educational Television Center network (NET). By that time, I had done a few spots on the Grand Ole Opry with Gary and Randy with me along with two or three other pickers, including Charlie Daniels, who had played on several Flatt & Scruggs recordings.

I invited Bob Dylan, Joan Baez, the Byrds, Doc Watson, and the Morris Brothers to take part in the documentary, and they all accepted the invitation. I had met Bob at a party hosted by Johnny and June Carter Cash. I had known Joan since the 1959 Newport Folk Festival. Gary had introduced me to the Byrds in 1968 when he brought them out to the house for a jam session. Doc and I had become friends during the recording of the Flatt & Scruggs *Strictly Instrumental* album. I had worked with Wiley and Zeke Morris in 1939. Bill Monroe also appeared during a jam session filmed backstage at the Opry.

The ninety-minute documentary was filmed in Tennessee, California, New York, North Carolina, and Washington, D.C. It was titled *Earl Scruggs: His Family and Friends* and aired to great reviews. Columbia released part of the music soundtrack to the film under the same title as the documentary.

By the time the documentary was released, Gary and Randy were signed to Vanguard Records. They had made a few concert appearances, mostly on college campuses, playing a mixture of rock and traditional country music. They were also touring with me when I did concerts, and I in turn performed as their guest on some of their shows. We blended our music, and the combination of acoustic and electric instruments was different from anything I'd ever heard before. The audience reaction was great wherever we played.

Word was getting around about those shows, and I began receiving a lot of great offers from concert promoters all across the country. Gary and Randy were still in school; Gary was in his senior year at Vanderbilt University, and Randy was in his senior year of high school. Because of their school commitments, neither they nor I were performing concerts year around, but when they graduated in the spring of 1971, we hit the road in earnest.

One of the stops for the Revue in the summer of 1971 was in Boulder, Colorado. John McEuen, a member of a young group called the Nitty Gritty Dirt Band, lived near Boulder at that time and came to the show. Gary had arranged for us to meet the Dirt Band in the fall of 1970 when they were in Nashville doing a concert at Vanderbilt. After our show, John came to the motel where we were staying, and we picked and talked into the early morning hours.

Earl and John McEuen backstage at the Grand Ole Opry House, 2003.
– Photo by Louise Scruggs

I told John that I would soon be recording an album with some younger guest artists along with the Revue. Linda Ronstadt, Arlo Guthrie, and Tracy Nelson of the group Mother Earth had already committed to the project. The album would be called *I Saw the Light (With Some Help from My Friends).* I asked John if the Dirt Band would like to take part in it, and he said he was sure they would all want to be on the album.

John was very interested in traditional music, and the talk turned to the possibility of me someday recording with them as well. I told him I would like that opportunity and also mentioned to John that maybe the Dirt Band should consider recording an album with some of the older artists of that day. He seemed surprised at my suggestion and asked if I was kidding. I said, "I don't kid around about music." It was there that the seeds for the album *Will the Circle Be Unbroken* (Volume I) were sown.

A week later, John's brother, Bill McEuen, who produced the Dirt Band's records at that time, called me and said that John had told him of our conversation. Bill told me the band wanted to record an all-acoustic album with guest artists that they had in mind, including me, who got their start in the earlier years of country music. He asked if I would help them get Maybelle Carter, Roy Acuff, and Bill Monroe to sign on for the recording, and I told him I would be happy to make the calls.

Maybelle and Roy accepted the invitation, but Bill declined, telling me he thought his fans would not "appreciate" him playing with "those kind of people," referring to their long hair and ventures into rock music. I told the Dirt Band of Bill's refusal and suggested that bluegrass artist Jimmy Martin could fill Bill's slot in their plans. They agreed, and Jimmy quickly accepted their invitation to be on the album. Merle Travis and Doc Watson also agreed to take part.

The Dirt Band also wanted fiddle, Dobro, and upright bass on the project. I recommended Vassar Clements to play fiddle, Norman Blake to play Dobro, and Roy "Junior" Huskey to play bass.

A couple of rehearsals were held at my house, and Gary and Randy sat in on those sessions. The Dirt Band invited Gary to sing background vocals and Randy to play guitar on the album.

Circle was recorded in Nashville in August 1971 and was released in 1972. It eventually spawned two more volumes released in 1989 and 2002 and I've taken part in all three projects.

1971 continued to be a busy year, and the Revue was evolving and establishing its own identity. At that time, Gary sang most of the lead vocals and played electric bass and harmonica. Randy played acoustic and electric guitars and would later learn to play fiddle. Jody Maphis, son of entertainers Joe and Rose Lee Maphis, started out in the group playing rhythm guitar and soon made the switch to drums. Vassar Clements played fiddle in the band. Bob Wilson, a session player who had played on the last couple of Bob Dylan albums, toured with us playing piano. In February 1972, Josh Graves, who had played Dobro in Lester's new band, the Nashville Grass, for the past three years, left Lester's group and joined the Revue.

By that time, I had already put out three albums on Columbia, two of which featured guest artists, and I felt it was time to release an Earl Scruggs Revue album. The Revue was booked into Kansas State University, and the concert was recorded. Looking back, *Live at Kansas State* is one my favorite Revue albums because I believe it captured the spirit and enthusiasm of both the band and the audiences that we were playing to at that time.

The Revue performed on many college campuses during its years, and we also played at a few music clubs around the country, especially in the earlier years. Back then, some of the better known clubs would book nationally known acts in for a week at a time with two shows a night and sometimes three shows on the weekends. We would have an opening act and then do a seventy-five to a ninety-minute set. The club would turn the house after the first show, and we would then play to another audience. The shows were generally sold out.

Music critic Robert Hilburn of the Los Angeles Times wrote of us, "The group is quite simply the best, most assured combination of traditional and contemporary music ideas that I've seen."

Another music critic, John Wasserman of the San Francisco Chronicle wrote, "I doubt there is another band in any form of American popular music that is better, man for man, than the Earl Scruggs Revue."

Not only were we blending acoustic instruments with electric instruments and drums, and playing both traditional and contemporary material, our audiences were looking at the stage and seeing two generations of musicians working happily together. My first full-time professional job was in the 1940s. Gary and Randy had begun their professional careers in the 1960s. I can't begin to remember how many times people would come up at the end of a show and tell me how much they wished that their own family could have as much fun together.

My youngest son, Steve, started playing rhythm guitar with the Revue in the summer of 1972. His touring with the band was mostly limited to summer months until he finished his high school years. He later taught himself how to play piano and switched over from rhythm to keyboards in the group. He also taught himself to play saxophone, which he played on a couple of blues numbers that we did in our concerts. Steve also played banjo and would often pick a banjo instrumental during our shows. At that point in the show, I would switch over to guitar and follow Steve's number by playing guitar on a couple of songs.

The 1972 concert at Kansas State University had been a great success, and we were invited back for another concert in January 1973.

The university billed the concert as *Earl Scruggs with Family and Friends* and also booked the Nitty Gritty Dirt Band, Joan Baez, the Byrds, Doc and Merle Watson, Tracy Nelson & Mother Earth, Ramblin' Jack Elliott, and David Bromberg to appear. The concert was filmed and would later be released as a movie titled *Banjoman*.

In the 1970s, most recording artists had albums released more frequently than they do now. In the five years spanning from 1973 to 1977, I had ten albums released. One of my favorites, *Dueling Banjos*, was an all-instrumental album. Gary, Randy, Josh, Vassar, Jody, and I recorded it in two three-hour sessions in one day of March 1973. It wasn't like we hurried through the songs; most of the tunes were ones that we had been doing on stage, and we were doing a lot of concerts, so we were well rehearsed, you might say. The tracks on the album were mostly first or second takes.

Ten days later, we were in Los Angeles recording the soundtrack for a movie called *Where the Lilies Bloom*. It was quite an experience. The band sat in a large recording studio, and the segments of the movie that required music were played in front of us on a small movie screen. The movie's director would cue us in during each scene where he wanted the music to begin, and we played each number at the tempo needed in order to end each musical piece where he wanted the music to end. Columbia released the soundtrack as an album when the movie was released in 1974.

Revue album cover: Earl, center; clockwise from top Josh Graves, Randy Scruggs, Gary Scruggs, Jody Maphis, and Steve Scruggs

The album *Anniversary Special* was recorded and released in 1975 and celebrated my twenty-fifth year with Columbia Records. It featured many guest artists including Johnny Cash, Joan Baez, Billy Joel, Bonnie Bramlett, Loudon Wainwright III, Roger McGuinn, Charlie Daniels, Dan Fogelberg, and Doug Kershaw.

It seemed to me that nothing could go wrong until September 28, 1975. That day was nice and clear, a perfect day for flying; I decided to fly my plane from Nashville to Murray, Kentucky for a concert that the Revue would be playing that night at Morehead State University.

169

Murray is about a two-hour drive northwest of Nashville, and the band left in the bus around noon for the date. Louise flew up with me. After the concert was over, Louise chose to ride back to Nashville on the bus. I told her I would see her at the house when the bus returned home.

As it turned out, I didn't make it home that night; I had crashed during my landing approach at the small airport where I kept my plane. My left wrist, left ankle, and nose were broken, and the head injury I suffered caused me to have retrograde amnesia, so I have no memory of the crash. The airport runway is near a river—I most likely had tried to land and ran into fog. I probably tried to abort the landing and the plane had stalled. I was off the road for over five weeks.

Because of the injuries, I had to miss the Country Music Association's award show, which was held a couple of weeks later where the Revue had been nominated for the Best Country Instrumental Group of 1975. The group also won Billboard magazine's Best Country Instrumental Group award for that year, and the movie *Banjoman*, premiered in November at the Kennedy Center in Washington, D.C. A soundtrack album from the movie was later released under the same title.

In addition to the many college dates we were playing, the Revue performed at a lot of music festivals. We were by no means a rock band playing rock music, but our show always went over well in rock and pop venues.

Some of the rock and pop acts that we shared a stage with included the Eagles, Fleetwood Mac, the Byrds, the Grateful Dead, Linda Ronstadt, James Taylor, the Beach Boys, B.B. King, and the Nitty Gritty Dirt Band.

We weren't a bluegrass band either, but we played several bluegrass festivals in our day and were well received by those audiences as well.

I was often asked to categorize the style of music that the Revue played. I never saw the need to pigeonhole the band, so my answer was always the same, that we played "Earl Scruggs Revue" music. We didn't limit our songs to come from any one particular musical style, and our audiences were diverse as well.

The Revue performed concerts in forty-eight of the United States, missing only Alaska and Hawaii. We also played in most of the Canadian provinces and in England and Bermuda. With my sons Gary, Randy, and later Steve in the band, there were not many personnel changes during the years of the Revue. Josh and Vassar, for examples, both left the group to begin their own well-deserved solo careers.

In the spring of 1980, Randy told me that he wanted to get off the road. He and Steve had invested in a recording studio in Nashville, and Randy felt he needed to spend more time in the studio and pursue a career in producing records.

The Revue performed its last concert in North Carolina in September of 1980, and the Revue's album *Country Comfort* was released around the same time.

The title for that album came from a song written by Elton John and Bernie Taupin that we had recorded earlier in the year. That song, by coincidence, had been one of the very first songs recorded by the Revue. Our original version of "Country Comfort" had only been released as a single, never showing up on a Revue album. It seemed like we had come full circle.

~

I went into semi-retirement when the Revue disbanded, doing only an occasional show over the next several years.

In 1981, I took part in a made-for-television movie titled *Return of the Beverly Hillbillies.* I recorded three albums on Columbia Records between 1982 and 1984. Columbia also released a Revue album titled *Super Jammin'* in 1984 that contained mostly previously released material.

Despite my plane crash in 1975, I still loved flying and I bought another plane in the mid-1980s. I flew short runs, often as a volunteer carrying blood for the Red Cross to small towns in Tennessee, Kentucky, Georgia, and Alabama. I continued to pilot the plane up until a few years ago.

I've also stayed involved with Gibson Instruments and have worked closely with the company in the design and promotion of several different Earl Scruggs signature banjo models.

I've never been known for my public speaking, but in the summer of 2001 I was asked to make a speech and present an award. There's an annual three-day event held in Murfreesboro, Tennessee called "Uncle Dave Macon Days" in honor of David "Uncle Dave" Macon, who some say was the first true star of the Grand Ole Opry.

Uncle Dave had lived near Murfreesboro. He was born in 1870 and passed away in 1952. Each year an award is given to someone who has dedicated his or her time, love, and energy to keeping old-time country music alive. I was asked to present the award that year to Eddie Stubbs who is a deejay on WSM and is also one of the Opry announcers. It came as a big surprise to Eddie, for he had no idea he was going to be so honored.

Eddie is a walking encyclopedia when it comes to country music, and I'm willing to bet that I'm his number one fan. It gave me a great deal of pleasure to be the one making the presentation to him. It was also fun for me to be there that day and reflect on what Uncle Dave had meant to me early on in my professional career.

Uncle Dave was one of my favorite people to visit with when I was on the Grand Ole Opry with the Blue Grass Boys in the 1940s. Sometimes the group and Uncle Dave toured together, and it was always a barrel of fun for me to be around him. He never learned to drive an automobile, so when he was on the road with us he would travel in our car. Uncle Dave loved to entertain people with his singing, banjo playing, and comedy routines. The number of old-time tunes he knew amazed me. Despite all his fame and fortune he never got away from his simple, down-to-earth life style and he endeared himself to many fans. His slogan was "I don't put on; I put out!" and that he did.

Uncle Dave had a tendency to call people by the wrong name or to give them nicknames. He called me "Ernest." One of his classic comments to me was, "Ernest, you play good in a band but you're not a bit funny, are you?" meaning of course, I had no comedy routine. In those days there were a lot of banjo pickers who doubled as comedians—Uncle Dave for one, Snuffy Jenkins, Stringbean, "Grandpa" Jones. The list goes on and on.

Another Uncle Dave comment was "You pick good in a band, but you don't sing a lick, do you, Ernest?" I did sing baritone harmony with the band, but the comedy and singing remarks did have a ring of truth to them since I had devoted most all of my attention to playing the banjo while growing up. But, for Uncle Dave to say that he admired my banjo playing was as satisfying as "writing home for five and getting ten."

Another wonderful friendship that had started for me in my Opry years in the 1940s was with Beecher (Pete) "Bashful Brother Oswald" Kirby. I had been greatly inspired by Roy Acuff and his Smoky Mountain Boys even before I made it to the Opry. Oswald, or "Os," (pronounced "Oz") played a fine old-time frailing style 5-string banjo and was the comedian in Roy's band. Os was also the best Dobro player I'd ever heard in that day and time, playing with a two-finger style. I loved the sound of his Dobro, and his fill-in licks behind Roy's singing fit Roy's voice like a glove. Os was featured on the Dirt Band's *Circle 1* album, backing up Roy and playing a couple of solo numbers. We often visited one another and spent many good times sitting around picking and talking. Oswald passed away in October 2002 at the age of ninety.

I lost one of my dearest and closest friends when John Hartford passed away in June of 2001. I met John in late November 1955 when he came from his Missouri home to visit me while I was recuperating from the car wreck. He was eighteen years old and pretty shy and didn't say much at all after introducing himself. Someone else had dropped by to visit, and John stayed and listened to our conversation. The other person left a couple of hours later and John said, "Well, I'll get out of your hair but before I leave, would you mind if I asked you some questions about Scruggs-style?" I told him to ask away, and he proceeded to pull out of his briefcase a notebook with eight pages filled with questions front and back that he had written down and wanted to ask me. John's visit ended up lasting ten hours, and our friendship had begun.

John moved to Nashville in 1965 and soon signed a recording deal with RCA Records. Besides writing the classic "Gentle on My Mind," he played great banjo, fiddle, and guitar. He loved old-time music and also became a licensed riverboat pilot. He moved to Los Angeles in 1968, where he wrote for and appeared on the CBS *Smothers Brothers Comedy Hour.* He later appeared frequently on *The Glen Campbell Goodtime Hour.*

John moved back to Nashville in 1971, and we often visited one another when we were both in town. When my son Steve passed away in September of 1992, I was crushed and felt like I had a big hole torn into my heart. I didn't even think to pick up a banjo for a long time. John would come visit me every chance he had, and he was a great help to me in dealing with my loss.

After eight months or so had gone by, John showed up one night and said, "Well, I brought my fiddle along in case you might want to pick a little bit." I slowly got back into playing that night.

I still didn't pick a lot for the next few years. I didn't feel good in general, and my back hurt more often than not. I was told I needed hip replacement surgery; my old artificial hips had simply worn out.

I entered the hospital in October 1996, and the surgery was done. While in the recovery room, I suffered a heart attack. By-pass surgery was performed; I had six blocked arteries. I was lucky—the doctors told me that if I had not been in the recovery room with the medical staff on hand when the heart attack happened, I would have surely died.

∼

A year after the surgeries, I felt like a new man. For the past several years I've stayed active with recordings and concerts. I've been a guest on several artists' albums including Dwight Yoakam, Patty Loveless, the Chieftains, the Nitty Gritty Dirt Band, Loretta Lynn, Béla Fleck, Marty Stuart, and Tony Trishka.

Fiddler Glen Duncan (foreground) and Earl in concert with the Chieftains at the Ryman Auditorium in Nashville
– Photo by David Schenk

I've also enjoyed doing concerts billed as Earl Scruggs with Family & Friends and have been a guest on other artists' concerts including Dwight Yoakam, the Dixie Chicks, and the Chieftains.

In 2001, I recorded my first album in seventeen years. It's titled *Earl Scruggs and Friends,* and several guest artists joined me on the project.

I re-recorded "Foggy Mountain Breakdown" for the CD, and the featured musicians on that track are my sons Gary and Randy along with Glen Duncan, Steve Martin, Vince Gill, Marty Stuart, Albert Lee, Paul Shaffer, Jerry Douglas, and Leon Russell. We all won a Grammy award for Best Country Instrumental Performance of 2001, and it marked the second time that "Foggy" had been honored with a Grammy.

Front cover of "Earl Scruggs and Friends" CD

I've been fortunate to receive quite a few awards during my career. One of the awards I'm most proud of is one that I did not win.

In June of 1999, Louise and I attended the International Fan Club Organization's annual show in Nashville. IFCO was founded in 1967, and it presents its annual "Tex Ritter Award" to honor a person who has worked hard to keep country music and its traditions alive. Marty Stuart presented the plaque in 1999, and I was on stage with him when he announced that year's winner was Louise.

Louise was stunned when she heard her name called out, and I was overjoyed for her. She made a name for herself in what was once literally a "man's world" as far as the business end of country music was concerned.

Earl and Louise
– Photo by Dan Loftin

Hazel Smith, a country music journalist, has said that Louise was the first woman to hold a position of power in the country music business world when she began booking and managing Lester and me in 1955. I'm not so sure our act would have lasted for as long as it did without her efforts.

The mid-1950s to the early 1960s were lean years for many country music artists. Groups were disbanding, and some artists were firing their bands and using whatever local pick-up musicians they might happen to find while touring from town to town. Much of the music that is now known as "bluegrass" was fading away from many of the larger country radio stations.

A lot of people blamed the popularity of Elvis Presley and rock 'n' roll early on in those years for the decline in country music record sales. The blame later shifted to the folk boom. It's easy to look back now and point some of that blame to mismanagement and bad business decisions made by some of those country music artists.

Louise's managing skills kept things happening for Lester and me during those times. She negotiated with record label executives, concert promoters, and television producers. And she kept thinking of ways to keep alive the interest in our music. She also deserves a lot of credit for the success of the Revue years.

I feel fortunate to have had Louise taking care of my business interests for all these years. I feel even luckier that she's my wife.

Louise, Gary, Randy, and other family members were with me on February 13, 2003 when I was inducted into the Hollywood Walk of Fame. Many others were there to help me celebrate the event including Gibson CEO Henry Juszkiewicz, my long-time agent D.J. McLachlan, and musicians Dwight Yoakam, John McEuen, Keb' Mo', and Jessi Colter. Actors Kevin Nealon, Fred Willard, and two of *The Beverly Hillbillies* cast members, Donna Douglas, who portrayed Elly May Clampett, and Max Baer, Jr., who played the part of Jethro Bodine, also joined in the celebration.

My star was placed in the sidewalk on Hollywood Boulevard near the Roosevelt Hotel where I used to stay when I was in Hollywood to film *The Beverly Hillbillies* shows. Speeches were made, and Henry displayed a new Gibson model banjo called "The Earl" for the crowd to see. That was a very exciting day for me, and I could not help but think about all that had happened during the course of my career.

I've heard it said that the banjo was in danger of becoming a forgotten instrument before I made my debut on the Grand Ole Opry in late 1945. I would like to think that the 5-string banjo is still alive and well and will continue to be heard in today's and tomorrow's music.

The Beverly Hillbillies television show remains popular to this day, thanks to the many reruns of the series. In 1998, The American Film Institute included Bonnie and Clyde in its list of the Top 100 greatest American movies of all time, ranking it number twenty-seven. I'm happy and proud to have played a part in both *The Beverly Hillbillies* and *Bonnie and Clyde.*

In March of 2001, I was invited along with other members of the Country Music Hall of Fame to attend a pre-opening party at the Hall of Fame and Museum's new building in Nashville. The festivities included some picking and singing, and I led off the program with "Foggy Mountain Breakdown."

When the party ended, Tony Brown, an executive with MCA Records at that time, came up to me and said, "Do you realize you played the first song to be performed in this new building?"

It hadn't really occurred to me until Tony brought it to my attention, but looking back, I'm glad it was "Foggy" that I had played.

On January 6, 2004 the Country Music Hall of Fame and Museum threw a surprise party for me to help me celebrate my 80th birthday. Later in the year, Columbia Records released a double CD titled *The Essential Earl Scruggs* that contains forty recordings spanning the years 1946 to 1984.

Front cover of "The Essential Earl Scruggs" CD

Country music has evolved over the years, and many changes have occured since I got into the music business. I'm flattered that there are still many fans and bands dedicated to holding on to and preserving the string band sound that became popular in 1946 and later became known as "bluegrass" music.

I'm also excited to see younger artists such as the Dixie Chicks, Alison Krauss & Union Station, and Béla Fleck, incorporating the banjo into their more modern sounds of these early years of the 21st century.

Music has brought me much joy over the years, and I feel very fortunate to have been able to earn my living by making music. I've always taken the music very seriously but never to the point of not having a whole lot of fun with it.

I'm particularly thankful for and honored by the many people who refer to three-finger banjo picking as "Scruggs-Style."

12 A BRIEF HISTORY OF THE 5-STRING BANJO By Louise Scruggs

THERE IS NO MUSICAL SOUND MORE DEEPLY rooted in American history than that of the five-string banjo. It was played by many thousands of people all across America in the last half of the nineteenth century, and yet by 1940, the national interest in the instrument was virtually non-existent.

The five-string banjo is a unique instrument in the way it is strung, having four long strings and one short "drone" string. It also has a unique history. The direct ancestor to the banjo originated in Africa and has been referred to by several different names, including "banjar." The body of the banjar was most often an open gourd with a skin head stretched over it. The body was extended with a wooden neck, and the earliest banjars had as few as one string and as many as three. Some of the instruments were plucked, and some were even bowed. Strings were made from gut or hemp.

Africans brought it to colonial America during the days of slavery. By the end of the eighteenth century the banjo had evolved into a four-stringed instrument. Thomas Jefferson made mention of the strange instrument in his *Notes on the State of Virginia,* published in 1785. Jefferson wrote "The instrument proper to them *(the slaves)* is the Banjar, which they brought hither from Africa."

Joel Walker Sweeney is widely credited for an innovation made in 1831 to the four-string banjos of Jefferson's era. He added another string, and the five-string banjo was born.

He was also an entertainer and did much to popularize the five-string banjo. Sweeney was born in Appomattox, Virginia in 1810, and at an early age, organized his own Appomattox band. He composed many songs based on the melodies created by the slaves he knew.

Billed as the "Banjo King," Sweeney was a hit on the New York stage after a wagon tour through the South. He eventually toured England where he appeared before Queen Victoria for a command performance.

Joel Walker Sweeney
Courtesy of the History Division of the
Los Angeles County Museum

In the 1840s, Sweeney is said to have encouraged a drum maker in Baltimore, Maryland, called the Boucher Company, to begin manufacturing banjos with a drum-like wooden rim as the body. One of those Sweeney banjos is now in the possession of the Los Angeles County Museum in California.

That banjo was still a far cry from today's five-string banjo. It was fretless, open-backed, and made before the advent of metal strings, which would not come along until the late 1850s. The banjo head, of course, was made of skin.

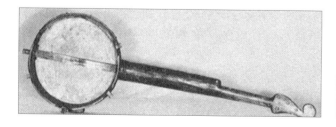 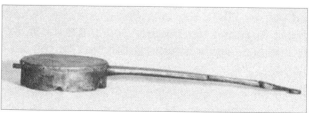

Photos of the Sweeney banjo
Courtesy of the History Division of the Los Angeles County Museum.

During his lifetime, Sweeney was the foremost of the blackface minstrels and has been called the "Father of American Minstrelsy." It has been said that his touring company was the very first of a long line of minstrel shows, which continued as popular entertainment up until the 1890s.

No other instrument in the world was strung like the five-string banjo, with its four long strings and one short drone string. New playing methods were developed that are unique to the instrument. Thousands of now unknown Americans developed their clawhammer, frailing, and two-finger playing styles during those early decades of five-string banjo history.

The banjo went west in covered wagons and was enjoyed by different ethnic groups throughout the nation. Soldiers on both sides of the American Civil War also contributed to the spread of its popularity. There were soldiers who brought their banjos with them to the war and taught others to play. When the war ended and the soldiers went back to their homes, knowledge of the banjo was spread far and wide.

Different players had different methods of playing. Many of them used four or five different tunings and various frailing and two-finger playing styles to play different songs. Little music was written for the banjo in those times. Instead, a tremendous amount of lore developed and was passed on from one player to another. Old folks taught the young ones, and players swapped style secrets.

In a nation of rugged individualists, the banjo was an appropriately individualistic instrument. The popularity of the banjo was important in perpetuating and preserving many songs that might otherwise have been forgotten. In addition, a special body of banjo music began to develop, and it, too, is now part of America's folk music heritage. For the most part, the writers of that music are unknown, as are the early innovators of the principal old-time playing styles.

The first frets were added to the banjo's neck in the late 1870s. Resonators, tone rings, and plastic heads would eventually follow.

Toward the end of the nineteenth century, instrument companies were manufacturing banjos in different sizes for "banjo orchestras" in hopes of capitalizing on the instrument's widespread popularity.

Throughout the nineteenth century, the five-string banjo held its place in the hearts of America, but in the early twentieth century its popularity declined. The advent of jazz was one major factor for the decline. Jazz musicians altered the banjo and the method of playing it in order to adapt it to the new jazz combos on the rise.

The fifth string was dropped, the neck was shortened, the head enlarged, and heavier gauge strings were used to make it louder.

The resulting four-string, or tenor banjo, was favored in jazz bands and was generally plucked and strummed with a straight pick. The old finger-picking and clawhammer styles were abandoned along with the fifth string. The banjo was expected to produce enough volume to be heard through a brass section. In some cases, the changes went even further, and some banjos were reduced to mandolin size and strung with eight strings. Such instruments did not sound even remotely like the five-string banjo. The innovations almost sounded the death knell for the five-string banjo, and only a few bands and natives in remote regions of the South kept the old traditions going.

In the 1920s when commercial recording companies put out their earliest folk discs, some of the remaining old-time five-string banjo players were recorded. Those records, once looked upon as beneath the notice of "cultured" people, are now among the most important sources of American folk music. Before country or folk music became highly commercialized, those performers played true folk songs in their own native style. Most of the early master discs have been destroyed or lost over the years, and the recordings that survived are now rare, precious, and sometimes very costly collectors' items.

By 1930, the four-string banjo's popularity was fading out. It was rarely used in jazz or popular music bands, having been replaced for the most part by the guitar. As for the five-string instrument, fewer and fewer people knew how to play it.

By the early 1940s even country music bands, or "hillbilly" bands as they were called at that time, were dropping the five-string banjo. The banjo players who remained playing on radio were usually billed as a single attraction and only rarely included in musical groups.

Three players from that era, David Macon, David Akeman, and Louis Jones are of particular note.

David "Uncle Dave" Macon was a rotund minstrel with gold teeth and a big gold watch chain, whose uninhibited performances with the five-string banjo were one of the Grand Ole Opry's best loved attractions in the early days of the Opry.

Uncle Dave, also known as "the Dixie Dewdrop," was born on October 7, 1870, in Smartt Station, Tennessee, in Warren County. His father was a hotelkeeper in Nashville, Tennessee who catered to the theatrical profession. Uncle Dave learned to play the banjo by watching performers who stopped at the hotel.

In 1920, he and "Uncle" Jimmy Thompson, the first fiddler heard on radio, joined a vaudeville show on the RKO circuit.

Uncle Dave's favorite tunes to play were "Eleven Cent Cotton and Forty Cent Meat," "Keep My Skillet Good and Greasy," "Bile Them Cabbage Down," and "How Beautiful Heaven Must Be."

Uncle Dave Macon

Uncle Dave traveled all over the country, playing and singing wherever there were people to listen to him. In 1925 at the age of fifty-six, he joined the WSM Barn Dance in Nashville, which would later become known as the Grand Ole Opry. He became its first singing star and its biggest single attraction in the Opry's early years.

Uncle Dave died on March 22, 1952 after a short illness. He was inducted into the Country Music Hall of Fame in 1966.

George D. Hay, a great fan and close friend of Uncle Dave, was the first announcer of the Grand Ole Opry. He joined WSM in Nashville after leaving WLS in Chicago, Illinois where he had worked on the National Barn Dance. It was on November 28, 1925 at eight o'clock in the evening when Hay, then thirty years old, presented himself as "The Solemn Old Judge" and launched the WSM Barn Dance.

His only artist that night was the elderly and long-bearded fiddler named "Uncle" Jimmy Thompson, who claimed he knew a thousand fiddle tunes. He played an hour that first night and didn't want to stop. Shortly thereafter, musicians began coming to Nashville to perform on the program.

It was "Judge" Hay who gave the WSM Barn Dance the more colorful title of the Grand Ole Opry in 1927 following a three-hour presentation

of the NBC Music Appreciation Hour conducted by Dr. Walter Damrosch. Hay opened the show by saying, "We have been listening to music taken largely from Grand Opera, but from now on we will present 'The Grand Ole Opry.'" He then called on Deford Bailey who performed a country version of his "Pan American Blues" on his harmonica.

Judge Hay believed in and respected traditional music. If he enjoyed an artist's performance, he would blow his then-famous steamboat whistle. During his years on the Grand Ole Opry, if an artist or group seemed to be playing too far out for his musical tastes, he was quick to say, "Keep it down to earth, boys, down to earth."

It is fitting that George D. Hay was inducted into the Country Music Hall of Fame in 1966 along with his friend Uncle Dave Macon.

George D. Hay visiting Uncle Dave at his home

David "Stringbean" Akeman was born in Annville, Kentucky in 1915. Stringbean eventually earned his nickname because of his lanky appearance. He was also known as "String" and described as "the Kentucky Wonder."

Stringbean grew up on a farm along with his seven brothers and sisters. His father played banjo, and String learned to play both two-finger and frailing styles on the five-string.

His musical career began at the age of eighteen. His first radio experience was on radio station WLAP in Lexington, Kentucky. He worked three years with Charlie Monroe's band, the Kentucky "Pardners," in Greensboro, North Carolina.

In 1942, String became the first banjo player for Bill Monroe and the Blue Grass Boys, playing his two-finger and frailing styles. He left that band in 1945 and would later become a member of the Grand Ole Opry working as a solo act.

Stringbean toured with many entertainers and appeared on NBC network radio programs for twelve years. He later became a regular on the *Hee Haw* television show, which premiered in 1969. He was a close friend of Uncle Dave Macon who willed Stringbean one of his banjos.

String's easygoing manner, rustic humor, and bizarre costumes consisting of pants that belted just above his knees and worn with extra-long shirts made him a great favorite with the Nashville entertainers and his many fans.

Stringbean in one of his stage costumes

He would often acknowledge his audiences for their applause by twirling his little hat in a comedic manner at the end of a song. His catchphrase was "Lord, I feel so unnecessary."

String was known by many people to not trust in banking institutions. He would often carry a large amount of cash stuffed in his pockets and was not shy about flashing the money around for others to see. It was rumored that he kept a huge stash of money hidden somewhere in his house, and that rumor contributed to his tragic death.

On the night of November 10, 1973, String and his wife, Estelle, returned home from an Opry performance and surprised two burglars who were not expecting them to be back until later in the night. The burglars shot and killed String. Estelle tried to flee and was gunned down in the yard, shot in the back.

Louis Marshall "Grandpa" Jones, another member of the Grand Ole Opry who was also String's neighbor and best friend, found the bodies the next day. The murderers were later captured, tried, convicted, and sentenced to life in prison.

Grandpa Jones was born in Niagara, Kentucky in 1913. His musical experience began at the age of eight when he learned to play the ukulele. In 1929 at the age of sixteen, he won an amateur contest in Akron, Ohio and got a job performing on an Akron radio station the very next day. He played straight roles and sang ballads and novelty songs in the early days of his career.

In 1936, while working on a radio station in Boston, Massachusetts, Grandpa began doing comedy routines in his act. It was a singer named Bradley Kincaid who gave him the nickname of "Grandpa," which reflected his older-sounding voice. Although he was only in his early twenties, radio listeners began calling in to ask just how old "Grandpa" was. Grandpa then began wearing a fake mustache, fake bushy eyebrows, and makeup-drawn wrinkles whenever he performed in public in order to make him appear much older than his tender years.

Grandpa Jones

In 1937, he formed his act, "Grandpa Jones and His Grandchildren," on radio station WWVA in Wheeling, West Virginia. It was also in 1937 when Grandpa became interested in the 5-string banjo for the first time. Until then he had played only the guitar in his performances. He began learning a frailing style of banjo and after a few weeks he was able to incorporate the banjo into his act for a few numbers. The banjo would later become more of his trademark instrument than the guitar.

Grandpa first performed on the Grand Ole Opry in 1946 and became a member in 1947. "Eight More Miles to Louisville," "Old Rattler," "Mountain Dew," and Jimmy Rodgers's "T for Texas" became signature recordings for him. He later became a regular on the *Hee Haw* television show in 1969 along with his friend, Stringbean. Grandpa's "Hey, Grandpa! What's for supper?" routine became a regular fixture on that show.

Grandpa was inducted into the Country Music Hall of Fame in 1978. He passed away in February of 1998. His last performance was on the stage of the Grand Ole Opry.

Uncle Dave, Stringbean, and Grandpa were each unique in their own way. Uncle Dave was outgoing and, at times, outlandish. Stringbean, with his tall and lanky appearance, was rather quiet and reserved in his performances and sang in a lonesome voice. Grandpa tended to "shout" his upbeat songs in a boisterous manner.

One thing that the three had in common besides the five-string banjo was that they were all comedians. In fact, it seems that "hillbilly" banjo performers from the 1920s until the mid-1940s were expected to be comedians. That stereotypical image would change in late 1945.

By that time, instrument companies were no longer making banjos except on special order, and the demand for the instrument was very limited.

Earl Scruggs, born on January 6, 1924 in the southwestern Piedmont section of North Carolina, started playing banjo at the age of four and learned to play three-finger style banjo at the age of ten. During the next few years he developed and finessed a playing style that transcended other three-finger picking styles being played at that time. His style of playing would later be imitated throughout the world.

He introduced to a huge radio audience what soon became known as "Scruggs-style" picking on the Grand Ole Opry in December of 1945 when he joined Bill Monroe and the Blue Grass Boys. Earl's hard-driving style of picking radically redefined Monroe's old-time hillbilly music that Monroe and other string bands of that era were playing before Earl joined the musical mix.

The new and more exciting sound would several years later become known as "bluegrass" music. Perhaps no other musical instrument is as closely associated with bluegrass music as is Scruggs-style five-string banjo.

Scruggs-style picking spread rapidly, and in the early 1950s the demand for five-string banjos was so great that instrument companies began to manufacture them again.

Earl decided to leave the Monroe band in early 1948 and soon after teamed up with another ex-Blue Grass Boy, Lester Flatt, for a partnership that lasted twenty-one years. Over the course of that time, Earl and Lester achieved international fame.

Earl's innovative spirit proved to be not limited to musical stylization. During the early to mid 1940s, Earl worked in a thread mill near his home in North Carolina where he learned many intricacies of machinery. The knowledge was later directed to the banjo. In 1952, he invented what became known as "Scruggs tuners," which allowed him to de-tune his banjo while playing a tune without having to do so by ear with standard tuning pegs.

Early publicity photo of Earl with the Gibson RB-11 that he purchased in a pawnshop in 1941

In the late 1950s and throughout much of the 1960s, what became known as the "folk boom" further increased awareness of the five-string banjo. Even Hollywood got in on the act in the 1960s with television's *The Beverly Hillbillies* and the movie *Bonnie and Clyde,* exposing Earl and his picking style to a vast audience.

Earl founded the Earl Scruggs Revue after the Flatt & Scruggs partnership ended in 1969. The Revue was largely a family affair that included his three sons Gary, Randy, and Steve.

Not content to be confined to one style of music, Earl and the Revue played an eclectic mixture of musical styles including traditional, country, blues, and rock. They were one of the pioneer acts in what came to be known as "country-rock" music.

Earl has won numerous awards and accolades during his music career. He was inducted into the Country Music Hall of Fame in 1985 along with his former partner, Lester Flatt.

Earl, Lester, and Bill Monroe were individually inducted into the International Bluegrass Music Association's Hall of Honor in 1991 in that Hall's inaugural year.

In 1992, the 41st President of the United States, George Herbert Walker Bush, presented Earl with a National Medal of Arts Award.

Earl was inducted into the North Carolina Music and Entertainment Hall of Fame in 1996, and in 2003 he was honored with a Star in the Hollywood Walk of Fame.

Music critic Walter Carter, in an article written for the Gibson website titled "Earl Scruggs Can't Get Enough Picking," wrote, "The most profound measure of Earl Scruggs' influence is the simple fact that the five-string banjo is the only instrument on which the overwhelming majority of players copy the style of just one man. 'Scruggs style'—the driving, three-fingered roll that Scruggs perfected in the 1930s—defines the five-string banjo. Scruggs has done everything a man could ever hope to do with a musical instrument, but he's not about to hang it on the wall and rest on his accomplishments. In an interview at Gibson's Original Acoustic Instruments division, where Gibson makes all the Earl Scruggs banjo models, the master revealed that his driving force today is the same as it was in 1934."

Perhaps no history regarding the development of the five-string banjo and those who have brought it to the public's attention would be complete without mentioning Pete Seeger. Pete did so much to help popularize the instrument among urban folk song enthusiasts during the folk boom of the 1950s and 1960s. When he heard that this book was being written, he sent the following message:

"They say there's nothing new under the sun. Tens of thousands of years ago probably some early man first plucked a rhythm on a string and made it louder by crossing it over a drum head. What do you bet?

"But the plunky, twangy, rippling tones of today's 5-string banjo is the creation of the country musicians of the Southern states of the U.S.A., and chief among them is Mr. Earl Scruggs. The style of music they created is going to be heard in many lands, wherever people love its bright sound, unlike that of any other musical instrument. 'Round and 'round this old world, ring, ring, the banjo!

"I'm sure glad to hear that Earl Scruggs is putting out a book about his kind of banjo picking. There will be millions of people wanting to buy it, and I'm one of 'em."

*Parts of this chapter were printed in the following publications:
© March 1961, Tennessee Folklore Society Bulletin
© 1963-1964 December, January issue of SING OUT!

A gigantic Gibson banjo headstock hangs over a window at the Gibson store and workshop inside Opry Mills Mall in Nashville, Tennessee.

– Photo by David Schenk

HOW TO BUILD A BANJO By Burt Brent

To fully understand your banjo, you should become familiar with its construction. A banjo is a unique instrument in that there are many variables in its construction and parts, which can affect the tone and the ease in which the instrument can be played.

Many automobile owners are dependent upon their favorite mechanic for every little thing that goes wrong with their car, as they only know how to turn a key, step on the gas, or hit the brake. A repair or adjustment is costly, as well as inconvenient. The exact same principles apply to the banjo. If you understand the "anatomy and physiology" of the instrument—in other words, its construction and mechanism of its parts—you will appreciate the instrument and respect it, as well as saving yourself the expense and inconvenience of leaving it at a music shop for weeks or months at a time. There is also much self-satisfaction in being able to make these repairs and adjustments yourself.

This, then, is the main importance of this article. Secondarily, it will teach you inlaying, fancy decorative type instrument work, gold-plating, etc., if you care to try some for yourself, as most banjo players do at one time or another.

Building a Banjo Neck

Unfortunately, the art of decorative musical instrument making has been lost through the evolution of our modern mass production age, but there are still many musicians that desire the old-time, artful instruments. It is for this reason that I have compiled these articles on inlaying, neck, and decorative shell-building, so that you may have an instrument suited to your taste. The techniques described are partly mine, but they mainly have been passed down to me by friends with the same interest.

Many serious banjo players, at one time or another, get the urge to make their own banjo neck, or to try some inlaying of mother-of-pearl. There are two main problems that will confront you, if you have such desires; first, learning certain tricks and short cuts that make it quite easy to do, and second, finding out where to buy the necessary materials and equipment. This article will try to provide the necessary information.

Woods

The best wood, in that it is hard and has a beautiful pattern to its grain, is curly maple. Unfortunately, there are several drawbacks. First, this wood tends to warp and twist unless it is properly seasoned and kiln-dried. (Be sure to specify the above requirements when ordering.) Second, it is difficult to obtain a piece that is large enough. Other woods that are good to use are the various hard maples, birdseye maple (if you want an unusual pattern), walnut, and mahogany.

Gluing the Block

I advise laminating the neck, as well as setting a steel rod or bar, to prevent warpage. However, you may have a piece of curly maple large enough to make a neck, and won't want to spoil the curly pattern with laminations.

The best glue to use is weldwood resorcinol glue, available in large hardware stores. Use as many clamps, wood vices, etc. as are available to get sufficient pressure for perfect jointing. The temperature of the room and clamping pressure time is specified on the glue container.

An attractive laminating pattern to try is shown below:

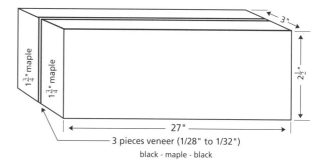

Fig. 1

Then, planing the top and being sure that it is perfectly flat, laminate it in the same manner:

Fig. 2

Incidentally, black and colored veneers are available under the name of "rainbow veneers." You may want to incorporate other colors besides black into your banjo. Beware of gaudiness, however. Some old banjos had green and orange veneers, and I would recommend looking at one before attempting the use of bright colors. You may like it, or you may not.

Next, draw the following pattern on the side of the block using a straight-edge where possible:

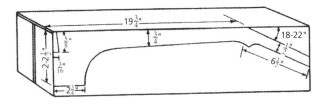

Fig. 3

Heel height varies with the height of your shell.

The notch for the tension hoop will have to be carefully cut and fitted to your banjo, but approximate dimensions are supplied.

Cutting Out the Rough Shape

Using a band saw, make the following cuts:

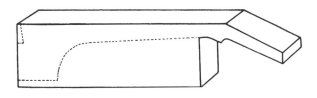

Fig. 4

Leave the block as shown above, so the peghead may be worked on with the advantages that will be explained later.

Laminating the Peghead

Glue the same three veneers on top of the peghead so it looks like this:

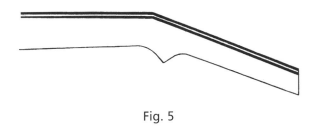

Fig. 5

In gluing veneers like this, use a 1/2- or 3/4-inch board above and below the peghead with a layer of waxed paper between the boards and peghead. The reason for this is to avoid gluing them to the peghead, as with pressure, glue will be forced through the veneer. Using this technique allows for even gluing pressure to veneers:

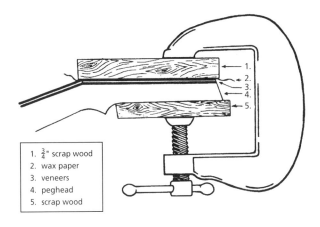

1. ¾" scrap wood
2. wax paper
3. veneers
4. peghead
5. scrap wood

Fig. 6

Setting Steel Bars and Rods

The easiest strengthening method is the use of steel bars. Hardware stores carry them, and the standard size is 3/16" x 1/2". Also available are L-shaped bars. Using two of them together, a T-bar is formed.

Borrow a router from someone, or using one at a woodshop, cut a groove in the block exactly the same size as the bar. This groove will extend into the peghead where the bar will have to be cut flush (giving strength to the peghead). The groove in the peghead will later be hidden with another piece of veneer. If a T-bar is to be used, adjust the level of the router bit and make several more cuts.

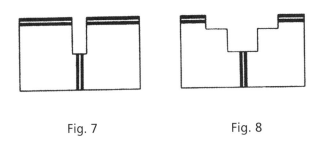

Fig. 7   Fig. 8

Routing the Block for Straight and T-Bars

Inserting the two L-bars to make a T-bar, glue them in with a strong epoxy glue (again, available at most hardware stores) (See Fig. 9).

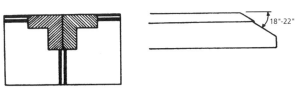

Fig. 9   Fig. 10

Refer to Fig. 29 at this time to get a preview of a cross-section of the finished neck.

The end of the bar will have to be cut at the same peghead angle in order to fit flush (See Fig. 10). The bar should not extend all the way into the heel, but should be 1 1/2" shy of the end of the heel (Fig. 11). Fill the space in front of it with wood. This allows for the attachment of the neck to the shell:

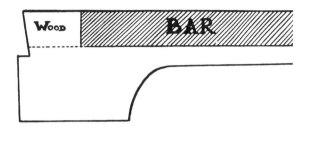

Fig. 11

Setting an Adjustable Rod

Some people prefer to put in an adjustable rod, so that possible bowing of the neck can be corrected.

In most hardware stores you can obtain the 1/8" threaded rods that you need. Put a slight bend on one end, and weld a washer and nut in place on the end. Then, after routing the groove, set in neck *without glue:*

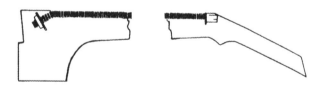

Fig. 12 ADJUSTABLE ROD

A slot will have to be cut for the washer to fit into. This holds the rod when tension adjustment is made at the opposite end.

An Allen nut is at the peghead end and is adjustable by the use of a wrench. A plate will have to be put over the peghead to hide this nut and groove.

Preparing the Peghead and Fingerboard

Next, glue a piece of veneer on the top of the peghead to hide the routed grooves. This veneer should match the wood used in the fingerboard. A hardwood should be used, and ebony is the hardest and prettiest for this purpose. If an ad-

justable rod is used, leave a 5/8" x 1" opening in the peghead, which will later be covered by a plate:

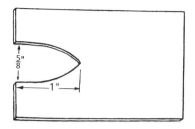

Fig. 13

When the fingerboard is glued on, it should be 1/8" from the end of the block, to allow a place for the nut:

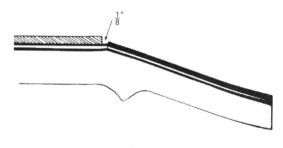

Fig. 14

Making the Fingerboard

Using a 3/16" piece of ebony or rose-wood, cut out the pattern and sand the edges straight and smooth, using sandpaper attached to a hand sander. The pattern can be traced from a good banjo, or if one is not available, the following pattern can be used:

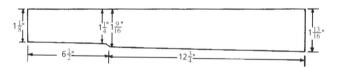

Fig. 15

Glue this fingerboard on *very carefully, centering* both ends over the groove for the bar. Remember, the end near the peghead should be 1/8" from the end of the block, allowing a place to set the nut (See Fig. 14, 16). A white glue should be used for this.

Use a board and waxed paper again to obtain adequate pressure and don't use too much glue this time. After clamping, wipe off all excess glue that oozes between the fingerboard and block, or else it will be difficult to remove after it is dried, and gluing of the ivoroid binding will be difficult.

Use white glue for the above operation, because being water soluble, it can be steamed and the fingerboard can be removed if this ever becomes necessary.

After this is dry, you must determine that your fingerboard is flat. Lay it on a perfectly flat formica counter or other surface and check. If it is not *perfect*, now is the time to correct it by the following methods:

Glue construction-type sandpaper of a medium grade onto a *flat* wood surface (it may require several pieces of sandpaper). Now turn the block upside down so that the fingerboard rests on the sandpaper. Run the block back and forth, occasionally checking the fingerboard against the perfectly flat surface you have chosen and repeat the process until you are satisfied that your fingerboard is perfectly flat.

Cutting Fret Slots

There are several methods of tracing out the fret patterns. Copy a good standard banjo pattern, or design the pattern yourself by the following method:

The distance from the nut to the bridge is called a scale. Measure this distance, multiply it by 1/17.835, and the resulting figure will be the distance at which the first fret is placed from the nut.

Now measure the new scale (distance between bridge and first fret) multiply it also by 1/17.835. This will give you the distance at which the second fret is placed from the first, and so on, for all the frets. In other words, the chromatic scale at which frets are placed is a decreasing logarithmic progression of 1/17.835. Draw the lines on the fingerboard with a pencil. To insure perfectly perpendicular lines, use a T-square.

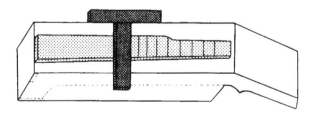

Fig. 16

The best method I can think of for cutting perpendicular slots of uniform depth is by the following method:

Purchase a guitar-maker's saw or a similar saw blade. The blade is 1" x 5" and is very fine. Using this saw blade, make the following set-up:

1. Cut two pieces of hardwood 1/4" x 1" x 10".

2. Drill holes through the wood pieces and blade, then fasten them together with bolts and nuts. Cut off the excess bolt, so that the blade is protruding below the wood by 3/8":

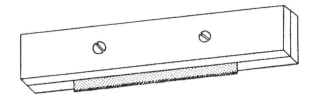

Fig. 17

3. Make two wood clamps using 1/4" x 1" x 5" hardwood with perfectly straight edges. Use bolts and wing-nuts:

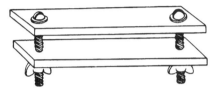

Fig. 18

4. **To cut a groove** (fret slot):

   a. Place one clamp over the block and tighten when its edge is lined up with the pencil marked fret.

   b. Place the other clamp on and slide it next to the tightened clamp.

   c. Drop the saw blade into the slot between the clamps.

   d. Tighten the other clamp.

   e. Gripping the wood ends of the saw, slide it back and forth (cutting the groove) until the wood of the saw rests against the wood clamps, as illustrated.

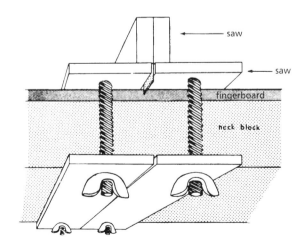

Fig. 19

Your groove will be ⅛″ deep and perfectly straight, cut perpendicular to the surface of the fingerboard.

Incidentally, the block should be placed in a wood vice while sawing for stability and for free use of both hands on the saw.

Frets are available from most instrument repair shops or banjo companies.

The slot you just cut may not be wide enough to set a fret. If not, the grooves can easily be widened by a few strokes from the proper size coping saw blade. Experiment on a scrap of wood to be sure of the right size blade. The fret should go in fairly easily upon hammering. If the slot is not wide enough, the fret won't go in. If it is too wide, the fret will slip out and white glue must be applied to hold it in place.

Do not put the frets in at this time, however as it is necessary to first put in your inlay (also at a later time). Also, the frets would be nicked during shaping of the neck if you put them in now.

Cutting Out the Peghead

Next, cut out the peghead shape, using a bandsaw. The block, resting flat on the bandsaw table, will allow the same bevel to be cut on the entire peghead. Be sure that the peghead base is slightly wider than the fingerboard, to allow for the ivoroid binding on the fingerboard to make the neck and peghead of equal widths at their junction (See Fig. 21).

My favorite peghead shape is the old mastertone fiddle shape, shown in the photo below. You may want to design your own shape, however.

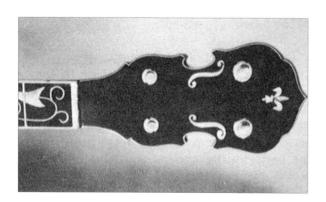

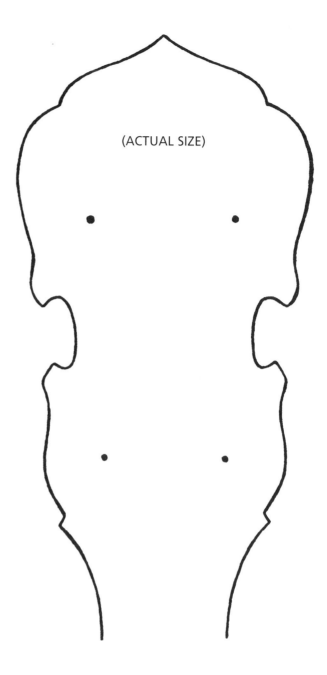

(ACTUAL SIZE)

Fig. 20
MASTERTONE FIDDLE-SHAPED PEGHEAD

Cutting the Banjo Neck Shape

Next, lay the block on its side, and finish cutting out the neck shape, including the notch for the tension hoop. (Use a bandsaw.)

Now, with the fingerboard pointing up, cut out the neck, allowing a ⅛″ margin around the fingerboard where the binding will fit in, as shown in Fig. 21. Again, use the bandsaw:

Fig. 21

Then, glue the same three veneer laminations to the bottom of the heel for decoration.

Now, shape the banjo neck with rasp files. Again, it is advisable to put the neck in a vice while working on it. *Don't* clamp onto the fingerboard!

The Heel

Before shaping the heel, make a heel plate with the following pattern:

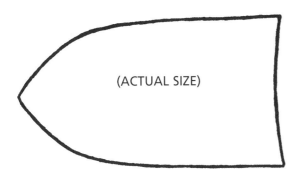

(ACTUAL SIZE)

Fig. 22
HEEL PLATE

Cut the heel plate out of the same type wood as the fingerboard, 1/8" thick. Bind it with ivoroid binding.

Method for binding is as follows:

1. Cut an appropriate sized piece of binding off the strip, then dip it into hot water for a few seconds until it begins to curl.

2. Quickly apply it to the side of the "heel plate" and hold till it cools. You can bend the binding while it's warm until you are satisfied that the shape is nearly correct.

3. Glue it on with household cement. When dry, sand the edges flush with the wood.

Now, trace this heel plate pattern on the bottom of the banjo neck (Fig. 23). Using your files, shape the heel up to your pencil mark. Do not glue the heel plate on at this time.

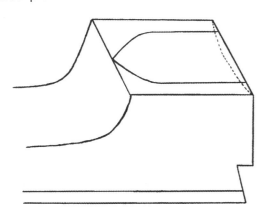

Fig. 23

Incidentally, the peghead can be bound in the same manner described for the heel, but it is a tedious job and it is difficult to cut the peghead out of veneers.

The neck will now have to be fitted to the shell.

From above, cut the neck in the same curve as the shell, using a bandsaw (See Fig. 23).

Then use a file to round the inside of the neck attachment so that it fits the shell at the proper angle (3°). To determine when you have the right angle, tape a straightedge across the fingerboard, hold it to the shell and note that the protruding yardstick should be about 3/8" above the drumhead where the bridge is (about 7" from the attachment of the neck).

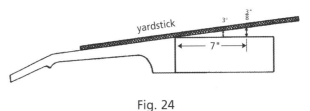

Fig. 24

Round the part of the neck in the notch that fits against the tension hoop, so that the whole neck fits tightly against the shell and tension hoop.

At the same time, note that a straight line down the middle of the neck must bisect the head equally. Determine this with a straight edge. If it is not centered, trim neck attachment with a file until the correction is made:

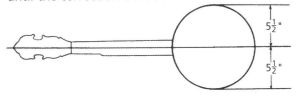

Fig. 25

How to Attach the Neck and Heel Plate

Before gluing the heel plate on, drill two 1/4" holes into the neck for two threaded rods which can fit into these holes. Then drill a hole down through the heel through the two rods, but not through the fingerboard. Through this hole place a 1/8" screw.

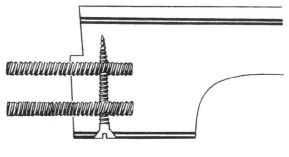

Fig. 26

The neck can be attached to the shell with two large hexagonal nuts. Be sure that the two rods are far enough apart so that the hexagonal nuts can be turned and tightened!

The heel plate can now be glued on.

Fitting the Pegs

Drill the holes carefully into the peghead, using an electric drill. It is best to have the pegs beforehand to insure correct fitting.

A non-slip fifth-string peg with a setscrew is the best standard non-mechanical fifth which still looks conventional and traditional. The hole should be drilled under the fourth fret, centered in the side of the neck. Tap it (purchase a tap at your hardware store with the same size threads as the thread found on your fifth-string peg). Now, the threads of the peg will screw in without splitting the neck. Remove the pegs after fitting them, so that they don't interfere with finishing.

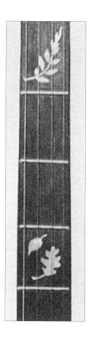

Inlaying Mother-Of-Pearl

You can make you own inlays, or else buy pre-cut inlays.

To make your own inlays, you need flat sheets of pearl (which you can grind out of abalone shell, or purchase).

Make your own inlays by cutting them out with a jeweler's saw, and filing with a small set of "needle files," while the pearl is held by a small vice.

Inlaying Technique

Practice on a scrap piece of wood before trying to inlay an instrument.

Design your whole fingerboard pattern on paper before you start inlaying.

1. Make the inlay (or use pre-cut inlays).

2. Center it between the fret slots.

3. Trace its outline with a fine pencil sharpened with sandpaper. Another fine tracing method is:

   a. Fasten the inlay to the fingerboard with a drop of contact cement.

   b. Spray the wood with a fine coat of shellac.

   c. Blow a sprinkle of talcum from your hand across the still tacky shellac, let it dry for a minute.

   d. Remove the inlay, and a perfect outline remains.

4. Routing the wood to the same size and depth of the inlay may be done with a small scalpel and fine chisels, but this is difficult for ebony inlaying. Far superior is the use of a small hi-speed electric drill that has a variety of uses. If you are working with ebony, buy several carbide bits that can be purchased from a dental supply company. They will not burn out as fast as others do.

5. After routing the space for your inlay and fitting it, glue it in place by the following method:

   a. Make a pile of fine sawdust of the same type wood into which you are inlaying by sanding down a scrap of that wood into a box.

   b. Mix some of the sawdust with a small amount of white glue.

   c. Fill the space with this mixture, then press the inlay into it, allowing the mixture to ooze up through any spaces. Be sure that you don't set the inlay below the surface of the fingerboard.

   d. Allow to dry for 24 hours, then sand flush with a fine sandpaper or emery paper, sanding lengthwise along the fingerboard.

   e. If an inlay is to cover several fret spaces, cut it into its respective pieces, rather than leave it whole, so that the fret may be hammered in without breaking the inlay (Fig. 27).

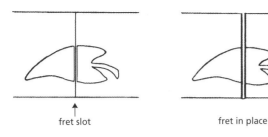

fret slot   fret in place

Fig. 27

Fancy vines can be inlaid by using pewter or 3/16" copper wire for the vine, pearl for the leaves.

The method below discloses how I inlaid the vine in the photograph.

1. Cover the slotted fingerboard with two layers of masking tape.

2. Draw the lines on the masking tape with pencil where the frets are located.

3. Trace the inlays with fine pencil on the tape.

4. Draw the vine.

5. Using a fine scalpel, cut along the pencil lines, then peel the tape leaves or flowers off. Trace around the vine, cutting a double line wide enough for the pewter wire. Peel this out, using a pin.

6. Now the whole thing can be sandblasted to the proper depth. (The sand bounces off the tape, but erodes the wood.)

The results are fine, and only a minimal amount of trimming with your high-speed drill will be necessary to fit the inlays into place.

As you make your inlays, and while the fingerboard is being blasted, be careful to keep the inlays in order and not misplaced. I have found an easy way to do this: simply fasten several strips of masking tape to a board, sticky side up. Stick your inlays to the tape, in order, as you make them. The fret spaces can be labeled on the tape to further simplify matters.

7. The tips of the vine's tendrils should be filled to a point before inlaying.

8. An example of this type of inlaying is seen in the photograph of a neck I recently made. Other fingerboards are shown in photographs to give you ideas of what has been or can be done.

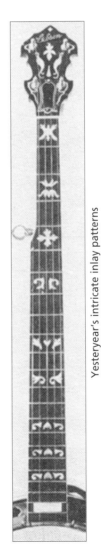
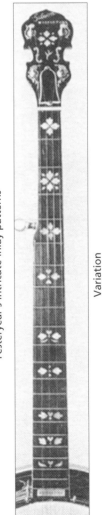
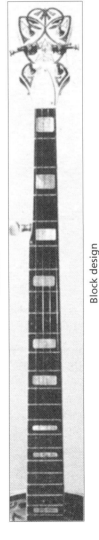

Yesteryear's intricate inlay patterns

Variation

Block design

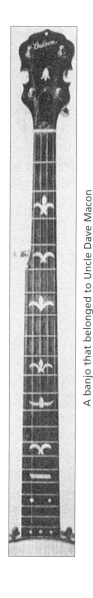

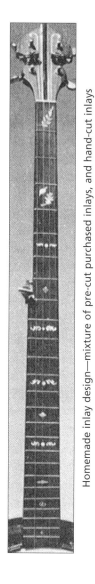

A banjo that belonged to Uncle Dave Macon

Homemade inlay design—mixture of pre-cut purchased inlays, and hand-cut inlays

Pearl and abalone vine, unfretted fingerboard

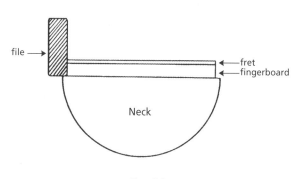

file → fret
fingerboard

Neck

Fig. 28

Binding

Now glue the ivoroid binding in the groove by the same method described for the heel plate. The neck can now be sanded smoothly, going from medium to fine grade sandpaper.

OTHER FANCY IDEAS FOR YOUR BANJO NECK

Carving the Heel

Carving a heel such as the one in the photograph, is not difficult.

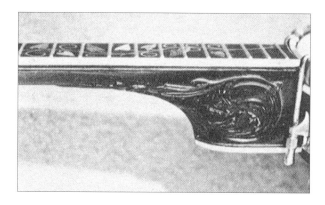

Draw the pattern on paper, cut it out, then pin it on the neck. Trace it with a pencil, then turn the paper around, pin it to the other side and trace it there. Then use your scalpels and chisels to carve. Several examples of carving are shown in photographs to stimulate your imagination.

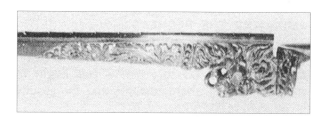

Engraving Mother-of-Pearl

Engraving veins into pearl leaves in your vines, initials, etc., can be attractive, and is fairly easy to do. Obtain a "graver" (a small sharp steel knife-like tool) from a jeweler supply, and practice on scrap pieces of pearl. After inscribing the pearl, which is done with a smooth, firm stroke, rub black jeweler's wax across the pearl and wipe off the excess. Only the engraved depressions will remain black.

Setting the Frets

1. Cover the head of your hammer with several layers of masking tape to cushion it and to prevent nicking the frets.

2. Tap the frets into place, clipping them off evenly at the edges of the fingerboard, using a wire-cutter.

3. When they are all placed and clipped, run a metal file in the groove where the ivoroid binding will go, as shown in Fig. 28. This will leave the frets flush with the fingerboard.

Position Dots in the Binding

Drill small holes in the binding at the required positions (1, 3, 5, 7, 10, 12, 15, 17, 19, and 22). Fill the holes with a mixture of white glue and ebony dust. The result will be black position dots.

Another technique is to inlay abalone dots in the binding as shown in the photograph.

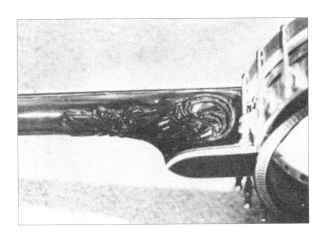

This will test your patience, as they are difficult to cut out of pearl. Run a hand sander obliquely across the edges of the fingerboard, thus beveling it and the frets:

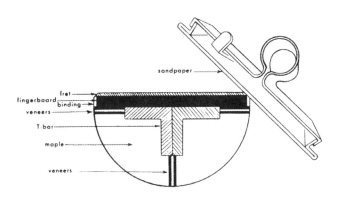

Fig. 29
CROSS-SECTION OF THE NECK;
beveling with a hand-sander

Laminating the Peghead

The undersurface of the peghead can be beautifully laminated. Do this before you begin to round the neck. I attempted this, and the results can be seen in the photograph.

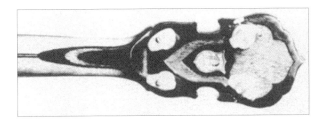

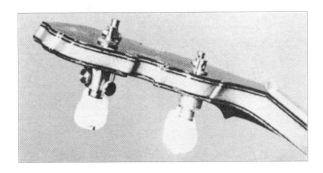

After the neck is finished, place the nut, made of bone, (bought at any stringed instrument shop) with a drop of white glue after shaping it. The string grooves should be cut with a 3-cornered file.

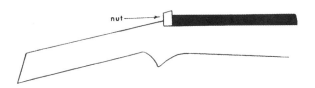

Fig. 30

Fifth-string nuts and hooks can be obtained from various manufacturers. A screw can be substituted for a fifth-string nut, but is unsightly.

Finishing the Neck

A good finish on the neck is important. In addition to adding beauty to the instrument, it protects the wood and also allows you to slide your hand back and forth smoothly and rapidly while playing.

Preliminary Work

1. Sand with fine sandpaper, fill all cracks with wood filler, and cover fingerboard with masking tape.

2. "Washing": dampen a rag with lacquer thinner, go over the neck once.

3. Spray (do not use brush!) two or more coats of clear lacquer on the neck, until the grain is filled. Wait until the lacquer is 3/4 dry before spraying each additional coat. Under normal drying conditions this will be about 15–20 minutes.

4. You are now ready to apply one of four types of finishes: solid, opalescent, clear, or sunburst.

Solid Finish

1. After completing above steps, spray solid color of your choice (opaque lacquer). The number of coats of this solid lacquer depends on how many defects, blemishes, etc., that have to be covered.

2. When 3/4 dry, spray 3 or 4 coats of clear lacquer at regular intervals.

3. Wait twenty-four hours to insure thorough drying.

4. Using wet emery paper, "water-sand" the "orange-peel" (uneven surface) effect off of the lacquered surface of the neck to get a perfectly smooth surface.

5. Spray two more coats of clear lacquer at regular intervals.

6. Wait twenty-four hours.

7. "Compounding": use fine abrasive compound. Rub the neck with the compound, using a cloth, until a glass finish is obtained—the "orange-peel" effect will disappear.

8. "Waxing": wax the neck using a fine wax.

Opalescent Finish

1. Repeat preliminary work steps through "step 3"—spray two coats or more of clear lacquer before tinting process.

2. The opalescent tint: mix clear lacquer 50-50 with lacquer thinner.

3. Add and mix oil stain (cherry or mahogany oil stain). Necessary proportions: 2 oz. stain to one pint lacquer-thinner mixture.

4. Spray the opalescent tint you have mixed on to the neck, according to how much you want to tint the wood. (The less you spray, the more the grain of the wood will show through.)

5. Repeat the rest of the process as for solid finish (begin with step 2).

Clear Finish

Same as above, except eliminate the opalescent tinting with the oil stain.

Sunburst

1. The same process is used as for the other finishing methods, except that "sunbursting" is substituted for the spraying of solid or opalescent tint.

2. Sunburst types

    a. Oblong: for necks

    b. Circular: for guitar bodies, banjo resonators

3. Process

    a. Spray yellow stain in middle (neck or body).

    b. Use opalescent tint mix of various mixtures—1 1/2 oz., 2 oz., 2 1/2 oz. stain to one pint lacquer and spray from center toward the periphery, using the thicker (and darker) mixtures toward the periphery, finally ending up with a black stain.

4. A general finishing hint is to keep lacquer buildup to a minimum to prevent cracking.

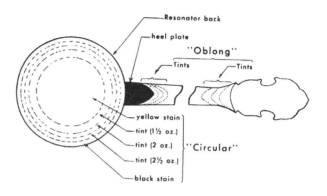

Fig. 31
SUNBURST FINISHING

Gold-plating

The finishing touch to a fancy instrument, in many artists' and musicians' eyes, is gold-plating of the metal parts. To have this done commercially is costly, but you can actually plate your small metal parts (brackets, pegs, etc.) on your kitchen stove.

Purchase some gold-plating solution and some zinc rods from a dental supply company and obtain a small Pyrex bowl. The solution can be used over and over, so one pint goes a long way.

Remove the grease, fingerprints, etc. from the object to be plated by immersing in a weak acid medium, or a safer method around the home is to warm some water with a small amount of baking soda and detergent and cleanse the object, then dry it without touching it again. Three minutes or so will do the job. Heat the gold solution on your stove in the Pyrex bowl until vapor begins to rise from it. Drop the object into the solution and touch the zinc rod to it. In about three to five minutes the object will be beautifully plated.

Building A Decorative Banjo Shell

Using Weldwood resorcinol glue, glue and clamp together layers of various fancy hardwoods until a block 1' x 1' x 2" is formed. I made the following block, shown in the illustration.

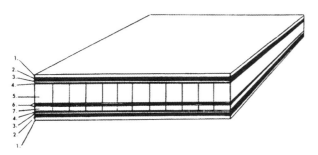

1. ¹/₈" maple
2. ¹/₈" rosewood
3. ¹/₂₈" mahogany
4. ¹/₁₆" maple
5. ³/₄" x 1" x 1' varying hardwoods
6. 3 layers of veneer
    (maple – rosewood – maple)
7. ¹/₄" x 1" x 1' varying hardwoods

Fig. 32
CONSTRUCTION OF THE BLOCK

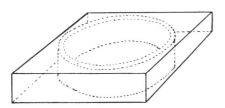

Fig. 33
CUTTING OUT THE SHELL

All the layers are 1' x 1' boards of varying thicknesses (¹/₂₈", ¹/₁₆", ¹/₈", ¹/₄", and ³/₄"). The layers with the squares (³/₄" and ¹/₄") consist of 1" x 1' strips of various fancy hardwoods (twelve of them constitute a layer that will be 1' x 1').

In clamping there is one problem: getting pressure from the sides, in order to form solid joints between these 1" strips. It may be accomplished by the following method:

1. The bottom layer (¹/₈" maple) should be 14" x 12", whereas all other layers are 12" x 12".

2. Screw down a strip of ³/₄" x 1 ⁷/₈" x 12" hardwood on both ends of the bottom layer of 12" x 14" maple, as shown in the illustration below (Fig. 34).

3. Glue all the layers together in order. The 1" x 1' strips must be covered with glue on all four sides. Use a large paint brush to apply the glue, as the block must be glued together rapidly. The brush should be washed out with water, before the glue dries.

4. Using clamps and sheets of waxpaper and scrap plywood (1' x 1' x ³/₄") for vertical pressure (as described in peghead veneer portion of the banjo neck chapter), apply the partial vertical pressure needed (don't tighten the clamps all the way at this time).

5. There will be ¹/₄" between the hardwood strips screwed to the bottom maple layer, and the rest of the block. To exert the horizontal pressure necessary for firm joints between the 1" strips, simply hammer in triangular wooden wedges, as shown in the illustration below. Then the clamps exerting vertical pressure can be further tightened.

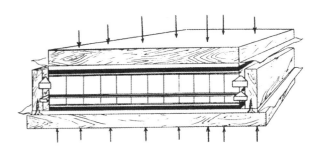

Fig. 34
GLUING THE BLOCK

When this is completely dry, remove the clamps, and using a bandsaw, cut off the excess of the bottom layer of maple, its ³/₄" strips and the wedges—you now have a 1' x 1' x 2" block.

Dry this block in your oven (with just the pilot light on) for several days, then let it sit around in a dry room for a week or more (as long as your patience holds out) to insure thorough drying.

Cutting Out the Shell (See Fig. 33)

1. Draw two lines across the block (from corner to corner) to find the center point.

2. Using a compass, draw an 11 ¹/₄" diameter circle on the block.

3. I was taught to make the outside cut with a router, as well as the inside cut, but since the outside is for show, I have found a quicker and easier method for clean results:

    Cut out this circle with a bandsaw. Then mount the circular block on a lathe baseplate. Put this on a wood lathe, and using a *sharp* straight lathe tool, cut a straight smooth edge. While it is still spinning on the lathe, use several grades of sandpaper to get a very fine finish. The final diameter of this block should now be 11".

4. If you have a tone ring to fit on the shell, cut the necessary notch in the block, while it is still on the lathe, using the straight sharp lathe tool, so that the side of the tone ring and shell are flush, as shown in the diagram below.

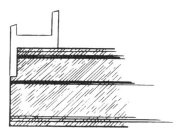

Fig. 35
FITTING THE TONE RING
cross section of the block
and an arch-top tone ring

5. Remove from the lathe and unscrew the base-plate from the round block.

6. Using a router, set the radius at 4 $7/8$", then cut the inside diameter out. (This will leave the shell thickness at $5/8$".) You probably won't be able to get a router bit longer than 1 $1/4$", so the best way to accomplish this is to drill a tiny hole through the block at the center point, using a drill-press, in order to help find the exact center on the other side. After routing a circle on one side, turn the block over, and rout a circle on the other side. You now have a shell $5/8$" thick. Don't throw the rest of that block away! It makes a beautiful bowl when turned out on a lathe. Here's what the finished shell will look like:

Finishing the Shell

Purchase a set of bracket holders and brackets, and drill the appropriate holes in the shell through which the bracket holders can be fastened with 3/4" bolts. Also, at this time, the holes for the neck attachment should be drilled into the shell.

Then fine sand the shell, and finish as described in neck finishing. Use a clear finish.

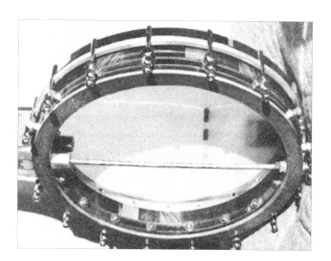

MAKING SCRUGGS TUNERS

Outlined below is a simple method of making cam-type Scruggs Tuners. You will need access to an electric tool workshop and a good deal of time. (I've used "mechanical" D tuners for many years and prefer them to cam tuners—*see page 20*).

1. MATERIALS NEEDED

a. 6" length of ½" x ¼" hard steel, available at most hardware stores.

b. Two plain banjo pegs.

c. Several "taps" also available at your hardware store. The sizes needed are: 4 x 40, $^5/_{64}$" to match bolt.

d. Two Lionel train transformer knobs.

e. Two small bolts, size $^5/_{64}$".

f. Two threaded bolt pieces, size 4 x 40.

g. Four headless nails.

2. PROCEDURE

Read through all of these instructions carefully and understand them fully before making the decision to drill into your peghead.

a. Using a hacksaw, cut out of hard steel the rough shape of the cam.

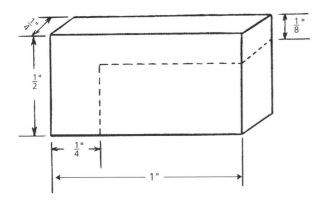

b. Trim with metal files.

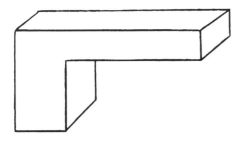

c. Round the end.

d. Drill a series of holes through the top of the cam.

e. Using "needle files" connect the holes, making a slot.

f. Shape the tip for appearances with the resulting cam.

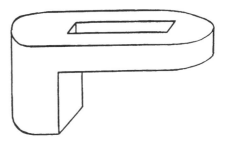

g. Screw a 4 x 40 bolt into a Lionel train transformer knob (which has 4 x 36 threads) so that the bolt jams and stays fixed in the knob.

h. Using a 4 x 40 tap, tap the string hole of the peg so that the bolt turns through it freely.

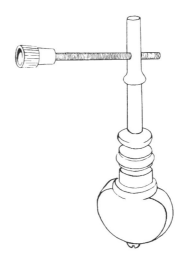

i. Drill a 5/64″ hole into the top of the peg (drill down about 3/16″). Use a vice and an electric drill press. Tap this hole to fit a tiny hexagonal bolt as illustrated (it should be about 5/16″ long).

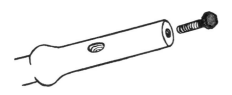

j. Screw the cam down to the peg, using the hexagonal bolt. Screw the other bolt through the peg until it rests against the cam (mark the exact spot).

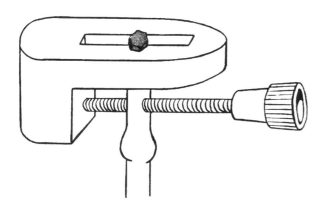

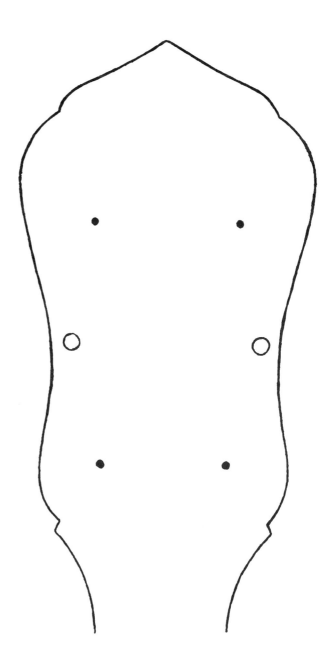

k. Drill a hole into the cam at the spot, which should just go into the cam about (1/16″–3/32″).

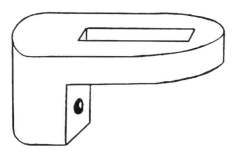

l. Drill holes in the peghead, centered between the other pegs (1, 2) (3, 4) and as far to the sides of the peghead as possible.

m. Mount the completed cams to the peghead using the photographs on the following page as a guide.

n. Without the cams touching the strings, put the banjo in D tuning. Swing each cam so that they push out the second and third strings, meeting them exactly perpendicularly; then, by turning the terminal knobs, tune the banjo into G (the second string tunes up two frets, the third up one fret). Now set two headless nails as shown in the diagram, which act as stops (drill holes first, so as not to split the peghead). Swing the cams back off the strings (you're now back to D tuning) and place two more nails as shown in the diagram. This keeps the cam from swinging all the way around when in D. The nails must be lower than the strings, or else they will stop the strings as they are stretched by the cams.

NOTE THE DIAGRAM. The second set of nails can be set so that the cams are still touching the strings when they are in the lowered position. Doing so will improve the action of the cams.

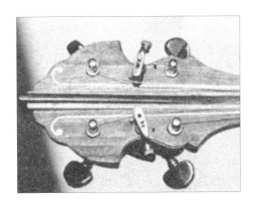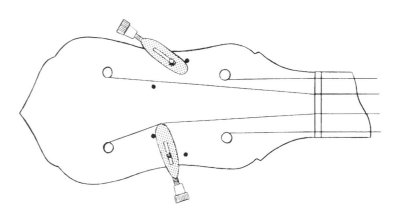

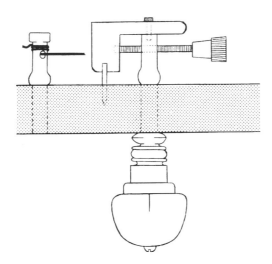

Information on how I set my tuners for certain songs that I play is in the "Scruggs Tuners" section in Chapter 2 on page 19, and also in Chapter 9 on page 67.

INDEX

AUDIO TRACK LISTING

1. Introduction
2. Tuning the banjo
3. Basic rhythm
4. Basic forward roll
5. Alternating thumb pattern
6. Mixing basic rhythm and alternating thumb
7. Basic sliding on the 3rd string
8. Basic sliding on the 4th string
9. Sliding with basic rhythm
10. Sliding with alternating thumb pattern
11. Sliding with basic rhythm and alternating thumb pattern
12. Chorus of "Cripple Creek"
13. Hammering-on
14. Hammering into basic rhythm
15. Alternating thumb roll and hammering
16. Hammers and slides with alternating thumb roll and basic rhythm
17. Forward roll modification and adding a C chord
18. Sliding and hammering in "Cripple Creek"
19. Pulling-off
20. Hammer pull-offs
21. Pulling-off in basic rhythm
22. Push-offs
23. Push-offs and alternating thumb pattern
24. Slides, pull-off, push-off, and alternating thumb pattern
25. Advanced version of "Cripple Creek"
26. Variation of the forward roll
27. Forward roll with a slide in "Cripple Creek"
28. Four forward roll variations
29. Reverse roll
30. Forward and reverse rolls in "Ballad of Jed Clampett"
31. Basic rhythm, alternating thumb and reverse roll in "Ballad of Jed Clampett"
32. Backward roll
33. Backward roll in first line of "Home Sweet Home" (C tuning)
34. Reverse roll variation (G tuning)

35. Adding a slide to another reverse roll

36. Forward roll emphasizing 2nd string with thumb

37. Forward roll with hammer on 2nd string

38. Double hammer on 2nd string and "Foggy Mountain Breakdown" roll

39. Hammer and a pull-off in a reverse roll

40. Fretting 1st string with previous exercise

41. Basic waltz rhythm and rolling waltz rhythm

42. Mixing basic and rolling waltz rhythms; adding slides

43. Setting tuners to open G and D tunings; "Flint Hill Special" opening

44. Tuning break in "Flint Hill Special"

45. 2nd-string tuner exercise

46. Harmonic chimes

47. Vamping full chord positions

48. Vamped rhythm pattern

49. Advanced vamping and rhythm

50. More syncopated vamped rhythm pattern

51. Vamped rhythm and muting

52. Vamping and hammering

53. Vamping with 4th-string lead-ins

54. Vamping an ending

55. C6 chord forward roll

56. Catchy backup lick

57. Boogie-woogie patterns

58. Backup lick on 1st and 2nd strings while muting other strings with right thumb

59. Mid-tempo fill-in licks using hammer-ons

60. Chokes, whole-step and half-step

~

Recorded by: Earl Scruggs
Edited by: Gary Scruggs
Mastered by: Brad Davis

GREAT BANJO PUBLICATIONS

FROM HAL LEONARD

Hal Leonard Banjo Method – Second Edition
by Mac Robertson, Robbie Clement, Will Schmid
This innovative method teaches 5-string banjo bluegrass style using a carefully paced approach that keeps beginners playing great songs *while learning*. Book 1 covers easy chord strums, tablature, right-hand rolls, hammer-ons, slides and pull-offs, and more. Book 2 includes solos and licks, fiddle tunes, back-up, capo use, and more.
00699500 Book 1 Book Only $7.99
00695101 Book 1 Book/Online Audio $16.99
00699502 Book 2 Book Only $7.99

Banjo Aerobics
A 50-Week Workout Program for Developing, Improving and Maintaining Banjo Technique
by Michael Bremer
Take your banjo playing to the next level with this fantastic daily resource, providing a year's worth of practice material with a two-week vacation. The accompanying audio includes demo tracks for all the examples in the book to reinforce how the banjo should sound.
00113734 Book/Online Audio $19.99

Banjo Chord Finder
This extensive reference guide covers over 2,800 banjo chords, including four of the most commonly used tunings. Thirty different chord qualities are covered for each key, and each chord quality is presented in two different voicings. Also includes a lesson on chord construction and a fingerboard chart of the banjo neck!

00695741 9 x 12.................. $6.99   00695742 6 x 9..................... $6.99

Banjo Scale Finder
by Chad Johnson
Learn to play scales on the banjo with this comprehensive yet easy-to-use book. It contains more than 1,300 scale diagrams for the most often-used scales and modes, including multiple patterns for each scale. Also includes a lesson on scale construction and a fingerboard chart of the banjo neck.

00695780 9 x 12.................. $9.99   00695783 6 x 9..................... $6.99

First 50 Songs You Should Play on Banjo
arr. Michael J. Miles & Greg Cahill
Easy-to-read banjo tab, chord symbols and lyrics for the most popular songs banjo players like to play. Explore clawhammer and three-finger-style banjo in a variety of tunings and capoings with this one-of-a-kind collection. Songs include: Angel from Montgomery • Carolina in My Mind • Cripple Creek • Danny Boy • The House of the Rising Sun • Mr. Tambourine Man • Take Me Home, Country Roads • This Land Is Your Land • Wildwood Flower • and many more.
00153311 ....$14.99

Fretboard Roadmaps
by Fred Sokolow
This handy book/with online audio will get you playing all over the banjo fretboard in any key! You'll learn to: increase your chord, scale and lick vocabulary • play chord-based licks, moveable major and blues scales, melodic scales and first-position major scales • and much more! The audio includes 51 demonstrations of the exercises.
00695358 Book/CD $15.99

O Brother, Where Art Thou?
Banjo tab arrangements of 12 bluegrass/folk songs from this Grammy-winning album. Includes: The Big Rock Candy Mountain • Down to the River to Pray • I Am a Man of Constant Sorrow • I Am Weary (Let Me Rest) • I'll Fly Away • In the Jailhouse Now • Keep on the Sunny Side • You Are My Sunshine • and more, plus lyrics and a banjo notation legend.

00699528 Banjo Tablature... $14.99

Earl Scruggs and the 5-String Banjo
Earl Scruggs' legendary method has helped thousands of banjo players get their start. It features everything you need to know to start playing, even how to build your own banjo! Topics covered include: Scruggs tuners • how to read music • chords • how to read tablature • anatomy of Scruggs-style picking • exercises in picking • 44 songs • biographical notes • and more! The CD features Earl Scruggs playing and explaining over 60 examples!
00695764 Book Only... $22.99
00695765 Book/CD Pack $34.99

Clawhammer Cookbook
Tools, Techniques & Recipes for Playing Clawhammer Banjo
by Michael Bremer
The goal of this book isn't to tell you how to play tunes or how to play like anyone else. It's to teach you ways to approach, arrange, and personalize any tune – to develop your own unique style. To that end, we'll take in a healthy serving of old-time music and also expand the clawhammer palate to taste a few other musical styles. Includes audio track demos of all the songs and examples to aid in the learning process.
00118354 Book/Online Audio..$19.99

The Ultimate Banjo Songbook
A great collection of banjo classics: Alabama Jubilee • Bye Bye Love • Duelin' Banjos • The Entertainer • Foggy Mountain Breakdown • Great Balls of Fire • Lady of Spain • Orange Blossom Special • (Ghost) Riders in the Sky • Rocky Top • San Antonio Rose • Tennessee Waltz • UFO-TOFU • You Are My Sunshine • and more.

00699565 Book/Online Audio... $27

Visit Hal Leonard online at **www.hal**